RUNNING A PUBLIC SAFETY LABOR UNION

A COMPREHENSIVE GUIDE TO PROTECTING THE PEOPLE WHO PROTECT EVERYONE

by Rob Heun

LRIS PUBLICATIONS
PORTLAND, OREGON

Published by Labor Relations Information System
3021 NE Broadway
Portland OR 97232
503.282.5440
www.LRIS.com

Heun, Robert. 1954 –

ISBN: 978-1-880607-27-5

Library of Congress Control No. 2014930036

Dedicated to those men and women who are often misunderstood, regularly second-guessed, generally underappreciated and always willing…

ACKNOWLEDGMENTS

I have often waded through pages of acknowledgments in books, and I have dutifully read every line and probably mispronounced the names of most of those folks acknowledged by the author. While I understand that no book is written without the assistance of others, this modest work exists only because of the assistance of two people with easily pronounced names.

First and foremost, I want to thank Debbie Frields Denman for her persistence, patience and professionalism. Only through Debbie's formatting, proofreading and subtle, yet firm, deadline reminders was I able to put my thoughts in readable, and hopefully useable, form. No one is more deservedly happy that this book is completed than Debbie, and rightfully so.

The only other person to acknowledge is Will Aitchison, who is the most intelligent individual I know. It was Will who suggested I attempt to write this book, it is Will who was the source of most of the ideas for organizing my thoughts, and it is Will who added so much quality content in such areas as social media, where my own experience was sorely lacking, and it was Will who ensured the book was less a regional perspective and more universally applicable to public safety unions. Will has always been there as a friend, consigliore, and "go-to-guy" when there was no one else to go to...

ABOUT THE AUTHOR

Rob Heun was a police union president for twelve years. He was a patrol officer, member of the Major Crimes Response Team, supervisor, Deputy Chief and eventually retired as Chief of Police. He has a Bachelor of Science from the United States Military Academy. He and his wife Michelle own and operate a small wilderness lodge in Alaska.

INTRODUCTION

Everything in this book is stolen. Everything. While writing it, I stole from police and fire unions all over the country. I stole from their contracts, their constitutions and bylaws, and from their experiences. I stole from attorneys, accountants, and trust consultants. I stole from books, though these are hopefully appropriately credited and footnoted. I stole comments and observations from cops and firefighters I've met on the job, at seminars and through telephone conversations. I stole from arbitrators and judges, and their decisions that ran from the insightful to the boneheaded. I even forced myself to steal a bit from Robert's Rules.[1]

If you bought this book thinking it would be a guide to running a police or fire union, you were partially misled. If you're a cop or firefighter, you know only too well that no one really runs one of these unions. We never consider ourselves stereotypical union officials. Through some idealistic notion, ego trip, or resolution that our public safety careers might have topped out, we sought and attained a leadership position among our peers. We have found that just by holding on and bumping a mass of Type-A personalities in the same direction is no less challenging than, and often very comparable to, the nastiest of domestic disturbances or the horsing of a hose without help.

That said, there is also something very rewarding in having a hand in ensuring that our professions are attractive to the "good" guys and gals. You know, the ones who not only seek to protect and serve for the right reasons, but who have the smarts to do it the right way. As we know, anyone who fits this category will say, probably more than once throughout his or her career, "Why do I bother?"

As union leaders, it is incumbent upon each and every one of us to be sure that when these folks do the great cost/benefit analysis of their lives, they have enough reasons to stand with us in a public safety career. Good wages, a work schedule that provides the needed time with family or in pursuit of off-the-job interests, and working conditions that include the means to provide for safety and self-actualization are all responsibilities that are all too often given lip service by management, but just as often, ultimately inherited by the union.

The whole reason this book was written is to help you run a police or fire union. The operative word is "union." That is sometimes a hard one to swallow for a group of professionals like us who are so proud of our individual skills and so sure of our individual judgments. Like I said before, our employers screen us for the traits that make the sacrifice of an individual perspective almost unbearable. But don't forget, we are also screened to be capable and willing to make the ultimate sacrifice for our community if that terrible time was ever to present itself. We don't want to and we shouldn't have to, but no one else in the community is compensated to do that. The only way to bet on the come is to keep the compensation high and keep attracting those with whom you'd be honored to have as back-up. That is the only way police and fire unions survive.

There's a lot in this book that I did or should have done as a union president. For what I did I am generally proud. For what I should have done, well, I wish someone would have written a book...

Rob Heun
January 2014

NOTES

[1] *Robert's Rules of Order* is the short title of a book containing rules of order intended to be adopted as a parliamentary authority for use by a deliberative assembly. Currently in its eleventh edition and published under the name *Robert's Rules of Order Newly Revised*, it is the most widely used parliamentary authority in the United States.

TABLE OF CONTENTS

CHAPTER 1

THE TEN TRUTHS OF UNION LEADERSHIP

There's a tremendous amount of personal and professional satisfaction in being a leader in a police or fire union. But never lose sight of the fact that we, screened by our employers to be individual thinkers capable of split-second, life affecting decisions, are often our own worst enemies. We tend to hang out with coworkers more than any other profession, and develop a jaundiced view of our own communities. We are driven by a basic need to better ourselves and our family's station in life, and over time, we assess the risks we take and compensation becomes very important to us. Ultimately, as the ones who actually do the dirty work, we know how to do it better, and we are frustrated that no one asks. So, as you refer to this book, keep in mind the Ten Truths of Union Leadership for public safety unions:

1. *We eat our own.* For having so much in common, it never ceases to amaze me as to how diversified the needs and agendas can be within one bargaining unit, and how willing to turn on each other we can be. One generation of employees feels they have been "sold out" by the older folks, who in turn think the newer generation expects too much and is willing to put in too little effort. Certainly a dash of ex-spouses and ex-professional partners lend an air of excitement and intrigue to what should be the rather dry job of protecting and advancing wages, hours, and working conditions.

2. *Member interest is directly proportional to wallet impact.* It's ironic. In good times, it's difficult to get a quorum at a union meeting. Yet it's precisely during the good times that so much critical planning for the future needs to be done. If you are going to get involved in this business, you also have to recognize that, as a rule, cops and firefighters will generally go along with the most boneheaded administrative and operational decisions, but will kick and scream if they think their compensation for putting up with those decisions is diminished or threatened in any way. Capitalize on the kicking and screaming. It's a great way to generate internal interest in the union, and actually it's a wonderful way to get new blood into union leadership positions.

3. *We are empowered by poor management.* Poor management usually makes for a strong union. Once again, there's an irony to this. Even the most hostile political leaders never realize that the best way to weaken our unions is to ensure solid operational and interpersonal leadership within a department. As it is, union leadership is often sucked into the leadership vacuum, thereby strengthening the informal chain of command and the union's credibility inside and outside a department. By ultimately invigorating the union itself, a chief can perpetuate his problems by not recognizing the power of the union and making decisions without union input.

4. *If you're in this business to hear someone say "thank you," get a different job.* Running a public safety union is one of the most thankless tasks imaginable. You can spend dozens of hours preparing for a mitigation hearing, turn a miracle in saving someone's job, only to watch his back gradually recede into the distance with not so much as a single word of appreciation. Union leaders, like the employ-

ees are motivated by something – sometimes money, sometimes power, etc... sometimes the greater good.

5. *You'll never please the ten-percenters.* No matter what you do, 10% of your membership will disagree with your actions. Usually, they're the same people, and they won't like it if you get a 5% raise or a 50% raise. Accept the fact that they exist, and that you won't make them happy. Above all, don't try to change your union's philosophies to please these people. You'll never achieve that goal, no matter what you do.

6. *You have to bring the dissenters in.* Simply because you can't please the ten-percenters doesn't mean you can't use them. Try to bring them into the organization. Put them on committees, even put one of them onto the bargaining team. You won't please them (See Truth #5), but you will quiet them, and minimize their effect on others.

7. *You must run the job, don't let the job run you.* The 1,001 things you have to do as a union leader can often seem overwhelming, and there will be days, many days, where it seems like all you're doing is running from thing to thing. Keep in mind that you were elected for a reason. Your membership thought that your vision and leadership were needed for the union. If you start to feel overwhelmed, take a step back, delegate, and bring your vision to your organization.

8. *Be true to your word, even if it hurts.* Every time you take a position on behalf of your union, your credibility is on the line. That's true whether you're dealing with your own members or with politicians, the employer's representatives, or the public. That means that if you make a deal, even an informal one, you should live up to your word. Your ability to reach beneficial agreements in the future is on the line.

9. *Know your audience.* Target audiences change, as does the packaging of the same message. For instance, if pending budget cuts might include layoffs, the underlying common message is that layoffs are bad. Your message to your members might be one of reassurance and unity. The message to the public might be an explanation of how layoffs will adversely affect public safety. Your message to politicians might take the form of a reminder that cops and firefighters vote, work for and contribute to campaigns.

10. *Start to groom successors early.* There are often unplanned turnovers in union leadership. These changes can be caused by health, member discontent, or even "management grazing," where the employer recognizes the leadership and organizational skills of a key union leader and offers a promotion or a plum assignment. Your job is to plan for that turnover. The moment you take over as president of your union, start thinking about who a good successor would be. Consider employees who have five to ten years on the job. Would they be good board members? Union executives? If so, reach out to them and bring them on board.

If you've been around for a while, you'll identify the truth in these ten basic premises. If you're just getting into it, keep your eyes and ears open, and do the job for the right reasons. And if you've got a personal agenda against an employer, get out now because over time your own members will see right through you.

CHAPTER 2

CONSTITUTIONS AND BYLAWS

Anything built to last needs a strong foundation. Whatever it was that motivated you to the task of building a union had to be formidable enough to force some unity of thought and purpose. Bottom line, you can't deal with an outside threat unless you have your own house in order. Let's get to building…

The most important document your union has, more important than even your collective bargaining agreement, is your constitution or bylaws. Let's start by getting the nomenclature down. Typically, governmental bodies have constitutions as their organizing documents, where businesses have bylaws. However, public sector labor organizations love to use the name "constitution" to apply to a document that is in fact nothing more than corporate bylaws. Some even call the document a "constitution and bylaws." Some unions have constitutions but no bylaws, and vice versa.

In this book, I'll use the term "bylaws" to describe the basic organizing document for your labor union. A good definition of a set of bylaws is: "The rules and regulations enacted by an association or a corporation to provide a framework for its operation and management. Bylaws may specify the qualifications, rights, and liabilities of membership, and the powers, duties, and grounds for the dissolution of an organization."[1] In theory, your bylaws are written on a blank slate, and you're free to fill them in to meet the needs of your organization. In practice, there may be external constraints on your bylaws. For example, locals of the International Association of Fire Fighters must have bylaws that do not contradict those of the International.[2] Along similar lines, the free speech guarantees of the federal constitution may dictate how the fair share provisions in your bylaws must be written.

In general, though, you have tremendous latitude in making the policy choices that will become your bylaws. Your bylaws can best be described as the synergistic catalogue of core rules that gives your organization its character and sense of self. The bylaws is a living, changeable document subject to amendment by a predetermined percentage vote of the membership.

Your bylaws define the organizational structure of the union, and set the specific duties of officers, election and recall procedures, and meeting protocols, and describe processes such as committee appointments and sanctioning of members. The bylaws specify membership eligibility, and may differentiate fair share and associate members from the general membership. While it is important that your bylaws are a legally-enforceable contract with your membership, it is even more important that your bylaws are a set of promises that you and others in your leadership have made to your membership as to how your organization will be run. Make sure you know what those promises are, and abide by them.

DEFINING SOME TERMS

Let's start with "Executive Board." That's a term that is unfortunately used in different ways by different labor unions. Some unions use the term to apply only to the union's officers. Other unions use the term to apply to the entire governing body of the organization. I'll use the latter approach in this book, and will use "officers" to describe the collection of the president, secretary, treasurer, and vice-president.

Let's also talk about the word "union." There is a bewildering variety of names used to describe public safety labor unions. Off the top of my head I can point to the Miami *Association* of Firefighters, the Police Officers *Federation* of Minneapolis, the Los Angeles Police Protective *League*, the Seattle Police Officers *Guild*, the Rochester Police Locust *Club*, the Fairfax *Coalition* of Police, and the Chicago Firefighters *Union*. In this book, I'll lump all of these names together, and will be using the term "union" to describe a labor organization with collective bargaining rights.

Interpretations Of The Bylaws

One of the most important provisions in your bylaws should be a statement as to who has the authority to interpret and apply the bylaws. That function should rest with your Executive Board. From my perspective, the Executive Board's interpretation of the bylaws should be final and binding. If you take the route of allowing the general membership to reverse a Board interpretation, you should make sure that the process is lined out in the bylaws, and calls for an informed general membership vote.

Amending The Bylaws

As previously discussed, a public safety labor union's bylaws must be a dynamic reflection of the rules that the membership, by agreement, is willing to adhere to for running the organization. The changes inherent in the nature of labor issues, the personality of the workforce, or simply the technological advances in the workplace all require that the membership be able to modify your bylaws. But how? Like all union elections, a referendum on changes to the bylaws must be handled in a manner above reproach and with constant credible oversight so that the changes that are implemented cannot be viewed as anything but reflective of the will of the membership.

The Threshold: A Majority Verses A Supermajority. At first, anyone with a modicum of historical perspective or, for that matter, anyone who sat through a junior high school citizenship class, will tell you that nothing short of a supermajority is appropriate for the modification of so important a document as bylaws. Maybe. Here's the catch. If there is a perceived need to modify the bylaws by the majority of the organization's membership, you can go on forever with a bylaw badly in need of change held hostage by a minority within the union. Here is a short war story that will illustrate my point:

In Anchorage, because of the community's location, most union members need to fly to the "Lower Forty-Eight" when dealing with family emergencies, since most of our members came to Alaska from other places. By the time an employee buys plane tickets and makes his or her way to the traditional family home or the location of the family emergency, quite a bit of money can be expended. Once upon a time, a group of well-meaning members in Anchorage decided that the union should have a role in shouldering some of the expense as a gesture of solidarity and support for the bereaved member. The resulting bylaw read as follows:

> "All Association contributions shall be made under one of the following categories:

> G. Bereavement: An untimely death in an association member's immediate family. The maximum contribution shall be $500.00."

What a magnanimous organization! We were all so smugly proud of ourselves that we took little notice that our action would have made Dr. Frankenstein proud. You see, not long after the bylaw went into effect, there seemed to be a rash of death and dying throughout the "Lower Forty-Eight." Did the Center for Disease Control fail to advise us of an epidemic of Biblical proportions? No. What did happen was that our well-informed members turned to the collective bargaining agreement language that addressed funeral leave, and they learned that during contract negotiations, we adeptly got the Municipality to identify the term "immediate family" when used in the context of funeral leave. According to the contract:

> "Immediate family shall be defined as spouse, son, daughter, mother, father, sister, brother, grandmother, grandfather, grandchild, mother-in-law, father-in-law, brother-in-law, sister-in-law, daughter-in-law, son-in-law, step-father, step-mother, step-son, or step-daughter, or any other family members permanently residing with the employee…"

So, the Executive Board at first felt compelled to give everyone who claimed the bereavement contribution the maximum allowable $500.00 without debate. Then, the pandemic of death from the "Lower Forty-Eight" hit…or possibly the word got out. Anyway, after voting down requests for backdated contributions for deaths that occurred before the bylaws change was initiated, the Executive Board could not bring itself to give anyone less than the $500.00 maximum allowable contribution because it could not put a value on one person's alleged need in the hour of grief versus that of another. So every time there was a death in the family, in state or out of state, the union rubber stamped the decision and cut a check for $500.00. It especially hurt when we had two employees who were married, and were compensated twice for the same death. Many of us felt like we were paying out bounties on relatives. After tens of thousands of dollars paid out over five years, our treasurer had enough and, with the help of our attorney, drafted a bylaws change that would end the madness.

Then came the vote. An overwhelming majority voted to do away with the bereavement provision. The only problem was that the vote fell just short of the supermajority needed as described by another bylaw in our Constitution which very clearly stated:

> "Proposed amendments to this bylaws must be read at a regular or special general meeting of the Association. This bylaws may be amended by two-thirds of the members voting in the election. Written balloting subsequent to the meeting at which the amendments were read shall be required in elections to amend this bylaws. Such balloting shall be completed within two weeks of the meeting."

So, there we were. Most members saw that the bereavement provisions were creating an unforeseen liability for the Association and it was in the union's best interest to change the bylaw. But, there is always a minority who will vote with their guts, or their wallet, or just because they think they should vote without taking the time to become fully informed on the issue. It was this minority that held the union hostage to a well-intended, yet poorly thought out bylaw. How did the union get out of this box? Well, the next thing the Executive Board referred to the membership was a proposal to end the supermajority requirement for constitutional amendments, and allow a majority vote to change the constitution. THAT amendment passed by a supermajority. Then, the Executive Board sent back to the membership a proposal to end the bereavement provisions, which passed by the simple majority now required for constitutional amendments.

To avoid getting stuck in the same predicament, I recommend that a simple majority of those voting be enough to amend your bylaws.

How Amendments Can Be Proposed. Amendments to the bylaws can be proposed in two ways: directly from the membership or from the Executive Board. The same review/ratification process should be used without regard to the origins of the proposal.

The bylaws should set up a review process for proposed amendments before those amendments are submitted to the membership for vote. I like to see the proposal go to the Bylaws Committee. The committee will meet with whoever is proposing the change, and potentially could suggest different wording for the proposal. The full Executive Board should then weigh in, voting on what position it will be taking on the proposal. As a last step, proposed constitutional changes should be referred to the union lawyer for review.

Then, in terms of voting on the proposed change, I recommend that all votes on constitutional changes be handled by written ballot. Here's some sample language:

> "Proposed amendments to this Constitution must be read at two scheduled, consecutive regular or special general membership meetings of the Association. These bylaws may be amended by a majority of the members voting in the election. Written balloting subsequent to the final meeting at which the amendments were read shall be required in elections to amend these bylaws. Such balloting shall be completed within two (2) weeks of the meeting."

Note that there is a necessity of two scheduled consecutive meetings for readings of the proposed changes. Two meetings allow for thorough discussion and the flexibility to schedule a debate following the second reading at the second meeting. The time limitation for balloting provides ample opportunity to get the word out about the changes, while precluding the option of a floor vote. Floor votes on bylaws changes should be avoided at all costs because they can be manipulated by "stacking" the meeting and not getting a true picture of the wishes of the general membership.

WHO ARE THE MEMBERS OF YOUR UNION?

Membership in police and fire unions is highly regulated by state statutes. These are continually subject to the review and exploitation of politicians.[3] The law that controls your bargaining will have articulated what kind of union "shop" is allowed. There are three possibilities. Closed shops, which mandate union membership, are illegal for public sector employees. Open shops allow employees to freely choose to join or not to join the union representing the bargaining unit. Typically, a union in an open shop environment has an obligation to represent all bargaining unit members, whether they choose to join the union or not. Agency shops, which are more the norm for public safety employees, require that a designated bargaining unit represent the interests of all bargaining unit members, but allow for "fair share" provisions. Fair share members, those who choose to not join the union, must pay for their fair share of the costs of negotiating and administering the collective bargaining agreement.

With that backdrop, here's a summary of the different possibilities for membership status, and a union's rights and responsibilities with respect to each.

Regular Members. These are the full or part-time permanent employees who have elected to join the union. Regular members pay the full dues as determined by the bylaws, have a right to vote in all union elections, and can run for and hold elected office within the union.

Fair Share Members. If a member of a bargaining unit refuses to join your union, there is nothing you can do about it. However, many state collective bargaining laws allow "fair share" membership, where non-members can (and should) be assessed the fair share of the cost of negotiating or maintaining the collective bargaining agreement from which the individual derives a benefit. The Supreme Court has given clear guidance as to how to determine what can be charged against fair share members, and has further provided strict guidance on how the fair share funds are utilized.[4] In essence, the Executive Board must determine the individual's fair share of the costs of negotiating and maintaining the collective bargaining agreement. This can occur only after an independent auditor has examined the union's detailed budget for the year.

The accounting must separate and detail the funds used for ideological and non-contract-related purposes as opposed to those strictly considered for bargaining and maintenance of the contract. Funds that are neither clearly for ideological purposes nor for negotiating or administering the contract, must be categorized and placed in escrow. The funds identified for negotiating, maintaining, and administering the contract may be used immediately by the union. The amount in escrow can only be used after fair share members have had an opportunity to register their objections through an approved appeal process.

Here's an example of the sort of accounting a union should make available to fair share members:

Account	Description	Amount	Chargeable
105	Contract Printing	$453	Yes
107	Arbitration Fees	$10,092	Yes
114	Attorney Fees	$98,209	Yes
116	Annual Picnic	$5,029	No
118	Political Contributions	$409	No
204	Office Manager Salary	$35,204	Yes
310	Rent	$5,984	Yes
	Total	$155,380	
	Total Chargeable	$149,942	
	Percentage Chargeable	96.5%	
	Regular Dues	$92.50	
	Fair Share (96.5%)	$89.26	

Your bylaws should describe the process by which the fair share members are provided a copy of the budget along with an explanation of the fair share assessment that is to be deducted from their paychecks, and a clear description of the bylaw outlining the procedure to register an objection to the amount deducted, including reasonable and articulated timelines. Your bylaws must provide that disputes over fair share assessments be resolved by an arbitrator, and that the arbitrator's decision will be binding on the union and the member. The union must bear the cost of the arbitration.[5]

Your union cannot discriminate against someone because of his or her fair share status. In other words, you cannot consider fair share status in making the decision as to whether to represent an individual. However, you can exclude fair share members from participating in the internal processes of the union, and from receiving any of the benefits for which they do not pay. For example, fair share members need not be allowed to vote in union elections, including elections for Executive Board members and contract ratification elections. Because they do not pay for them, fair share members need not receive non-bargaining benefits such as the right to attend the union picnic, disability insurance the union may offer, or even to receive flowers in the hospital should they get sick.

Associate Members. An associate member is someone who is not a member of your collective bargaining unit, but is still interested in joining your organization in some capacity. The most common associate members are retirees. Some unions even allow members of the public to become associate members. The idea behind allowing associate members is two-fold. Associate members help build your community of interest, and the dues they pay also add a bit to the union's coffers.

While some unions do not allow associate members, I like having them. Associate members with a vested interest in the success of the police or fire union can be invaluable resources for highly visible public relations events, charitable endeavors, public education, and political action that are beneficial to the union. If you're going to have associate members, you absolutely must line out what their rights are (or more appropriately, what their rights aren't) in your bylaws. In no case should associate members be allowed to vote, run for union office, or attend any meetings in which sensitive information is discussed.

Religious Objectors. State collective bargaining laws that allow fair share membership almost always allow an exception for those holding *bona fide* religious beliefs that have as one of their tenets non-membership in a labor organization. So-called religious objectors are usually required to pay an amount equivalent to union dues to a non-religious charity mutually agreeable to the objector and the union. Note that I used "*bona fide*" to describe the religious beliefs that are necessary to trigger religious objector status. We're not talking about the First Church of Elvis here. Religious objector cases are few and far between, and often involve Jehovah's Witnesses.

NOTES

1 *West's Encyclopedia of American Law*, edition 2. Copyright 2008 The Gale Group, Inc.

2 http://www.affi-iaff.org/docs/IAFFConstandbylaws.pdf; http://www.iaff4173.com/Union%20Documents/bylaws%20NEW%20LAKELAND%20VERSION.pdf.

3 While politicians can be the greatest threat to a fair organizing and bargaining process, those who become educated and nurtured can prove the greatest defenders of police and fire unions. This will be discussed later in Chapter 13, "Political Activity and Using the Media."

4 There is a three-part test that determines whether the costs of certain activities can be charged against fair share members: Whether the activities are germane to collective bargaining activities; whether the activities are justified by the government's vital policy interests in labor peace and avoiding "free riders"; and whether the activities do not significantly add to the burdening of free speech that is inherent in the allowance of an agency shop. Will Aitchison's assessment of procedures that account for the use of fair share funds include (1) an obligation to provide adequate explanation of the basis for the fee; (2) the provision of a reasonably prompt opportunity to challenge the amount of the fee before an impartial arbitrator, and (3) the establishment of an escrow for the amounts reasonably in dispute while such challenges are pending. Will Aitchison, *The Rights Of Law Enforcement Officers, 6th Edition*, LRIS, (2009) p. 82.

5 *See* Appendix A, "A Model Constitution," Article III, Section 5 for sample language and process of appeals dealing with fair share members.

CHAPTER 3

UNION OFFICERS

The union's bylaws should clearly lay out the structure for authority within the union. These bylaws must make it clear who runs the day-to-day business of the union, who sets the philosophical direction for the union, and who has the authority to decide the issues pertaining to the limitation or expansion of the union's duty of fair representation. There should be a clear differentiation between the executive, legislative, and administrative functions within the organizational structure.

Who should run the union is a hotly-debated topic among police and fire employees, who for the most part have been chosen for their public safety jobs as a result of their propensity to be individual thinkers, apt at quick decision making and taking action. While these traits are dream ingredients for activist organizations once a direction is determined, these very same characteristics make it difficult for dues-paying members to relinquish control of their labor destinies to others of no less ardent opinions.

That said, no amount of words on any amount of paper will provide instant credibility to any authority within the union unless it is developed and nurtured by those empowered on paper. Police officers and firefighters are as demanding a bunch as you'll ever meet, and when you mix in a smattering of dispatchers, clerks and other support staff who might be included in the bargaining unit, you have a volatile combination of potentially divisive interests and bad feelings. The leaders of successful public safety unions must be flexible, fair, principled, and at times, just as hard-headed as their constituents. How this leadership is organized and structured in executive, legislative, and administrative realms is key to the effectiveness and survival of the police or fire union.

Executive Functions. The executive functions of the union are shared by the four (sometimes five) elected executive officers. These executive positions are president, vice-president, secretary, treasurer, and sometimes, sergeant-at-arms. What follows is a suggested breakdown of the duties for each executive position, duties that should be clearly described in the union's bylaws.

President. The president is the chief executive officer of the union, and ensures that all business is conducted in accordance with the union's bylaws and the policy decisions of the Executive Board and the general membership. Once the president is elected, this lucky individual inherits a laundry list of non-delegable duties. Although he can delegate the execution of certain duties, subject to the predetermined limitations set forth elsewhere in the bylaws, responsibility remains his alone. The president should be an *ex-officio*[1] member of all committees, call for regular and special meetings, preside at general membership meetings, and have the right to vote as a tie-breaker in Executive Board and general membership meetings. Typically, the president has the authority to appoint or remove shop stewards and members of committees. Generally, the president must obtain Executive Board approval before making decisions such as procuring office space for the union, and engaging professional and technical services such as legal counsel, labor representation, accounting, and other services.

The president should be an ex-officio member of all committees.

One responsibility usually given to the president is that of negotiating and signing contracts on behalf of the union. Public safety unions enter into a variety of contracts. Probably the most important of these are the agreements with professionals such as attorneys and CPAs who provide services to the union. Other contracts include everything from internet service contracts to janitorial services. The union's bylaws should call for the president to be able to conditionally negotiate contracts, but should retain for the Executive Board the right to approve contracts before they are signed.

Though certain of the president's responsibilities cannot be delegated, the execution of these responsibilities can be delegated if the delegation is not prohibited by the union's bylaws. For example, it is not unusual for bylaws to make the president a member of every committee. That does not mean that the president cannot delegate to another the president's position on a particular committee.

The president's term of office should ideally be two years, and in no circumstances should exceed three years. This allows the opportunity for fresh blood to at least be given the opportunity to run for the presidency. You can make arguments on both sides of the question of whether the president's and vice-president's terms should be staggered in alternate years. The case for staggering is that if the president is defeated and a new president elected, having the vice president remain in office provides valuable continuity and stability for the organization. The argument against staggering is that individuals should be allowed to run for the two top positions in the union. Having seen the disruption that occurs when a whole slate of incumbents is defeated, I favor staggering.

The bylaws should provide for a period of time, ideally six months in length, when an outgoing president assists the incoming president. After this period of time, the outgoing president should assume a non-voting seat on the Executive Board for one year. This seat on the Executive Board is designed to provide the outgoing president with all the duties, responsibilities, and benefits of any Executive Board member except actually voting on policy decisions. Even when the most bitter of election campaigns is waged, this type of bylaw provision within the Constitution ameliorates the impact of leadership transition on the bargaining unit.

Vice-President. Vice President Dan Quayle once said, "One word sums up probably the responsibility of any vice-president, and that one word is 'to be prepared'." The vice-president assists the president and carries out all the delegated duties of the president when the president is absent or there is a vacancy in the office of the president. The vice-president can and should be instrumental in coordinating the internal affairs of the union, affording the president time to deal with external issues such as lobbying and educating politicians and elected or appointed bodies, and interacting with the police or fire administrations in the interests of the union. Such internal coordinating efforts can include shop steward assignment, education, and the monitoring of grievances. As stated before, the elections for vice-president should be staggered with that of the president.

Secretary. The union's secretary is primarily responsible for keeping the union's records. This means the responsibility for taking correct and impartial minutes of the proceedings at each meeting of the Executive Board and the general membership, maintaining collective bargaining notes, balloting results, grievance files, and other records of the union.

If your union chooses to maintain electronic records, it is imperative to ensure that there are appropriate measures in place for the backup and security of those records. The secretary and the president should be earmarked for this responsibility. Off-site backup is a must; no less than once a week, the union's electronic files should be backed up off-site. This may mean simply copying the files to a flash drive or setting up an automatic upload from the union's computers to a backup site on the Internet. For larger unions, there are companies with secure servers and the appropriate liability insurance to organize and maintain backup copies of electronic files.

The minutes of formal meetings must be preserved and are subject to inspection by the general membership at all times. As a rule, minutes of meetings are posted and distributed to the membership immediately upon approval of the draft minutes by the Executive Board. Once approved and posted, the minutes of meetings are kept on file for the life of the union. Minutes of executive sessions of the Executive Board should be separately maintained from minutes of regular Executive Board meetings, and access to minutes of executive sessions should only be available to current Executive Board members.

If the union is sued, the union's minutes are often placed into evidence and used as the basis for questioning of Executive Board members and union officers regarding decisions made in the past. This possibility is reason enough that Executive Board and general membership meetings should not be electronically recorded and verbatim minutes made of the recordings. Comments made during a heated discussion of an issue might not translate the intent of the statement when pulled out of context and twisted to meet the needs of an opposing attorney. Moreover, electronic recording of meetings tends to stifle the nature of discussions and tends to make individuals not only wary of their comments, and may actually motivate certain Board members to "play to the tape." Bottom line: Do not record any meetings or discussions pertaining to the internal business of the union.

> *Do not record any meetings or discussions pertaining to the internal business of the union.*

The secretary should oversee the activities of the elections and balloting committee. Ballots should be kept until the challenge period and challenge process outlined in the bylaws is met.[2] The secretary is then responsible for certifying and posting the ballot results. A record of the outcome of each ballot issue or election should be kept on file for the life of the union.

One of the most important responsibilities of the union secretary is that of tracking grievances[3] and ensuring adherence to the time parameters outlined in the contract agreement. The secretary must construct and maintain an updated file for each grievance, ensure shop stewards are working their assigned grievances through the grievance process, arrange for and coordinate witnesses for arbitration, and archive every resolved file and arbitrator's decision for future reference.

The secretary should also be in charge of the union's "reminder system" for processing grievances, described in more detail in Chapter 9.

Even unions that do a good job regarding the duty of fair representation of their members will not avoid lawsuits. Many times an antagonistic administration will refuse to process a grievance to arbitration, or a disgruntled member will feel that he or she did not get "their dues worth" and file suit against the union. When these situations occur, it is the secretary who usually saves the day with factual filing and organized record keeping.

The election of the secretary should be staggered with that of the treasurer, and coincide with that of the vice-president.

Treasurer. Taking nothing away from the hard working union secretary, the treasurer's position is arguably the most underrated, thankless, and important job in the police or fire union. Hardly ever does anyone run for this position unless gently coerced by someone who is already in office.

As the chief financial officer of the union, the treasurer is responsible for the receipt and deposit of union funds into accounts or investments in the union's name. While the types of accounts or investments chosen by the union are a matter of policy for the Executive Board, it is the treasurer who shepherds the funds and must be able to articulate the status of the investments and the nature of the expenditures regularly to the Executive Board and the general membership. The treasurer is the primary point of contact for all financial entities with which the union contracts, including investment advisors, accounting staff, banks, and auditors.

Your bylaws should specifically lay out the treasurer's duties, and should also set forth parameters that provide for the tracking and accountability of the treasurer's actions. These parameters should include a schedule for audits of the union's books,[4] the presentation of monthly reports to the Executive Board, and quarterly reports to the general membership. In this day and age, there is no reason why your treasurer should be doing the union's books by hand. There are any number of good, relatively simple bookkeeping programs out there – Quickbooks, Simply Accounting, Peachtree, Sage Business Vision, and Microsoft Small Business Accounting are the most popular – and the first thing a new treasurer should do is learn how to use whichever of these programs the union has purchased.

One of the most effective safeguards of union monies is that the bylaws mandate that all withdrawals of funds deposited in union accounts or investments require two signatures. The two signatures should be officers of the union, one of whom should always be the treasurer, if available.

The union treasurer is also the custodian of all union properties. The bylaws should specify that an inventory of the union's property should take place each time a new treasurer is elected. The election of the treasurer should coincide with that of the president, and be staggered with that of the secretary.

Sergeant at Arms. Some bylaws still call for the office of Sergeant at Arms. The sergeant at arms typically has only one function – maintaining order at union meetings. In modern public safety organizations, this role is usually assumed by the president, or in case of a serious problem, by the burliest member of the Executive Board.

Full-Time Officers. There comes a stage at which a labor organization has grown enough to require full-time officers. What is that level? I'd suggest that when you hit 500 members, the work of the union has grown to the point that you need a full-time president. Roughly with each additional multiple of 500 members, you should consider adding another full-time union officer.

When you hit 500 members, the work of the union has grown to the point that you need a full-time president.

To have full-time union officials, the collective bargaining agreement must call for the officials to be released from their normal jobs. In the best of all worlds, the release would be with full pay and benefits. Some employers agree to full-time release, recognizing that they too benefit in a variety of ways from having a full-time union officer, whether it be through the prevention of grievances or through the facilitation of communication. More commonly, employers insist that unions repay some portion of the wage and benefit costs for union officers on release time. In some cases, the repayment takes the form of a union leave bank, where union members contribute a portion of their accrued leave to the "purchase" of the release time.

If you have full-time union officials, there are some details you need to take care of. Should the union official track his time? Should he receive overtime if he works more than 40 hours in a week? Should the union official strictly account for vacation and sick leave usage? All of these involve policy considerations for the union, and the rules as to how they are treated should be included in the bylaws.

Compensation for Officers. There is great debate over whether union officers and board members should be compensated and, if so, how much. The compensation for union officials is all over the map. Some unions pay their officials nothing extra. Some wait until the end of the year and then rebate the dues the union official paid over the course of the year. Some pay a supplement equivalent to a percentage of the union official's normal salary, and others pay a supplemental flat fee. From my perspective, union officials should receive *something* for the hundreds of hours they devote to the union; otherwise, you'll be excluding some good people who would otherwise seek union office. Setting that supplemental amount as a percentage of salary makes the most sense, if only because a percentage-based supplement need not be revisited every year and thus avoids the inevitable debates on the "right" amount of compensation.

NOTES

[1] "*Ex officio*" is a Latin term meaning "by virtue of office or position." *Ex-officio* members of boards and committees, therefore, are persons who are members by virtue of some other office or position that they hold. For example, if the bylaws of an organization provide for a Committee on Finance consisting of the treasurer and three other members appointed by the president, the treasurer is said to be an *ex-officio* member of the finance committee, since he or she is automatically a member of that committee by virtue of the fact that he or she holds the office of treasurer.

[2] See the example of bylaws for balloting and challenges, Article V, Section 8 in the "Model Constitution" in Appendix A.

[3] An example of a grievance filing form is found in Appendix B.

[4] See Chapter 12, "Finances and Fundraisers."

CHAPTER 4

THE EXECUTIVE BOARD

As the legislative branch of the union, the Executive Board possesses all the legislative and policy-making authority of the union, except the authority to amend the bylaws. The Board also makes binding interpretations of the positions the union will take on the meaning of contract language, and creates committees whose members are usually subject to appointment by the president. Only votes of the general membership can reverse determinations made by the Executive Board.

The structure of the Executive Board, the election process, the length of members' terms, and recall procedures should be clearly addressed in the bylaws. A union's bylaws should provide flexibility for the Executive Board in its decision making. I recommend a bylaw that grants the Board the right to exercise discretion on a particular case or issue, and provides that the exercise of discretion does not constitute a binding past practice.

Regarding the representational structure of the Board, there has been much debate and experimentation as to how best ensure fair representation of the general membership. Many smaller police and fire unions, blessed with limited diversification in the job classifications held by the general membership and the resultant focused community of interest that engenders, opt for at-large Board members. The election of at-large Board members is a straightforward, clean, and simple procedure with available Board seats going to the highest vote-getters. The drawback to this method inevitably is that minority members, such as detectives, non-sworn clerks, or dispatchers, sometimes feel that they are under-represented.

The other structure for an Executive Board is a unit or job-specific representation. This can vary from a certain number of seats specifically designated to be filled by a group of members from a specific job classification, such as "two seats shall be filled by detectives," or "non-sworn members shall secure 20 percent representation on the Board at all times," to the entire board (except officers) being selected on a unit-specific basis. While these structures might successfully address the potential disenfranchisement of minority members, I think they're ill advised. They can exacerbate problems in a large and diverse bargaining unit. They tend to foster provincialism within the Executive Board, where Board members are supposed to act along lines that are beneficial to the overall union. Of course, as unions get larger – over 500 members, for example – unit or job-specific representation becomes necessary to ensure that all employees have some representation on the Executive Board.

The size of Executive Boards often varies proportionally to the size of the union. There is a level, though, beyond which Executive Boards should not grow. C. Northcote Parkinson, probably the foremost scholar on bureaucracies, once said, "Deliberative bodies become decreasingly effective after they pass five to eight members." A limitation like this may be difficult to achieve with even a mid-sized public safety union, particularly with a variety of constituencies all feeling underrepresented. However, the closer you can come to eight members, the better, and heaven forbid, don't have more than 15 board members. Board meetings will become nothing but endless talk sessions.

As the legislative branch of the union, the Executive Board possesses all the legislative and policy-making authority of the union, except the authority to amend the bylaws.

Deliberative bodies become decreasingly effective after they pass five to eight members.

The bylaws should specify the quorum for purposes of conducting business. Robert's Rules suggest that the quorum "should approximate the largest number that can be depended on to attend any meeting except in very bad weather or other extremely unfavorable conditions." I like a bit clearer rule – if 50 percent of Board members are present, you've got a quorum. If there's no quorum, the Board cannot take official action on any issue. If you start an Executive Board meeting with a quorum, and during the course of the meeting you lose your quorum, business can't continue to be transacted. This is called the problem of the "disappearing quorum."

Preparing for Board Meetings. A productive Executive Board meeting requires advance planning, mostly on the part of the president. No less than a week before the meeting, the president should prepare and circulate an agenda. In putting together the draft, the president should consult the draft minutes of the prior meeting to see if any items need further work, and should also add to the agenda any issues that have arisen since the meeting that require Executive Board discussion. The president should assign starting times for all agenda items; depending upon the Board's ability to stay on schedule, it may be necessary to also assign ending times for each discussion.

No less than a week before the meeting, the president should prepare and circulate an agenda.

The president should circulate the agenda to all Board members along with electronic versions of any materials the Board will be considering on agenda items. In the circulation letter, the president should ask for suggestions as to changes in the agenda. Now for the hard part. Executive Board members actually have to read the agenda and attachments before the meeting. Nothing brings an Executive Board meeting to a dead halt more quickly than having to stop while Board members catch up on reading they should have done before the meeting.

If the Executive Board will be considering any grievances at the upcoming meeting, the president should notify each grievant in writing as to the time their grievance will be considered. As described in Chapter 9, each grievant should be invited to make a presentation to the Executive Board.

Consent Agendas For Executive Board Meetings. It's surprising how few public safety unions use consent agendas. Consent agendas can cut significant amounts of time from Executive Board meetings, and are an efficient way of running a meeting.

Here's how a consent agenda works. In constructing the agenda, the president collects all non-controversial issues into a single agenda item. A sample consent agenda could look something like this:

CONSENT AGENDA

Item 1. Donate $100 to Memorial Fund.

Item 2. Donate $50 to American Cancer Society.

Item 3. Accept reports from Bylaws and Public Relations Committees.

Item 4. Approve purchase of new printer for $224.

When the Executive Board meets, one of the first items for consideration will be the consent agenda. A motion will be made and seconded to approve the consent agenda. Each Board member will then have the opportunity to remove particular items from the consent agenda. If an item is removed, it becomes a separate agenda item. All items left on the consent agenda are then voted on as a group, and are inevitably approved. Not only do you avoid multiple votes, but you greatly reduce the need for unnecessary discussion of relatively unimportant agenda items.

Voting At Executive Board Meetings. It is somewhat surprising, but many bylaws do not specify how many Executive Board members must vote for a motion in order for it to pass. Most public safety unions have adopted the practice that a majority of the Executive Board members present at the meeting (not the Executive Board as a whole) is necessary for any motion to carry. I recommend you put this standard in your bylaws.

Communication With The Executive Board And The General Membership Between Meetings. With almost every union member having a personal e-mail account, there's no reason not to give periodic updates between meetings to the Executive Board and the general membership (in Chapter 18 I'll cover social media). Of course, with any "broadcast" e-mail, you should be careful of what you say, since there are few guarantees that your e-mail will not end up in the chief's hands. However, that's no reason to avoid providing general information; giving updates on when bargaining sessions are occurring; circulating arbitration, labor board, and court decisions involving the union; and providing other timely information. Make sure you use personal e-mail addresses to communicate about union issues; there are no privacy guarantees in the employer's e-mail system.

Use personal e-mail addresses to communicate about union issues; there are no privacy guarantees in the employer's e-mail system.

Executive Board Conflicts Of Interest. There are some pretty simple rules Executive Board members should follow when facing a vote that poses a potential conflict of interest. Here they are in summary form:

1. If you have a conflict of interest, get out of the room. Don't stay for the discussion of the issue and the vote, and for heaven's sake, don't participate in any discussion. The moment you feel you may face a conflict, promptly note the conflict for the minutes and recuse yourself from the discussion.

2. Recuse yourself even if there's a possibility of a conflict of interest. Will you financially benefit from your vote on an issue? Will your seniority be affected, or important working conditions you face? If your spouse and/or your significant other works for the employer, will he/she be directly impacted by the vote? If any of these are true, you've got a conflict of interest.

3. Use the "rule of necessity" sparingly. An exception to the normal rules for conflicts of interest exists, known as the "rule of necessity." Under the "rule of necessity," if so many Board members have potential or actual conflicts of interest that the Board won't have the necessary quorum for the vote, Board members with conflicts of interest can vote after recording their conflict of interest for the

minutes. If there's no real need to invoke the "rule of necessity" – for example, if the necessary number of Board members would exist if you postponed the issue until the next meeting – don't use the rule and avoid even the perception of a conflict of interest.

The Board Should Not Hire Members or Relatives. High on the list of things your Executive Board should not do is to hire members or relatives for union work. Sure, it's tempting. You know the firefighter on your rig well, and are confident he'd be the right person to do the sheetrocking needed in the union office. Or that your cousin would be great for the job of the union's paid administrative assistant. Or that one of your members is starting off in the barbecue business and would be great for the union picnic, or has become a CPA and would be interested in the union's work. Resist all of these temptations. There are too many things that can go wrong, and then what are you left with? A disaffected member and an Executive Board with a bad taste in its mouth.

Training the Board. The training and retraining of your Executive Board should be a top priority. While periodic out-of-town training is a good idea in terms of getting an infusion of new ideas and hearing more of a national perspective, don't overlook your local training opportunities. Many public safety unions use their labor lawyers to conduct an annual one-day class for Executive Board members and shop stewards on the basics of union representation. Some colleges have labor education centers that offer low-cost training in union issues, and some state labor boards hold annual public training sessions.

While you're at it, build a good library for your Board to read. There are some good basic books out there that should be in the library of any public safety union. They include at least *How Arbitration Works*, by Elkouri & Elkouri, plus *The Rights of Law Enforcement Officers* and *The Rights of Firefighters*, both by Will Aitchison.

CHAPTER 5

ELECTIONS AND BALLOTING

One of the times a public safety union is most prone to internal divisiveness and external observation is during voting. Union elections are bellwethers of the organization's philosophical direction and priorities. Smooth and credible balloting is absolutely necessary in order to insure the integrity of the process.

Union elections should be run by an elections and balloting committee. The committee has essentially two responsibilities: Making sure that all candidates for office are eligible, and conducting elections.

As part of its responsibilities, the elections and balloting committee is responsible for ensuring that only qualified members in good standing are allowed to vote, and that they vote only once. If elections are held in person, this means the committee should use a sign-off sheet listing the alphabetized names of members in good standing. As each member votes, the member should sign the sheet and list an identifying number such as a badge number or social security number. If mail ballots are used, the committee should make sure that a "two envelope" balloting system is used, where the ballot is placed inside a non-identifiable envelope that is in turn inserted into an envelope signed by the member. All committee members should be present when the envelopes are opened.

Increasingly, unions are turning to on-line voting in elections. There are a number of commercially available on-line balloting services.[1] If the union uses on-line balloting, the elections and balloting committee should oversee the conduct of the election and the performance of the on-line balloting company.

Ballot Propositions. Unions vote on many things that fall under the general heading of "ballot propositions." Perhaps the most common are proposals for constitutional changes and assessments. It's a good idea to use the same ballot form every time ballot propositions are sent to the membership. The form I like states the proposition at the top of the ballot, leaves a place for the member to vote yes or no, and then states at the bottom of the page the Executive Board's recommendation on the proposition. Here's an example of a ballot proposition:

> *Union elections should be run by an elections and balloting committee.*

Question: Should the Association amend Article 1, Section C of its Bylaws to allow retirees to become Honorary Members of the Association?

_____ Yes   _____ No

Executive Board Recommendation: On January 5, 2014, the Executive Board voted by a 7-1 margin to recommend that membership amend the Bylaws to allow retirees to become Associate Members. The Board believes that retirees will broaden the community of interest for the Association. The proposed amendment specifically states that Associate Members will have no voice or vote on any Association matter.

Candidate Elections. The bylaws should specify election dates as well as the dates on which successful candidates take office. The bylaws should specify how ballots will list candidates – usually either randomly or alphabetically. There are two lines of thought as to the threshold for winning a candidate election. Some prefer a plurality vote, where the individual receiving the most votes in an election is declared the winner. Others prefer a majority vote, where a runoff election is held between the two highest vote-getters if neither receives a majority vote in the first election. Whichever approach you follow should be specified in your bylaws.

No more than one half of the Executive Board should be elected in any one year so as to ensure the stability and the preservation of institutional memory and knowledge. To ease with transitions in office, I recommend that there be a period of ten days between the counting of the ballots and the assumption of office.

Vacancies In Office. Your bylaws should make provisions for filling vacancies in office for the remainder of unexpired terms. Most unions look at how much time is left in the member's unexpired term. If more than six months remain on the unfulfilled term, then an election would be held; if less than six months remain in the term, then the Executive Board would fill the vacancy. The bylaws of some labor unions require the Executive Board to select the next-highest vote getter in the previous election for the position; the bylaws of others allow the Executive Board the discretion to select any eligible member for the position.

Transitions After An Election. Usually, when an incumbent is unelected, the transition from the old to the new goes smoothly. But not always. I've heard accounts of a treasurer spending election night erasing his computer, including all union financial records on the computer, and of recently-unelected officers refusing to even communicate with their successors as to simple matters. Unfortunately, there's no way to prevent these sorts of things from occurring. The best you can do is to make sure you have solid procedures and back-up systems in place so that any transition-related harm to the union is only temporary.

Recalling Executive Board Members. Until your first serious problem crops up, you may not realize how much your bylaws need a provision allowing you to recall and suspend Executive Board members. The possibilities as to what can go wrong are numerous. You can have a Board member who has been stealing from the union, relating Board discussions to management, assisting someone in suing the union, or is simply not attending any meetings.

There should be two ways of initiating a recall election. The Executive Board should have the ability to call for a recall election. Do keep this in mind – the Board simply initiates the recall election. It is the union's members who actually vote in and decide the recall election. In addition to a Board-initiated recall election, your bylaws should allow a recall election to be called by a petition signed by a percentage of the membership. The recall vote, and any petition for a recall, should be among those eligible to vote for the Board member. For example, if the Board member is elected from the Traffic Division of a police department, only Traffic Division members could sign a recall petition or vote in the recall election.

Your bylaws should make provisions for filling vacancies in office for the remainder of unexpired terms.

Beyond recall, you need to have the ability to temporarily suspend Board members pending a recall election. In cases of serious misconduct where there is the very real possibility of ongoing harm to the union, the Board member must be removed from office while the recall process is unfolding. This is one of the places where I believe a supermajority vote should be required from the Board. Since suspension from office is so serious, I recommend that suspension be supported by 3/4 of the Board members voting on the issue. Of course, the member who is being considered for suspension should not vote on the suspension motion.

Contract Votes. The best procedures for contract ratification votes require at least 14 days' notice of a vote, and mandate that at least two informational meetings be held no less than one week before the vote. Some unions mandate that members have to attend an information meeting in order to vote. Though that sort of requirement is controversial, I like it. It ensures that those voting on the contract will at least have a chance to hear an explanation of the proposed contract terms.

There is a distinction between agreements that modify the contract and agreements that interpret the contract. Modifications of the contract must be voted on by the general membership. Interpretations of the contract often result from a grievance settlement short of arbitration. Contract interpretations are within the purview of the Executive Board and need not be voted on by the general membership.

There is a distinction between agreements that modify the contract and agreements that interpret the contract.

Absentee Ballots. There are two schools of thought on whether to even have absentee ballots. I like having them, particularly if your union has in-person voting. The procedures for absentee balloting should be set only in your bylaws, and in general should be the same procedures used for mail balloting.

Ballot Protests. Though it's rare, ballot protests do occur, so it's important to set up a procedure to handle them in your bylaws. I recommend that your bylaws require that any protest regarding the conduct of balloting or certain ballots be made in writing within 72 hours. Challenges should set forth the exact nature and specification of the protest, and the claim as to how the practice or ballots affected the outcome of the election.

Once a ballot challenge is received, the elections and balloting committee should hold a special meeting to hear all sides of the issue. The committee should then make a recommendation to the Executive Board, which in turn should call a special meeting to resolve the protest. The Executive Board's decision should be only subject to appeal at the next regularly-scheduled general membership meeting, with the decision by vote of the general membership being final and binding. There is no way around it – balloting challenges are messy and can rise to crisis proportions, so a very specific and irreproachable challenge procedure in the bylaws is imperative.

Votes On Political Endorsements. Political endorsements are best dealt with as the result of recommendations by the union's political action committee (PAC) to the Executive Board. Avoid debating and voting on political endorsements before the general membership. Instead, advise the members of the choices made by the PAC, the criteria on which the choices were made, and emphasize that dues money is not being used in support of any political campaigns. For more discussion on political activity, see Chapter 13.

NOTES

[1] For example, see http://www.votenet.com/.

CHAPTER 6

MEETINGS

Meetings fall in three categories: General membership, Executive Board, and emergency or special meetings of either the general membership or the Executive Board. These meetings should all follow some common procedures.

General Membership Meetings. Regularly-scheduled general membership meetings should be held at least quarterly. Because police and fire departments are 24/7 operations, there is always the chance the members working odd hours might never have the opportunity to attend a general membership meeting. This situation should be avoided because it might lead to misinformation being repeated (and believed) and eventual disenfranchisement of the members not able to attend the meetings. A good way to avoid this is to ensure that the bylaws allow the flexibility to schedule meetings on a rotating basis to accommodate as many members as often as possible.

Ideally, general membership meetings should be held in a union hall. Some unions are not so lucky as to have their own place, so they are forced to utilize some centrally-located facility capable of holding the expected number of attendees. Some state and municipal laws prohibit union meetings at the police or fire department, but some are silent on the issue, and the use of the department facility is often at the discretion of the agency head. In any case, I'm not fond of unions using department facilities, if only because of the security issue. Better that the union borrow or rent a meeting room.

The union's bylaws should provide that agendas for regularly-scheduled general membership meetings be posted for at least a week in advance of the meeting. While most bylaws provide for the agenda to be set by the president, it is prudent to encourage input from the Executive Board and the general membership prior to the posting of an agenda. The agenda items should focus on updates on budget, grievances, lawsuits, and any other timely issues of broad interest to the general membership. General membership meetings are excellent times to solicit help in filling committees and volunteers for community service projects in which the union is involved.

As mentioned in the previous discussion about Executive Boards, a quorum is the minimum number of members who must be present at a meeting for the union to transact business. In setting your quorum for general membership meetings, don't get too optimistic about attendance. I favor stating the quorum in alternative terms such as: "The quorum for a general membership meeting shall be 20 members or 10% of the membership, whichever number is lower."

In reality, a healthy police or fire union will conduct most of its business transactions at the Executive Board level, but there will always be decisions of such importance or timeliness that must be brought before the general membership. Here is where it can get a bit sticky. There is always a danger that any special interest element within the bargaining unit can stack a meeting, assuring a quorum, and ramrodding through an action that is not on the agenda and might not be in the interest of the whole association. Your bylaws should prohibit floor votes on matters of policy that are not on the agenda for the meeting. Instead of floor votes, I recommend that the bylaws allow the membership to vote to refer policy

A healthy police or fire union will conduct most of its business transactions at the Executive Board level.

matters either to the next regularly scheduled or special general membership or Executive Board meeting.

Executive Board Meetings. Since Executive Board meetings deal with the enforcement and modification of union policy and philosophy and the routine transaction of union business, they should be held at least monthly. As I've mentioned earlier, building an agenda well in advance ensures the meeting is prioritized and structured to be efficient, and gives Executive Board members an opportunity to familiarize themselves with the materials prior to the meeting.

Executive Board meetings can range from two-hour updates to multi-day affairs, depending on the content and volatility of the issues discussed. A regular monthly Executive Board meeting for an organization of about 500 members can be expected to last about six hours. This hopefully includes time for visits and discussions by the Chief or his representative, updates from each Executive Officer, and prioritized policy discussions. If the full Executive Board is a part of the grievance screening process, always leave time for the presentation by the shop steward, the employer's case, and debate within the Board regarding the merits of the grievance.

When it comes to voting on issues during the course of an Executive Board meeting, traditionally the Chair of the meeting votes only in matters of a tie. Who should chair the meeting? Generally, police and fire unions will have either the president or the vice-president chair the meeting and thus have the power and responsibility of the tie-breaking vote. My druthers are for that person to be the president, who should also personify the will of the organization to the various outside entities with which the union must deal.

Special Meetings. Special or emergency meetings are a rarity, and are usually for the purpose of contract ratification or to deal with a crisis. The bylaws should give the president the ability to call a special meeting, and as well should allow a majority of the members of the Executive Board to call a special meeting. Some constitutions even allow a special meeting to be called by a specified number of members, usually at least 10% of the membership. Special meetings should be tied to the reason for which they are called, with no action allowed on any matter not listed on the agenda for the meeting.

No one hates meetings more than cops and firefighters. The unscientific dichotomy seems to be that no one HAS more meetings than cops and firefighters. There must be an understanding that a special meeting carries with it the connotation that it is indeed "special" and worthy of the time allotted to it. A word of caution: When a special meeting is called, the organization will be abuzz with excitement and expectation. Do not erode the level of importance or the sense of timeliness of the special meetings by making such "special" meetings routine.

Minutes. Minutes should be taken of all formal meetings of the Executive Board and general membership. I recommend that the manner in which minutes should be taken be a matter of policy set by the Executive Board.

What should go in the minutes? As little as possible. Minutes are the official records of the actions of your organization, not the thinking process of its members. About the only people who will read the minutes are Board members who will vote on approving the minutes and a member who is contemplating suing you. Your minutes should give as little fodder as possible to those in the second camp.

What should go in the minutes? As little as possible.

At a minimum, and really at a maximum, the minutes should reflect only the following:

- What body is holding the meeting (for example, whether it is an Executive Board, general membership, or special meeting);

- The date, time and place that the meeting was called to order;

- Who chaired the meeting;

- Who recorded the minutes;

- Who was present at the meeting;

- Whether or not the minutes of the previous meeting were amended or approved (or both); and

- What motions were made, who seconded them, whether the motions were carried; and who voted for or against the motions.

Draft minutes should be prepared and circulated prior to the next meeting of the body holding the meeting, and the approval of the minutes is ordinarily the first order of business at the meeting. Only after the minutes are approved should they be posted. The approved minutes should be kept on file by the secretary of the union.

Some unions electronically record meetings as an aid for the preparation of minutes. Don't do this! The electronic recording of meetings tends to stifle frank discussion and presents a potential boon for subpoena-happy attorneys. In a civil action, such recordings are a treasure trove of comments that can be taken out of context and used against your organization.

Executive Sessions. By their very nature, public safety labor organizations will sometimes be dealing with sensitive personnel issues, hearing updates and strategy briefings on pending or on-going litigation, or discussing other issues of business that could reasonably result in injury to an individual's character or reputation. The bylaws should allow the Executive Board to go into executive session to consider sensitive issues.

When a motion passes to move into executive session, all observers should be excluded from the room. A new set of minutes should be started, confined just to the executive session. No substantive votes should be taken in executive session, though unions will do formal or informal straw polls in executive session. Formal votes should be taken when the regular meeting resumes. When a motion to return to regular session passes, the executive session minutes should be closed and the normal minutes resumed with a notation of the time the executive session convened and was adjourned. When executive session minutes are finalized, they should only be available to Executive Board members, and not to the general membership.

Rules of Decorum. Books – no, volumes have been written on this one little subject. It is extremely important and appropriate for a bylaw to state how business will be conducted at meetings. That said, I must come clean and tell you right up front that I am predisposed to advise against including in the bylaws a requirement that Robert's Rules, Atwood's Rules, or any other stuffy, formalized procedures be named as the sole rules under which business will be conducted. Bottom line, no one knows what's in these books, and tying your organization's operations to a set of often arcane rules simply doesn't make sense.

Let me give you a simple example. We all know what a motion to "table" means, right? If a motion to table passes, all debate on the issue is suspended. But do you know that under Robert's Rules, before the matter can be taken up again, there must be a motion to "take from the table" whatever the issue is, and that that motion must first pass? And that if there is no motion to "take from the table," any decision made by the Executive Board is technically invalid?

Business should be conducted in a business-like manner. That is all that needs to be said. If there is no mention in the bylaws as to any specific rules of order, then it becomes a policy decision for the body as to how it handles business. Our Executive Board used a bastardized version of Robert's Rules that has evolved over the years (jokingly called Rob's Rules). Any procedural problems that came up were addressed immediately by a Board member making a motion. The members then voted on the motion, and the Board decided what procedure should be used to deal with the issue. This situation came up rarely, by the way, and as opposed to wasting precious time debating procedural technicalities, we got on with business.

> *Business should be conducted in a business-like manner. That is all that needs to be said.*

CHAPTER 7

COMMITTEES

There are many reasons to have an active committee structure in your union. With an active committee system, responsibilities are shared and more members become involved. Inexperienced members gain confidence while serving on committees, and committees are able to look at issues in greater detail than could the Executive Board. Committee members also bring different perspectives to an issue, leading to creative results. Not unimportantly, the more work done by a committee, the less that needs to be done by the Executive Board and the officers.

Think of committees as hammers…they could just as easily be used to tear something down as to build something, and there is always a chance that you'll bang your thumb. That said, I have always considered committees to be useful tools for unions, and a benefit to the union's ultimate decision-making process.

Got someone who is a "sniper?" That's the guy you never see or hear from regarding any issues until you have a general membership meeting, and in the most demeaning and accusatory tone he takes you or your Executive Board to task on needs that aren't being addressed or things that aren't being accomplished. Be a "counter-sniper." Put him on a committee and task him to provide a status report at the next Executive Board meeting or general membership meeting. The issue will either be addressed, on its way to being accomplished, or the criticism will suddenly die down. You can do this…if your bylaws provide the president the authority to appoint committees. But be careful…remember the Soviets. Committees killed the Soviet Union. It's true. Probably bogged down by Boris' Rules of Order or something.

Here are some suggestions for committees that should be considered for specific mention in your bylaws. Keep in mind that the language must be clear as to whether these committees SHALL be constituted, or MAY be constituted. If it is the intent of your organization that the committees SHALL be constituted, then by all means articulate that, in detail, in your bylaws. If the intent is that the committees MAY be constituted, I lean towards keeping those specific committees out of the bylaws, with clearly articulated authority for the president to appoint committees elsewhere in the Constitution under the president's duties. Specialized skills of members can be used to best advantage.

Let's start with the five committees that I recommend SHALL be constituted:

Bylaws Committee. A bylaws committee serves two functions. First, it should periodically review your bylaws to see if any changes are needed. The committee's second role is to review all proposed changes to the bylaws, and to make recommendations on the proposals to the Executive Board. It's a good idea to have bylaws committees work with members who want to propose bylaws changes, helping the members with the best way to wordsmith the proposal.

Elections and Balloting Committee. As I've mentioned in the discussion on union elections, the elections and balloting committee is in charge of all union elections. The committee is as important as any entity within the organization, because without credible election oversight there are no credible elections, and ultimately no credible leadership or policy. The elections and balloting committee is somewhat of an unusual beast in that its membership is constantly changing. This is due to the fact that no member of the committee can be a candidate for office while serving on the committee.

Finance Committee. The finance committee is an umbrella committee that works closely with the treasurer regarding the organization's present and future financial goals and priorities. The finance committee should be made up of individuals who have an interest and knowledge in financial matters as they pertain to the financial stability and growth of the union. Your constitution should be very specific as to what duties the finance committee will undertake. A broad span, such as audit coordination, budget projection and review, fundraising, and contributions might be appropriate for a small organization of committed members. A larger organization with membership exceeding 500 would do well to break down these overall responsibilities into more than one committee, possibly a finance committee responsible for audit and budget review and recommendations, and a fundraiser and contributions committee dealing with those more specific operations.

Contributions Committee. Public safety unions are besieged with requests for contributions. Everyone from local charities to members wanting to start a softball team to members' children who are involved in a fundraising effort will have their hands out to the union. Having a contributions committee can save the Executive Board a tremendous amount of time sifting through these requests. The contributions committee can track all union contributions over the years, evaluate current requests in light of the contributions history, and make recommendations to the Board on each request. Having the report of the contributions committee presented as part of the Board's consent agenda saves even more time, eliminating the need for the Board to consider individual contributions.

> *Having a contributions committee can save the Executive Board a tremendous amount of time sifting through these requests.*

Beyond a contributions committee, it's a great idea to set contributions limits in your bylaws. Having contribution limits not only reduces the tendency of the Executive Board to overspend, but also lets your members know what they can expect if they come asking for a contribution. Here's sample language setting contribution limits:

Contributions Policy

All Association contributions shall be made under one of the following categories:

A. **Professional.** Contributions to organizations for the purpose of improving law enforcement. The amount shall be determined on a case-by-case basis by the Executive Board.

B. **Association Athletics.** Contributions to athletic teams and events organized for the benefit of Association members. The maximum contribution shall be $600 and shall not exceed $30 per involved Association member. An additional contribution of up to

$500 may be made once during any three-year period for the purchase of equipment and/or uniforms.

C. **Hospitality Rooms.** Activities organized for the purpose of entertaining Association members and/or members of other public safety agencies with the provision of food and beverage. The maximum contribution shall be $500.

D. **Youth Activities.** Contributions to activities organized for the benefit of young people such as Scouts, athletic teams and School Safety Patrol. The maximum contribution shall be $400.

E. **Gifts to Individuals.** Gifts purchased for individuals as an expression of Association appreciation. The maximum expenditure per individual gift shall be $200.

There's one other thing you might think about with respect to contributions. Likely as not, your members participate in some sort of coordinated giving program such as the United Way. Why not channel the charitable instincts of your members in a way that benefits the union? A success story along these lines is the San Diego City Firefighters, Local 145 of the International Association of Fire Fighters. Many years ago, Local 145 set up what is known as the San Diego Firefighters Community Responsibility Fund, a charitable organization under Section 501(c)(5) of the Internal Revenue Code. Now, instead of making donations to United Way, firefighters donate to the Fund, receiving the same tax deductions as would otherwise have been the case. When the Fund distributes the money to charities, the gifts are made in the name of San Diego firefighters, building goodwill throughout the community. Setting up a corporation like this is straightforward, and should be part of your public outreach effort.

Political Action Committee (PAC). I know. Cops and firefighters hate politicians. After all, aren't all politicians our buddies and supporters until…? Well, that's the point of the PAC. The PAC can't (and shouldn't) buy influence. The importance of the PAC is that, through political endorsements, the union can achieve audiences with key policy makers regarding wages, hours, working conditions, and public safety issues. Any politician alive will want the support and endorsement of a reputable and professional public safety labor organization. After all, you are the "front line" folks for your community. So take the opportunity to educate and develop relationships with the elected officials. And if you're big enough, with many ongoing issues, hire a lobbyist to monitor and report back to your Executive Board regarding the shenanigans of those whom you have chosen to support and those whom you will soon work to send back to private life. Unfortunately, I have found, over time, that one politician can often embody both descriptions simultaneously.

Getting your members to donate to the PAC is as frustrating a challenge as any you will undertake. But what is true is that politicians hold the fruits of your professional future in their goody baskets. Like it or not, you need to let

The importance of the PAC is that, through political endorsements, the union can achieve audiences with key policy makers regarding wages, hours, working conditions, and public safety issues.

them know that you are watching. I have found direct deposit allocations from members' checks, $5 to $10 per pay period, can add up. Tell your members that for the price of a mocha or two they will find that issues near and dear to their wages, hours, and working conditions will suddenly begin to get more positive attention by elected decision makers. Set up phone banks to get your membership out in force, voting for those candidates who are most aligned with your interests. Finally, the law requires that you set up a process for donations to the PAC that is separate from the mix of general membership dues.

State and local laws regulating PACs might vary in breadth and focus, but as a rule your PAC should be a separate entity from your labor organization. The Federal Election Commission refers to labor union PACs as Separate Segregated Funds (SSFs) that can only solicit contributions from individuals associated with the connected or sponsoring organization. Basically, the feds recognize that your PAC will be a political committee established and administered by your union. Don't ever mix and mingle the monies collected by and for the PAC with those compelled to be collected from your members. There must always be a bright line between the PAC and your union, and the reality is (and the law ensures) that you will have members of your union who will not be contributing members to your PAC. A good overview and a list of the appropriate forms can be obtained at www.fec.gov for federal considerations. Check your state statutes for more localized guidance if you (*and you should*) plan to have your PAC active in state and local races and issues.

OTHER COMMITTEES.

I think it is imperative to establish the five committees I've described in the preceding passages. There are some other committees that may be important to you depending upon the size and purposes of your organization.

Public Relations Committee. In a perfect world, your union has a strategic plan in which a public relations strategy is an integral part. That said, the only perfect situations that most cop and firefighter unions run into are those that are perfectly messed up. Sometimes it is an issue gone public pertaining to contract negotiations, or more regularly, it's being asked to comment on a member who, either by criminal or unscrupulous actions, has caused embarrassment to your department and to your union. In most of these situations, the union is viewed as the entity that is somehow supportive of or responsible for the bad behavior. The public doesn't get the intricacies of due process or duty of fair representation, and it becomes important to have an understandable, pertinent and consistent message crafted and articulated by a credible representative of your organization. A public relations committee, with the board's oversight, can be valuable in creating the message, gauging public sentiment, and making recommendations for not only the content, but the method of delivering the message.

For those times when the union is not on the front page or being blamed for all the ills in the world, an active public relations committee can ensure the activities pursed by the union for the public good, such as charity basketball games, Big Brother and Sister partnerships, and other community-oriented initiatives get the kind of public notice they deserve in the media and throughout the community. A public relations committee just may be what your union needs to burnish your reputation in your jurisdiction.

Depending on the traditions of your union and its relationship with your department, there might be other committees that are more appropriate to the MAY designation. Think "Cost Containment," "Employee Assistance," Employee Death," "Leave Donation," and "Thanksgiving Turkey Delivery" (we actually had one of them). Many of these, such as "Cost Containment" and "Employee Assistance," are already within the function of the more sophisticated departments, but that doesn't preclude active union representation and influence in any of them. You usually won't find a "Thanksgiving Turkey Delivery Committee" at most departments, but we found it to be a great way to engage management, make the deliveries with our police cars, and garner lots of good PR through the efforts of our Public Relations Committee. It just MAY work for you.

COMMITTEE REPORTS

Committees should report to the Executive Board at each Board meeting. Even if the report simply says "no report," having a reporting obligation acts as a spur to the committee to do its job. I like to see written committee reports presented to the Board, though I'd settle for any report at all.

COMPENSATING COMMITTEE MEMBERS

Committee members can work long and hard hours, particularly those on your PAC. Should you compensate them? Most public safety unions do not, and as long as you don't get tired of twisting arms to get committee members, I wouldn't consider compensating committee members beyond buying them lunch during committee meetings.

CHAPTER 8

THE DUTY OF FAIR REPRESENTATION

In general, a union has one duty to its members – the duty of fair representation. The things you need to know about the duty of fair representation incurred by police and fire unions can be distilled into one word… PROCESS. Only through a fair, non-discriminatory, and consistent process can a union avoid a successful lawsuit for breach of duty of fair representation. Those same fair processes will maintain the credibility of the union in the eyes of the employees, and will let the employer know that the union takes its legal responsibilities seriously.

To best understand the duty of fair representation, a quick history lesson and discussion of the core reasons it exists should shed some light onto the issue.

Only through a fair, non-discriminatory, and consistent process can a union avoid a successful lawsuit for breach of duty of fair representation.

THE ORIGINS OF THE DUTY OF FAIR REPRESENTATION.

I'll bet every book on a union's legal responsibilities written since the late 1940s has a chapter or a major heading that says "The Origin of the Duty of Fair Representation." Yeah, I know, most folks' eyes glaze over when court cases start to get referenced, but this is important stuff.

It all began with the Supreme Court's decision in *Steele v. Louisville & Nashville R.R.*, 323 U.S. 192 (1944). In retrospect, the case itself is an almost unbelievable commentary on the times, and while the decision is most important to the labor crowd, I like to think it also helped to foster a moral imperative that sowed the seeds of social change. The five short paragraphs of concurring remarks by Justice Murphy challenging the Court to deal with the constitutional issue of discrimination are worth a quick read. But I will leave the social commentary to the social scientists and historians, and I will try to focus on the pure labor issue at the heart of the decision.

During 1941, the Brotherhood of Locomotive Firemen and Enginemen (BLFE) finalized a contract agreement with the Louisville and Nashville Railroad. Under the Railway Labor Act, the BLFE was the exclusive bargaining agent for all of the firemen employed by the railroad. While the railroad employed both white and African-American firemen, the union's constitution prevented the African-American firemen from joining the BLFE. At the time of the negotiations (1940-1941), the majority of the firemen working for the railroad were white. Part of the negotiated agreement ensured that no more than 50% of the firemen at each classification of service in each seniority district could be African-American. Further, until the 50% figure was reached in each seniority district, all new runs and all new job openings had to be filled with white firemen, and no African-Americans could be hired into any seniority district that they were not already working in.

As it happened, Mr. Steele, an African-American fireman, was employed in a "passenger pool" to which one white fireman and five African-American firemen were assigned. The jobs in the pool were eventually declared vacant due to a reduction in mileage on the route. Because of the negotiated agreement, the five black firemen were replaced by five white firemen with less seniority, and Steele was reassigned to a freight route that was more arduous and paid less. He was replaced again, and put on a switch engine, an assignment even less desirable than the freight route and even less remunerative. It was about now that Steele started to get angry. Steele, with a group of firemen who were displaced and reassigned in a like manner, filed a complaint with the union. Though Steele was not permitted to be a member, you have to remember that the BLFE was the exclusive bargaining unit for the railroad's firemen. The BLFE ignored Steele and his fellow African-American employees until he filed a suit. Then he was reassigned to a passenger service slot comparable to the one in which he had been forced out of eight months prior.

What The Court Said And How It Impacts Cops And Firefighters. After the case wound its way through Alabama state courts, the United States Supreme Court had to decide the core issue – did BLFE have any obligation to Steele and his compatriots, and if so, what was the nature of that obligation? You don't have to be a detective to figure out the answer, but, take just a second to put it into the context of the times. Realize that the Supreme Court did not rule that the color bar was illegal, after all, at this time, "separate but equal" was legal. But, while the BLFE did not have to admit African-American firemen to its rank and file, the Court did insist that the union represent them since the union was the exclusive bargaining unit for the firemen at the railroad.

The Supreme Court held that the negotiated agreement was unlawful, and found that a union must represent all members of the unit, not discriminate for invidious reasons; that is, for reasons that tend to cause animosity or resentment. While the Court accepted that there will always be legitimate reasons to discriminate among different groups of workers because of skill level, seniority, or the type of work engaged in, the language in the BLFE's contract discriminated on the basis of union membership and race. The BLFE therefore had acted against the interest of a large number of firemen, who, while not permitted to join the union, were entitled to representation by the BLFE.

While unions are given great latitude in what they bargain, they cannot act discriminatorily against any group of their members.

So what is key about all this that modern cop and firefighter unions need to know? Plenty. The Court's message was that while unions are given great latitude in what they bargain, they cannot act discriminatorily against any group of their members.

The Supreme Court expanded on this notion in *Vaca v. Snipes*, 386 U.S. 171 (1967). In *Vaca*, the union member had been on leave for six months from his job at a meat packing plant for a chronic high blood pressure problem. Two physicians had cleared Vaca to return to work, but the company doctor refused to allow him to return to his job, which included heavy lifting. As a result of the company doctor's evaluation, Vaca was terminated.

The union initially accepted Vaca's grievance and processed it toward arbitration. During the course of preparing for the arbitration, the union sent Vaca to another physician, at union expense, to build its case. The fourth doctor did not agree with Vaca's doctors, and the union chose not to pursue the grievance to arbitration. Vaca sued the company and the union, specifically claiming that the union's decision to refuse to take his grievance to arbitration was *arbitrary* and *discriminatory*.

Before getting into how the Supreme Court resolved Vaca's case, think about how many times have you heard the words "arbitrary" and "discriminatory," mostly together, and sometimes in the company of capricious and in *bad faith*? All are terms of art, with very specific meanings that reflect directly on PROCESS.

Arbitrary, in the context of our labor concerns, means that a decision was made impulsively, without due regard to the reasonable impact of facts on a particular issue. An arbitrary decision is one that is so far outside a wide range of reasonableness as to be irrational. Capricious means that the decision or action follows no predictable pattern or level of reasonable expectation, usually done "on a whim."

Discriminatory has morphed over the years to mean so many things to so many people, with the definition generally subject to the user's agenda. For our purposes, this term is best used if there is an indication that the decision or action is marked by prejudice or bias against a person relative to the way other employees or classes of employees are treated.

Bad faith is a term of art that infers or actually is a fraud, deception, or an intentional neglect of legal obligations. It is not a matter of poor judgment, but rather a breach of a contractual agreement that is fostered by conscious design and intent to mislead or deceive.

Vaca's assertion that the union should have followed through with its representation of his grievance forced the Supreme Court to decide what standards applied in judging duty of fair representation claims. In a decision that held that the union did not violate Vaca's right to fair representation, the justices set forth a pretty good guide to member and union alike regarding expectations for the duty owed.

First, the Court made it clear that a union is given broad discretion in its control over the grievance process. No union member has an absolute right that a grievance be submitted to arbitration. Again, the union must process all grievances in a like manner and give all the same due consideration.

No union member has an absolute right that a grievance be submitted to arbitration.

Second, no union breaches its responsibilities under a duty of fair representation because of the union's decision that a grievance is without merit. As long as the union acted properly in its decision-making process, a court should accept the union's determination on the substantive merits of the grievance. In other words, a union can be completely wrong in its assessment of the merits of a case and *still* cannot be successfully sued provided it uses appropriate procedures to consider the claim.

Third, the Court found that a union's decision to process, withdraw, or settle a grievance should be based on the individual merits of a particular grievance, and that only if the conduct of the union is *arbitrary, discriminatory* or in *bad faith* is the duty of fair representation breached. Pretty high threshold, don't you think?

The Supreme Court also held that it is only when the duty of fair representation is breached that a grievant (as opposed to the union) should be given the opportunity to prove that an employer violated the collective bargaining agreement. This is important: Unless there is contract language to the contrary, no individual can grieve an employer for an alleged contract violation.

Courts have elaborated on *Steele* and *Vaca* many times, but the basic standards for the duty of fair representation remain essentially unchanged. Simple negligence on the part of a union is generally insufficient to find that the union has violated its duty of fair representation. However, if your union simply goes through the motions, or, as the courts call it, gives "perfunctory treatment" to a grievant, that's where the trouble lies.

Bottom line: Each grievance deserves fair and equitable consideration before the body that determines whether or not a grievance will be accepted and processed by the union.

WHERE THE DUTY OF FAIR REPRESENTATION APPLIES.

The duty of fair representation applies only to the two areas where your union is the exclusive representative for employees, in the grievance procedure and in the collective bargaining process.

The duty of fair representation applies only to the two areas where your union is the exclusive representative for employees, in the grievance procedure and in the collective bargaining process. If the union is not the *exclusive* representative for employees in a particular forum, there is no duty of fair representation. So, if someone else can represent the employee (the employee's attorney, for example), the union has no obligation to even consider acting on the employee's behalf, and no duty of fair representation exists.

Here is a list of categories where the union most likely is not the exclusive representative for employees:

Pre-disciplinary Hearings. There are all kinds of misunderstandings regarding a union's responsibilities in regard to pre-disciplinary hearings. Chances are your union or association bargained only the *procedures* to be followed at a pre-disciplinary hearing, and in no way is the exclusive representative for employees in pre-disciplinary hearings. In most places, depending on state or local law, employees can engage their own attorney during the course of a pre-disciplinary hearing. That means there is no duty of fair representation in this environment.

Civil Lawsuits. From time to time, members will come to the union and ask the union to fund a civil lawsuit the member wants to file against someone else. It may be a police officer wanting to sue a suspect who has bitten, kicked, punched and/or spit at the officer. It may be a firefighter who wants to sue his supervisor for harassment. Since the union is not the exclusive representative for employees in filing civil lawsuits, there is no duty of fair representation and the union is under no obligation to even consider assisting the member.

Criminal Defense. Employees who are charged with job-related crimes occasionally ask their unions to provide them with an attorney. Every represented employee should know, right from the get-go, that criminal defense is an area in which the union will not (and should not) venture. No court on earth will determine that a union's duty of fair representation should extend into the realm of criminal defense.

Workers' Compensation Cases. The duty of fair representation does not apply to workers' compensation claims unless the union has negotiated for a collective bargaining agreement that creates the workers' compensation rights.

Pension Claims. Pensions are not normally a part of any public sector collective bargaining agreement. Using the same logic as above, unless there is specific language regarding pensions in your collective bargaining agreement, unions should stay out of pension dispute issues.

Promotional and Other Civil Service Issues. Usually, promotional criteria and the appeal process that accompanies promotional selections and issues are excluded from a collective bargaining agreement, thereby excluding promotional issues from a union's duty of fair representation.

MEMBER AGAINST MEMBER.

The prospect of having the interest of one dues-paying member against that of another is at best an uncomfortable subject for a union to deal with, and at worst, it can border on an internal war that can irreparably damage the cohesiveness of the association. Let's try to address some of the situations you might face in regard to "family feuds" where the duty of fair representation can be applied no matter which side of the issue is involved.

Seniority Cases. Almost by definition, every seniority dispute benefits at least one union member and harms at least another. A good example of this occurred in my former department.

Our chief decided to do away with the job classification of corporal, believing that corporals and sergeants really do the same job. The chief created one new supervisor classification, into which all sergeants and corporals would be pooled, and for which he intended to pay the higher (sergeant) wage. Most of the present sergeants were actually younger employees who had spent just enough time as corporals before they put in for and received promotions to sergeant.

The chief recognized that the older, more experienced corporals were actually running the shifts. The old corporals were content, and though they didn't make the higher base salary that the younger sergeants were making, the overtime opportunities afforded them by their seniority as the younger officers "passed through" the corporal ranks on their way to sergeant was more than enough incentive to mark time as corporals. The chief turned to the union and said, "Tell me what you think the seniority of the employees in the new classification should be."

Both sergeants and corporals made their arguments to the union's executive board. The sergeants contended that the corporals had made a conscious decision to stay at that rank, while they, the sergeants, had chosen to sacrifice the seniority at corporal and move up to establish themselves as sergeants with appropriate position seniority in that classification. The corporals who had just been involuntarily promoted to sergeants argued that most of them had been on the force when many of the incumbent sergeants were still in high school, and that department seniority and not positional seniority should take precedence.

How is a union to proceed when it faces an issue like this? What the law on the duty of fair representation teaches us is that the union should listen to all sides and make its decision in a non-discriminatory fashion. And that's what our union did. It sided with the sergeants, and to be sure a bunch of corporals were very angry, but the one thing they couldn't claim is that the union breached its duty of fair representation.

Potential Conflicts Posed By The ADA. Under the Americans with Disabilities Act (ADA), the employer must "reasonably accommodate" an individual regarding his or her disability. There is an expectation under federal law that an effort at "job restructuring" and arranging "part-time and modified work hours" will be explored as part of the reasonable accommodation process. Here's the rub. What if the employer's obligation to reasonably accommodate an employee with a disability collides with its obligations under a seniority clause?

For example, let's say a police officer is a diabetic, and begins to show signs of night blindness. The officer's doctor suggests that assignment to day shift would be a reasonable accommodation. However, the collective bargaining agreement calls for shift selection by seniority, and the officer does not have enough seniority to successfully bid for day shift. What wins – the seniority clause or the ADA?

The Supreme Court has made life easier for unions, ruling that if a seniority clause is "bona fide" in the sense that it was negotiated for non-discriminatory reasons, the seniority clause will "trump" an employer's obligation to reasonably accommodate an individual with a disability.[1] The same is true if the employee is demanding an accommodation for religious beliefs (for example, no work from sundown Friday to sundown Saturday) and yet does not have the seniority to accomplish the assignment under the collective bargaining agreement.[2]

Member Against Member In Disciplinary Cases. Member against member conflicts come up in disciplinary cases from time to time, so you should be ready for them. Sometimes, one member may have witnessed the potential misconduct of a fellow employee, and may have some personal culpability herself. Remember, the employer disciplines and the union represents. It's your job to represent all members who face possible disciplinary charges.

The most troublesome member-on-member cases involve allegations of sexual, racial, or religious harassment, where both the complaining employee and the target of the investigation are members of the same union. When this occurs, a union should assign separate union representatives to each of the participants, and should erect a metaphorical wall between the representatives so that they do not communicate about the case.

Competing Interests Of Members In Negotiations. Inevitably, there will be times when competing interests at the bargaining table will result in some members realizing a benefit over other members. While this is often an unavoidable outcome in negotiations, that does not mean that the duty of fair representation has been violated. So long as the union's decision making on contract priorities was non-discriminatory, the fact that some members are helped and others are not (or perhaps even hurt) by a contract settlement does not amount to a breach of the duty of fair representation.

The fact that some members are helped and others are not (or perhaps even hurt) by a contract settlement does not amount to a breach of the duty of fair representation.

Processing Grievances To Avoid Duty Of Fair Representation Claims.

Once again, I capitalize the word PROCESS purposely to stress that there should be an established procedure that your union uses to consider grievances. This procedure, whatever it is, must be used for every grievance, every time. That does not necessarily mean that all grievances culminate in arbitration or settlement; what it does mean is that the union will use the same PROCESS to consider every grievance.

The key is consistency. Whenever an Executive Board or grievance committee hears a grievance, it should use the same procedures. And "same" means "same," no matter if the grievance is a lock-solid winner or a dead loser, no matter whether the grievant is a frequent flyer who's better at imagining grievances than actually working or is a solid citizen who's been wronged by the employer.

The procedures used by the union should be fair. That means that at a minimum, the grievant should be given the opportunity to be heard by the decision-making body of the union. The union also has a responsibility to guide the grievant through the established process – as far as the merits of the grievance take him.

In evaluating grievances, unions can take a lot of different things into consideration, including the following:

- The chances of success in arbitration.

- The cost of arbitration.

- The impact on the bargaining unit as a whole of losing the case.

- The impact on the union's collective bargaining posture.

- The union's evaluation of how the grievant will perform as a witness.

- The possibility that adverse precedent will result from the case.

There should be an established procedure that your union uses to consider grievances.

What Happens If You Are Sued?

Anyone with a map to the courthouse can file a suit. If your association has followed fair and non-discriminatory procedures, you're going to be okay in the eyes of the court or the labor board hearing the case. But if you don't have duty of fair representation insurance, then be prepared to spend thousands defending yourself against the suit. Don't count on being able to collect damages if your union is wrongly accused of a duty of fair representation violation. The real expenses coming from the duty of fair representation are the court costs and attorney fees, for which unions are inevitably not reimbursed.

Duty Of Fair Representation Insurance. Get out your checkbook. Now. This is one of those premium payments that you should write with a smile on your face. No one likes to write checks for insurance payments, but if you haven't read Appendix D yet, stop shaking your head, flip to the back of the book, and read it. Moral of that story: Even if you're right, you won't collect any damages or fees, and if you don't have Duty of Fair Representation (or Union Liability) insurance, you will pay big bucks just defending your association against discouraging and baseless lawsuits.

Duty of fair representation insurance today runs at about $15,900 per year for $1 million of coverage, with a $10,000 deductible. Pretty steep, but not so bad when you consider the possibility of combination court and attorney fees in the tens of thousands just to see a case through or to a point where the plaintiff's attorney throws in the towel. And if your union loses, remember that damages in duty of fair representation cases are compensatory only; that is, the intent is to make the individual whole, not to punish the union. This could include any back pay after the time the member brought the grievance to the union and the costs incurred by the member for pursuing the case. A sample duty of fair representation insurance policy is attached as Appendix D.

The Liability Of Union Officers For The Breach Of The Duty Of Fair Representation. Because the duty of fair representation is owed to members by the union and not individual union officers, Executive Board members cannot be held personally liable for any breach of the duty of fair representation by their union. Any liability for breach of duty of fair representation lies with the union alone.

An Employer's Liability For A Union's Breach Of The Duty Of Fair Representation. While an employer is not technically liable for a union's breach of the duty of fair representation, it may have to pay damages to an employee who successfully brings a duty of fair representation claim. What a duty of fair representation claim does is to allow the employee to directly bring the underlying contract violation claim against the employer. If the employee succeeds on that underlying claim, it is the employer, not the union, that will be responsible to make the employee whole for the losses suffered as a result of the breach. Only if the union's breach of the duty of fair representation adds to those losses (for example, by delaying how quickly the employee could claim that he was improperly discharged) will damages be apportioned between the employer and the union.

NOTES

[1] *U.S. Airways v. Barnett*, 535 U.S. 391 (2002).

[2] *Balint v. Carson City*, 180 F.3d 1047 (9th Cir. 1998).

CHAPTER 9

GRIEVANCE PROCESSING

The grievance procedure is the lifeblood of your collective bargaining agreement. Only through the grievance procedure can you effectively redress the employer's contract violations, and obtain remedies that include back pay, interest, and the equivalent of injunctions. It's your job as a union leader to make sure that grievances are filed in a timely and correct manner, processed expeditiously, and fairly considered by the union.

When processing a grievance, a union should keep the following basic tenets in mind:

- Time Limits!!! Follow them strictly, and hold the employer's feet to the fire on the times specified to respond to the grievance.

- The grievance procedure is vital to your union. It is the way you enforce your contract rights to the requirements of the agreement. Don't be lax in your use of the grievance procedure.

- Nothing about the grievance should interfere with the union's ability to represent its members. A union has the right to negotiate a settlement of a grievance with an employer, even over the objections of the grievant, as long as the settlement is in the best interests of the union as a whole.

- Unions need not process a grievance to arbitration if the prospects for success are limited.

- Time Limits!!! I know I mentioned it before, but it's worth saying twice.

What is an efficient grievance processing system that will ensure your organization's duty of fair representation responsibilities are met? There are many models to choose from. I recommend a simple system that not only ensures that the grievance is dealt with in a timely manner, but also "truth checks" the merits of any allegation.

Shop Stewards.

Your bylaws may or may not go into detail regarding shop stewards. While the determination of the number of shop stewards, and their particular benefits such as lay-off protections, might be addressed in the collective bargaining agreement, the bylaws should provide for a definition of the shop steward's selection process, role, and training. Your pool of designated shop stewards should reflect the job classifications and duties that are common to your union. Your general membership must feel that the shop stewards are empathetic with the workplace challenges encountered in your department.

The shop steward is the union's trench soldier. Oftentimes the shop steward is the first person your union member will turn to for clarification of information or will approach if they believe their contract (or civil) rights have been violated.

All the more reason the shop steward should be credible, trusted and trained. No matter what process your union uses to select a shop steward, these traits are foundational to the individual selected for the position.

Before getting into a more comprehensive discussion of the traits you want in a shop steward, a quick discussion of the process for filling the shop steward vacancies should be addressed. It really doesn't matter how your organization chooses to select shop stewards, but it is important that that selection process is understood by the general membership. The union president should have the authority to appoint the shop steward, and that appointment should be confirmed by the Executive Board. It's understood that the individual to be appointed will have already expressed an interest in the position, either through his or her own initiative (or that of their co-workers), or as the result of having been asked (or coerced…or begged) by the president. The aspect of the confirmation by the Executive Board allows the individual to be satisfactorily vetted by that body, and the ultimate responsibility for the selection is shared by the president and the Executive Board.

So, you've got your eye on someone who you think will make a good shop steward…that is, someone who can carry your union's ball after hours if need be; say, during the chaotic moments following an officer-involved shooting during a midnight shift. Is this someone you can count on to make the right choices when dealing with management? Is this someone who will be firm, fair and realistic?

First and foremost, you want a credible shop steward. The person must be a technically proficient, solid operator with street and organization credibility. A rookie rarely makes a good shop steward. A shop steward has to have the "been there, done that" swagger or bearing that will make the member actually listen to what he or she is being told. Also, the shop steward's credibility with management as an employee with a solid work history increases the potential that any points made regarding potential contract violations will actually be heard.

Union leadership must trust the shop steward. As alluded to before, this person might, under certain circumstances, be the sole embodiment of the union leadership. The trust must not only be in the form of trusting the knowledge the individual has in regard to the contract or work rules, but also there must be a strong trust in the individual that he will contact the appropriate union leadership at the right time for guidance, support and updates without going too far or acting inappropriately in his shop steward role.

Generally, people who have organizational credibility will understand that a good knowledge base is foundational to that credibility. It is a working knowledge of the contract and past practices (again, the seasoned veteran is the obvious choice here) that will make your choice an effective shop steward and a trusted agent of the union. Bottom line is the shop steward cannot fake it. They must be trained.

The shop steward cannot fake it. They must be trained.

Shop steward training must be an ongoing priority within your union. The knowledge base of contractual rights, past practices, civil rights, due process, duty of fair representation, and resource pools such as on-call attorneys, is imperative to the success of the credible, trusted and knowledgeable stable of shop stewards that will oversee the everyday implementation of your employees' rights and responsibilities. Appendix C to this book is a sample shop steward's training manual that covers each of these areas.

GRIEVANCE PROCESSING, THE PRELIMINARY STEPS.

Identify the contract violation. Even before the grievance is filed, assign a shop steward or other union representative to work with the grievant on the allegation to flesh out the exact nature of the contract violation. Most union members are not as conversant in the language and intent of their collective bargaining agreements as a trained shop steward or union official would be. The union representative should try to identify every possible contract violation. Remember, arbitrators will often refuse to consider contract articles that were not listed in the original grievance.

Sometimes, what at first blush appears to be a violation of the contract turns out to be an implementation of a management right. Remember, no collective bargaining agreement and no union can force management to manage wisely. Ultimately, the specifics of the grievance must be articulated strictly within the context of a contractual violation in order to have a chance to prevail.

> *The specifics of the grievance must be articulated strictly within the context of a contractual violation in order to have a chance to prevail.*

On other occasions, the employee may feel wronged, but there is simply no remedy through the grievance procedure. For example, if employees are covered by a statewide retirement system, a grievance procedure is likely to provide little relief for an employee who feels he or she has been given incorrect retirement information. Member-on-member gripes that do not involve contract issues are also not appropriate for grievances. It is important for a union to identify these non-contract disputes early in the process, and steer members to possible solutions other than the grievance procedure.

Have the shop steward or union representative conduct a thorough investigation. Cold, hard facts regarding the alleged grievance must be brought to light early in the process. Interview the principals. Interview witnesses. Ask hard questions, both of the grievant and of witnesses. Gather documentation. Sometimes time cards, police reports, daily activity reports, and even taped interviews are appropriate sources of information that will bring the merits of the grievance to light. Since police and fire departments are paramilitary organizations with defined chains of command, contact members of the chain of command who participated in the decision-making process that led to the alleged contract violation. Find out what their perspective is on the issue.

The union representative should also discuss the grievance with union officials. The representative should ask if there have been similar grievances in the past, and particularly if those grievances were sent to binding arbitration. If a question of contract interpretation is involved, the union representative should ask to be provided with all relevant bargaining history, including negotiations notes.

Try to resolve the pending grievance at the lowest level. Many contract violations committed by management (other than those resulting from disciplinary action) are often honest mistakes. The longer you are in the union business, the less surprised you are when you realize that supervisors and managers are generally ignorant of the provisions of collective bargaining agreements. Cops and firefighters being who they are, believe that management regularly conspires to violate contracts, when the reality is that most grievances result from a member of the chain of command making an ill-informed decision, and then being reluctant to reconsider that decision in an effort to save face. Much is to be gained if the shop steward or union rep discusses the potential grievance with the chain of command, even before a formal grievance is filed.

Prepare a Grievance Summary Form. Consistency is the hallmark of a good union grievance processing system. I recommend that with every potential grievance, the union representative complete a Grievance Summary form. The form acts as a checklist for union representatives while at the same time recording the most salient information about a grievance. See Figure 1.

> *Consistency is the hallmark of a good union grievance processing system.*

ACCEPTING OR REJECTING THE GRIEVANCE.

There are times when informal discussions about a potential grievance simply won't work. Both sides may be too philosophically, emotionally, or economically entrenched in their positions to reach resolution. It is at this point that the union needs to formally consider the merits of the grievance. In most organizations, that means filing a grievance and processing it through the preliminary steps of the grievance procedure while at the same time scheduling a meeting of the union's Executive Board or grievance committee, whichever makes decisions on whether to refer grievances to arbitration. In some organizations, grievances are not filed until after they have been accepted by the Executive Board or Grievance Committee. No matter which process you follow, there are some basic rules for writing and considering the grievance.

CONSIDERING THE GRIEVANCE.

When the grievance committee or Executive Board considers the grievance, I recommend a three-stage process.

Stage 1 – The Grievant. The grievance meeting should start off with a presentation by the grievant. The grievant can be assisted by a shop steward or can make a solo presentation, and should be given adequate notice of when the grievance meeting will occur. Sometimes grievants ask to be accompanied by their attorneys. I see no harm in this, provided the attorney isn't allowed to take over the meeting.

GRIEVANCE SUMMARY

Union Representative: _____

Grievant: _____ Job Title:_____
Home Address:_____Work phone _____
Home/cell phone _____Personal email address _____

What complaint did the grievant present?
_____
_____
_____

Date of Employer's Action: _____
Last Day To File Grievance: _____

With whom did union representative speak, and when?
_____
_____
_____
_____

Names and contact information for other witnesses: _____
_____
_____
_____

What other information may be important in the Board's consideration of this grievance?
_____
_____
_____

What contract articles are involved? _____

What is the appropriate remedy? _____
_____

Figure 1 - Grievance Summary Form

During the grievant's presentation, the union's aim should be to allow the grievant to say anything he or she wants that is relevant to the grievance. This is your member's day in court. The Executive Board or grievance committee should be respectful and considerate of the grievant, and allow the grievant as much time as necessary to present his side of the story.

Stage 2 – The Employer. The union should always invite management to make a presentation regarding the grievance. Often, the management perspective can be valuable when assessing the potential contractual breach. Sometimes the management presentation will preclude the grievance from being accepted once the entire story is heard. Also, there's a strategic advantage to hearing what management has to say – the Executive Board should be attentive to justifications or rationalizations for certain management decisions, and if the grievance has substantive merit, the union should craft the arbitration case using what was learned about the management mindset during the course of the presentation.

Not all management teams will see a benefit to making a presentation before a grievance committee or an Executive Board. Getting to the necessary give-and-take culture must be nurtured. Over time, management must perceive that its decisions are viewed as rational and responsible, and that making a presentation to the union is not a waste of time. The best way to engender this mindset is to not take grievances that are without merit, and to constantly search for a middle ground when it is possible and cost effective. Grievance presentations can be a foundation for better union to management dialogue that inevitably spills over to all facets of working conditions.

The presentations should be before the grievance committee or the Executive Board alone, with neither the grievant nor management present for the presentation of the other. Members of the committee or the Board should ask pertinent questions of fact, but should refrain from substantive discussion of the grievance's merits in front of either party. Oftentimes, the presentation of one party will raise questions regarding a previous presentation of the other party. Members who must vote on the merits of the grievance should request clarification of any conflicting facts pertinent to the issue.

Stage 3 - Discuss and vote on the merits of the grievance. Once all the presentations are complete, the grievant, his shop steward, and the management representative should be excused. It is a judgment call whether or not to ask the parties to remain available for clarifications that might arise out of the closed discussion. While the ultimate vote of committee or Board members must be noted in the minutes, closed discussion has always been the way to flesh out the merits of a grievance. Since some grievances involve potentially embarrassing and sometimes scandalous allegations, closed discussions, as a rule, generate the most unabashed and beneficial discussion.

The next step is for the chairman of the grievance committee or the Executive Board (usually the president or vice-president) to accept a motion whether or not to accept the grievance. Once the motion is seconded, the members will engage in a discussion regarding the substantive merits of the grievance. These discussions

The union should always invite management to make a presentation regarding the grievance.

Grievance presentations can be a foundation for better union to management dialogue that inevitably spills over to all facets of working conditions.

can take anywhere from a few minutes to several days, depending on the type of grievance and the potential outcomes. The meeting's Chair must use every tool at his or her disposal to keep the discussion on point and orderly. It is not uncommon for personal animosities or longstanding underlying issues to surface during the course of discussion, and the greatest challenge for the Chair is to assess what is appropriate for discussion and what is superfluous. The Chair should resist any requests to stifle debate by a request to "call for the question."

If the union attorney is present for the grievance presentation and subsequent discussion, the committee or Board members should make sure to get the attorney's opinion on the grievance. While most attorneys will (and should) refrain from recommending whether or not the grievance should be accepted, they should be asked to offer an opinion as to the potential success of the grievance in arbitration. The attorney should also articulate the strengths and weaknesses of the grievance as it pertains to the contract, past practice, and, when appropriate, the law. All of this discussion with the union attorney should take place in the presence of those who will be voting in regard to the potential grievance, and should most certainly take place prior to any voting. If the Executive Board ultimately does not accept a grievance, barring other provisions in a bylaw or collective bargaining agreement, the grievance is withdrawn. That leaves the grievant with no remedy for the alleged contract violation except a claim for breach of duty of fair representation.

FILING THE GRIEVANCE.

There is no magic to the form that should be used to file a grievance. At a minimum, the form should state the name of the grievant, the date the grievance is filed, the contract articles alleged to have been violated, how the contract has been violated, and what remedy is being sought. See Appendix B for a sample grievance filing form.

A few words to the wise about filling out grievances:

Get your lawyer involved. The arbitration casebooks are littered with examples of grievances that have been lost because of technicalities. Your lawyer may eventually be handling the grievance in arbitration; why not get him involved from the outset so you can make sure the grievance is being correctly written?

Be expansive about the contract articles you cite. The claims made in your grievance can always contract as you realize that some of them may be questionable. What an arbitrator will not allow to happen, however, is for a grievance to grow beyond what was originally written.

An arbitrator will not allow a grievance to grow beyond what was originally written.

Ask for the moon. Unless you've asked for a remedy in a grievance, an arbitrator won't give it to you. Though it might seem logical that any award of back pay should include interest, arbitrators won't even consider awarding interest unless you've requested it in the grievance. Do you want the employer to add hours to vacation accruals? Post a statement that it has violated the contract? Rescind new work rules? If you do, you need to request those remedies in your grievance.

The union can always be the grievant. Remember, the collective bargaining agreement is between the employer and the union, not the individual members of the union. That means the union can always be listed as the grievant. Some unions list the union as the only grievant in every grievance they file. There's nothing wrong with that.

Be concise. I know this sounds contradictory to the advise to "be expansive," but when you're writing your "statement of the grievance," be as concise as you can. The more you write about what happened, the greater the chance that you may get some individual facts wrong and thereby jeopardize the entire grievance. Some unions file disciplinary grievances with only a single sentence as the statement of the grievance: "The reprimand/suspension/discharge was not for just cause, was disproportionate to any offense committed, was imposed on the basis of unclear rules, and was not in keeping with the standards used by the employer in considering similar cases in the past."

> *The more you write about what happened, the greater the chance that you may get some individual facts wrong and thereby jeopardize the entire grievance.*

THE DETAILS OF GRIEVANCE PROCESSING.

Generally, the grievance should be filed by the union secretary so that appropriate records can be kept of the filing. Though not for everyone, I've found it good practice that every grievance that is filed and unresolved has a "hard-copy" file as well as an electronic file. The hard copy can be kept by the secretary in a secured filing cabinet and should be updated as the grievance proceeds toward arbitration. The file, hard copy or electronic, should contain notes regarding the person responsible for handling the grievance, conversations with witnesses, meetings with management, and a "to-do" list in preparation for arbitration. The date-stamped copy of the grievance filing must be in the hard-copy file to ensure there is adherence to any time parameters articulated in the labor contract, while e-mail responses from management serve the same purpose if the filing is done electronically. One of the draw backs of the hard-copy files is that they take up space and they have to be put back and not left laying around or stacked on a desk somewhere.

A union should use a reminder system for every grievance. The reminder system should produce reminders whenever action needs to be taken on a grievance. For example, let's say that all of the time limits in a grievance procedure are 20 days. The union has 20 days to file a grievance, management has 20 days to respond, the union has 20 days to advance the grievance to the next step, and so forth. If a grievance is filed on July 1, the union's reminder system should identify July 21 as the date when the grievance should be advanced to the next step. If the employer actually answers the grievance on July 8, the tickler should be reset to July 26 (to allow some leeway before the deadline expires).

The advent of easy-to-use electronic calendar systems such as Outlook or Google Calendar makes reminder systems a much easier proposition than was the case in the past. Individuals with basic computer skills can quickly set up a calendar for a union, and make the entries necessary for the reminder system. Some unions have gone even further, and have either purchased or written grievance processing software that has a built-in reminder system. Such software is available from companies such as the Internet Grievance System (www.griev.com) and Nova Software (www.unionez.net).

THE ROAD TO ARBITRATION.

Now that the union has accepted the grievance, preparations for arbitration must be made. Selecting an arbitrator is an important first step in setting up for a victory. A grievance procedure usually calls for a list of arbitrators to be provided to management and the union. The names are generally provided by one of three sources, the American Arbitration Association, the Federal Mediation and Reconciliation Service, and state or municipal labor relations authorities. The list of arbitrators contains an odd number of names. The first strike is determined by chance, usually with a coin toss, and is then alternated for fairness in future arbitrations. The parties work their way down the list until one name remains. The person whose name is remaining is the arbitrator with whom the hearing is scheduled.

This process is a good reason to research the arbitrators with whom you might be dealing. On-line information such as resumes at the arbitrator's personal web-site is a good place to start. Searching out any published arbitration decisions by a particular arbitrator is extremely valuable since it provides insight into the arbitrator's reasoning process and might be insightful as to whether or not the arbitrator possesses a union or management bias. Paid research firms also track arbitrators' decisions and should be a consideration for your bargaining unit. Word of mouth perspectives from other unions who deal with the same arbitrator pool are another good information source.

Continuing Settlement Efforts. As previously mentioned, settlements can be reached up to the end of the arbitration hearing. Sometimes a party will sense that the arbitration is not going well, and the case might not be as strong as initially perceived. Since the union will NEVER find itself in this position, let's consider what to do when the employer calls for a side bar conference outside the presence of the arbitrator.

Remember: Nothing in arbitration is guaranteed. So if you find yourself in a position where the employer is seeking to settle, don't blow it off. Even if you were to win the substantive issue in the arbitrator's ruling, you might not do as well as you'd expect on the remedy the arbitrator might award. Listen to the offer…and counter, of course. But if you get a guaranteed reasonable win that preserves your unit's bargaining rights and the settlement itself underscores a favorable interpretation of any potentially ambiguous contract language, go for it. Keep in mind, however, that many times offers such as this have a "non-precedent setting" caveat attached. This simply means that the parties cannot be held to the conditions of the settlement in a future grievance. When you receive an offer like this, you have to determine if this is a case that is strong enough to be won in arbitration and

Nothing in arbitration is guaranteed.

settle the issue once and for all, or is it in the bargaining unit's best interest to settle with a guaranteed, if not far-reaching, win.

If the prospect of a reasonable settlement presents itself, you should run it by the initial grievant. Keep in mind that once the Executive Board accepted the grievance, it became the union's grievance, and the member technically has no control over the terms of the settlement. But don't discount the interest that the aggrieved individual or group of individuals has in the outcome. Certainly, if there was a cash settlement of the grievance, it would go to the injured party who initially presented the grievance to the union. A reality of dealing with grievances is that the aggrieved member usually expects more in the line of monetary settlement in a make-whole provision than most settlements will produce. If the settlement includes provisions other than monetary ones, the conversation with the grievant is generally much smoother. It is in everyone's best interest to ensure a satisfied, dues-paying member, but remember the bottom line: If the Executive Board feels the settlement is reasonable, then the settlement can be consummated with no danger of duty of fair representation exposure.

TRACKING GRIEVANCE SETTLEMENTS AND ARBITRATION DECISIONS.

The value of tracking the grievance settlements and any arbitration decisions cannot be overstated. The signed deal (ALL grievance settlements should be signed and dated) should be filed, indexed, and stored. The same should be done with all arbitration decisions.

GRIEVANCE PROCESSING SENDS A MESSAGE.

Though there are times that you will swear that the same people keep filing grievances over and over, keep in mind that the entire bargaining unit watches how members and their concerns are handled by your union. If you feel that you are constantly dealing with the same folks, remember that these are probably the same folks who have actually READ their contracts. Oh, sure, you'll get the constant complainer who has a bone to pick with the chain of command, but most credible grievances or potential grievances eventually settle before they get to arbitration. You might identify a situation or two where there is specific intent to violate the contract by individuals in management, but by and large, if the chain of command realizes that they will be constantly challenged on contractual interpretation and held to the parameters of the agreement, they soon determine that it is inefficient and costly to commit contract violations.

By being vigilant, you send a message to the employer that you take the contract seriously, and a message to your members that you are protecting their bargaining rights.

What is key here is that the bargaining unit must be vigilant in regard to potential contract violations. By being vigilant, you send a message to the employer that you take the contract seriously, and a message to your members that you are protecting their bargaining rights.

CHAPTER 10

REPRESENTING A MEMBER IN A DISCIPLINARY INVESTIGATION

Police and fire departments are, by their organizational nature, paramilitary entities. As such, they are fertile fields from which disciplinary issues regularly spring. These issues span the spectrum of simple "punk attacks" or lapses in judgment by dues-paying members to serious violations of law by those who should know better.

As a union leader, you have assumed the responsibility to advocate for fair, lawful treatment of the alleged offender. Remember: Cops and firefighters have the same rights under the Constitution as anyone else. That makes it your responsibility to familiarize yourself with the tools available to you during the course of this advocacy, to include the rights provided under *Weingarten*, *Garrity*, *Loudermill*, any applicable bill of rights, and any other rights that might exist.

THE RIGHT TO REPRESENTATION IN DISCIPLINARY INTERVIEWS –

THE *WEINGARTEN* RULE.

Without getting into too much legalese, the *Weingarten* ruling is based on a case that came before the United States Supreme Court (*NLRB v. J. Weingarten*)[1] in 1975. Basically, when a private employer denied an employee's request for union representation during a disciplinary interview, the Supreme Court held that the right to representation was a necessary part of the collective bargaining process. Now, we all know that not everyone has collective bargaining. But for those jurisdictions that do, almost all state collective bargaining laws contain provisions similar to Section 7 of the National Labor Relations Act, which was the core issue in *Weingarten*. While the Supreme Court decision is not necessarily binding on state or local governments, most states' public employee relations commissions were quick to adopt the *Weingarten* rule. In other states, the right to representation can exist as a function of a statewide public safety officer bill of rights.

As the *Weingarten* rule has developed over time, three key aspects of the rule have emerged. First, *Weingarten* applies if the employee, not the employer, reasonably believes that the interview might result in a disciplinary action. The definition of discipline can be limited by a collective bargaining agreement in which "formal discipline" might be defined at any level between an oral reprimand up to and including termination. If the employee reasonably believes that any of these forms of discipline might result from the interview, then the right to representation exists. Keep in mind, though, that if an employer assures the employee that no discipline will occur, and as a result of those assurances the employee does not request representation during the interview, any discipline resulting from that interview will likely be overturned.

Second, the employee must request the union representation for the interview. Many employers, as a matter of course, will offer to accommodate the union representation preemptively, though they are not compelled to do so. Even still, it is vitally important to train your members to affirmatively request union representation during disciplinary interviews.

> *Weingarten* **applies if the employee, not the employer, reasonably believes that the interview might result in a disciplinary action.**

Third, the representation provided to the employee by the union cannot unduly interfere with the legitimate needs of the employer. Just what the threshold might be for unduly interfering with the legitimate needs of the employer is very much a gray area. Suffice it to say that if an employee's chosen union representative happens to be on vacation in the Bahamas for three weeks, it is possible that such a demand by the union could be construed as to unduly interfere with the employer's need to conduct a timely investigation. This does not mean, however, that the employer can dictate who will or will not represent an employee during a disciplinary interview. The key questions to ask are: "Would the employee suffer harm if his or her choice of representation is not honored?" and "What harm would the employer suffer if the interview were delayed?" An extreme example of this might be in the unusual case of an employee who has been through several previous disciplinary interviews and actions with a union rep for whom a level of trust and communication had developed. Bottom line, the representation is chosen by the member or the union, not the employer.

If the timing of the interview becomes an issue, a reviewing body might ask: "Why did the interview need to take place at such and such a time?" If it becomes clear that it was necessary for an interview to take place at that particular time, the next question that might be asked is: "How long has it taken for the employer to get to the interview?" Or better, "How long did it take for the employer to conduct the investigation?" If the investigation has been going on for six months, and for some reason the employer decides that an interview has to be conducted at a particular time, there would need to be a justification on the part of the employer regarding why, after six months, it is so necessary to the investigation that the interview be conducted at that time.

Since the *Weingarten* rule came about as the result of a ruling by the U.S. Supreme Court under the National Labor Relations Act, based on a dispute in a collective bargaining atmosphere, can *Weingarten* rights be waived by a union in that particular environment? They can indeed. I can't imagine the motivation for doing so, but cops and firefighters have done stranger things. But individual cops and firefighters must get over the illusion that "they don't need representation" because "they have nothing to hide." What about your buddy who chooses to invoke his rights under *Weingarten*? Does that infer that he has something to hide? If nothing else, an employee invoking his *Weingarten* rights will buy himself time to put his predicament in perspective with another party that has the employee's best interest at heart. And this is key: The employer has the department's best interest at heart, only the union rep has the employee's best interest at heart.

Remember, the employer does not need to be conducting a formal internal affairs interview for the right to representation to exist. Any time an employee reasonably believes that discipline could result from an interview, the employee has a right to union representation. Examples of common situations public safety employees find themselves in that will probably lead to, or are of themselves disciplinary actions, are vehicle accidents, sick leave denials, demotions, suspensions, discharges, and uses of force. Sometimes, an interaction between an employee and a supervisor might begin informally as a "spot correction" but morphs into some form of questioning. Once that happens, the right to representation arises. Only the employee's willingness to assert *Weingarten* rights will secure a guarantee of representation.

Speaking of rights, wallet-size rights reminder cards are invaluable. These laminated, two-sided cards should have specific guidance to employees if they are either informed that they are under investigation and told to provide an interview, or involved in a lethal use of force. Here are two samples you can use for your own rights reminder cards – one for law enforcement and one for firefighters:

Side One of Card:

LAW ENFORCEMENT ADVICE OF RIGHTS

IF YOU ARE BEING ASKED QUESTIONS WHICH COULD RESULT IN DISCIPLINE, BE SURE TO DO THE FOLLOWING

1. Request the right to have your union representative with you before answering any questions, and do not volunteer information before speaking with your union representative.

2. Make sure you are ordered to answer the questions.

3. Keep your answers to the point and very accurate. Be completely truthful in your answers. Do not speculate.

4. Do not volunteer to take a polygraph examination or drug test.

5. If you are told you are facing a criminal investigation, refuse to answer any questions until you have spoken with an attorney or a union representative.

Side Two of Card:

IF YOU ARE QUESTIONED ABOUT AN OFFICER-INVOLVED SHOOTING OR THE USE OF FORCE

1. Do not answer questions or write a report unless you are ordered to do so. An order to answer questions means your statements and the fruits of your statements cannot be used to criminally prosecute you.

2. Immediately request the presence of your attorney or union representative. Have the union representative or your attorney present when all questioning takes place.

3. Remember that the statements you make to your union representative may not be privileged; statements you make to your attorney are covered by the attorney-client privilege.

4. If you need to talk to a doctor, psychologist, or minister, do so.

Side One of Card:

> ## FIREFIGHTER ADVICE OF RIGHTS
>
> ### IF YOU ARE BEING ASKED QUESTIONS WHICH COULD RESULT IN DISCIPLINE, BE SURE TO DO THE FOLLOWING
>
> 1. Make sure you are ordered to answer the questions.
>
> 2. Request the right to have your union representative with you before answering any questions, and do not volunteer information before speaking with your union representative.
>
> 3. Keep your answers to the point and very accurate. Be completely truthful in your answers. Do not speculate.
>
> 4. Do not volunteer to take a polygraph examination or drug test.
>
> 5. If you are told you are facing a criminal investigation, refuse to answer any questions until you have spoken with an attorney or a union representative.

Side Two of Card:

> ### IF YOU ARE QUESTIONED ABOUT ANYTHING THAT COULD RESULT IN CRIMINAL CHARGES
>
> 1. Do not answer questions or write a report unless you are ordered to do so. An order to answer questions means your statements and the fruits of your statements cannot be used to criminally prosecute you.
>
> 2. Immediately request the presence of your attorney or union representative. Have the union representative or your attorney present when all questioning takes place.
>
> 3. Remember that the statements you make to your union representative may not be privileged; statements you make to your attorney are covered by the attorney-client privilege.
>
> 4. If you need to talk to a doctor, psychologist, or minister, do so.

PREPARING FOR THE DISCIPLINARY INTERVIEW.

Here are a few thoughts for union reps chosen to represent an employee in a disciplinary interview. Take the time to prepare prior to the interview. Gather as much information about the incident as you can before meeting with the member. Your knowledge of the incident will not only help you understand the reason the investigation is occurring, it will help keep the employee truthful during the interview.

Truth. Odd thing, truth. Employees guilty of the most boneheaded acts under color of authority have kept their jobs because they told the embarrassing (for some) truth, while others, while guilty of lesser violations, have been terminated because they lied during the interview. A good rule of thumb: The employer probably already knows the truth before the interview. So, meet with the employee who is to be interviewed. First and foremost, and continually, the union representative must stress to the employee the importance of being honest during the interview.

Now, listen to your member's account of what happened. The Michigan Education Association has put together a great pamphlet on representing members in the grievance procedure. One of the best parts of the pamphlet is the section that contains ten "commandments" for good listening, and eight ways to be a lousy listener. The advice bears repeating here.

There are ten commandments for good listening:

1. Stop talking!

2. Put the speaker at ease.

3. Show that you want to listen.

4. Minimize distractions.

5. Put yourself in the speaker's place.

6. Be patient.

7. Hold your temper.

8. Go easy on the criticism and argument.

9. Ask questions.

10. Listen "actively" (more on this later).

Now for the other side of the equation – the eight wrong ways to listen:

1. Editing – you hear only what you want to hear.

2. Rehearsing – you think about what you want to say while the other person is speaking.

3. Deriving – you focus on finding a hidden message, rather than listening to what the other person is saying.

4. Daydreaming – you let your mind wander.

5. Personalizing – you relate everything the person is saying to your own life.

6. Switching – you change the subject quickly as soon as the person stops speaking.

7. Arguing – you focus on finding something to judge.

8. Agreeing – you nod your head to everything in order to avoid conflict.[2]

Once the member employee is convinced that telling the truth is the only acceptable and effective means of surviving the disciplinary interview, work out certain rules with the member that will encourage him to follow your lead. For example, tell him that if you request a break, you are doing it for a reason. Let him know that a break sometimes provides the opportunity for the member to refocus and clarify his thoughts. Gauge the necessity for breaks. Ask for the break, and if it is denied, the request and denial are there on tape. Even the request for the break should send a message to the employee that he must give his answers more deliberate consideration.

Work out certain rules with the member that will encourage him to follow your lead.

The burden once again shifts to you, the union representative, to ensure that the rendition of the truth will be direct and concise. Tell the member before going in that if you find him rambling and being less than totally honest, you will request a break. Lay the groundwork with the employee for such breaks and "time outs" during the course of the interview (and later, don't hesitate to use them if you feel the interview is getting out of hand or your employee is being too flexible with the truth).

Public safety union lawyer Will Aitchison, who has trained union representatives for over 25 years, has developed a list of Ten Tips for Internal Affairs Interviews. It's a good idea to show your members a list like this, and to review it with them shortly before the interview:

1. **Prepare.** Don't go into an internal affairs interview assuming you can "wing it." You can't. You've been involved in too many cases before and after the interview, and things may be a bit garbled. Review all of your reports about the incident. If you can find the reports of others, review those as well.

2. **Talk Things Over With Your Representative.** Ideally days before the interview happens, sit down with your representative and go over the entire incident. The representative may ask you to run through your account once more, and one more time again, and may ask you some pointed questions. That's all a good thing. It will help prepare you for the actual interview.

3. **Tell The Truth.** Enough said.

4. **Listen To The Question, The Whole Question.** Don't turn your brain off halfway through the middle of a question. Let the interviewer finish speaking before you start to answer.

5. **Answer Only The Question That Was Asked.** If you're asked, "What's your date of birth," answer "July 2, 1980," not "July 2, 1980, in Portland, Oregon," or, heaven forbid, not "I was born on July 2, 1980, in Portland, Oregon. Shortly after I was born, we moved to Gresham, and later to Beaverton, where I went to Beaverton High School." Do not volunteer any information other than what was specifically

requested in the question. The investigator's job is to ask specific questions; don't make that job any easier by unnecessarily volunteering information.

6. **Don't Guess At What A Question Means.** If you do not understand a question, tell the investigator you don't understand the question. Don't overdo this, of course; it doesn't help if you say "Could you rephrase the question" 72 times during the interview.

7. **Don't Guess At Your Answers.** If you cannot remember something, you have only one answer: "I do not remember." If you have a vague memory, say something like "I don't remember all of the details. I think that this is the way it might have happened, but my memory could be faulty on this." If you are asked for a time or date, and you cannot recall the exact date and time, tell the investigator that your answer is an approximation.

8. **Beware Long Or Leading Questions.** A leading question improperly suggests the answer in the body of the question. Don't allow the investigator to try to put words in your mouth with leading questions. Instead of answering "Yes," use your own words to describe what your answer would be. Some investigators ask long or compound questions where a portion of the question may be inaccurate. Listen for these questions, and feel free to ask the investigator to break the question down into smaller questions. Do not accept the investigator's summary of your account unless it is 100% accurate.

9. **The Internal Affairs Investigator Is Not Your Friend.** The investigator has one job to do – find out what happened. Don't be misled into thinking that the investigator wants anything else, much less that the investigator will somehow influence the course of the investigation because you've suddenly become friends during the interview. It won't happen.

10. **Forget About Being Humorous.** It doesn't work. Worse, if a transcript is eventually prepared of the interview, the humor will not translate (at best) and may even give the wrong impression (at worst).

The folks representing the employer will undoubtedly have done interviews before. It only makes sense for agencies to put their police and fire investigators in internal affairs to capitalize on their interview and interrogation expertise. They have a job to do, and most of them do it well. And as the union rep, you have to function with the expectation that they *will* do it well. You can afford to do no less.

Recognize that, as the union rep, you have a right to obtain certain information. Identify the nature of the interview; that is, determine the allegations before the interview. Before the interview, you should review all the documentary evidence you can get your hands on with the member. Depending upon your state law or collective bargaining agreement, you may have a right to review all interviews, complaints, and physical evidence pertinent to the charges. Charges…it sounds so criminal. But keep in mind that termination is capital punishment when it comes to administrative actions, and like comparisons can be drawn for the lesser progressive disciplines. Property rights, liberty rights…all can be impacted by the due process that begins with the notification of the disciplinary investigation and the interview that follows.

It is critically important that you, the union rep, meet with the person who will conduct the interview of your employee…that's right, you own him, and you are responsible for his emotional and professional care and feeding until the disciplinary action runs its course. Now that you have willingly assumed this role, get with the person conducting the interview and work out some ground rules. Meet without the employee who is under investigation present. Do not tape record this meeting, but do a memorandum for record to yourself later regarding what was said. If you do not already have it in writing as a result of official notification by the employer, have the investigator articulate the specific charges. Clarify that the employee will, indeed, be ordered to answer questions. In addition to identifying the person or persons conducting the interview, find out who else will be present and why. Press for a reason for their presence, because in interviews an atmosphere of intimidation can play a pivotal role. Once this is done, enter into a discussion and set parameters for the interview that will preclude "fishing expeditions."

> *The purpose of the disciplinary interview is to obtain facts that might lead to discipline as they pertain to a specific allegation or misdeed.*

Remember, the purpose of the disciplinary interview is to obtain facts that might lead to discipline as they pertain to a specific allegation or misdeed. The union rep should never allow such an interview to turn into a feeding frenzy for folks with an axe to grind. Since most jurisdictions record disciplinary interviews as a matter of course, let it be known that you will be bringing and using your own recording device in addition to the one used by the employer.

WHAT A REPRESENTATIVE CAN DO DURING AN INTERVIEW.

Note the heading here…It doesn't read "What a Representative Can and Can't Do During an Interview" for a reason. Since *Weingarten* rulings are still evolving, an aggressive union rep won't consider what he or she *can't* do. Aggressive union reps will push their right to representation to the edge of the envelope, and will do their best to ensure that the interview goes as well as possible for their member.

Some of the most aggressive cops and firefighters get nervous when they're interviewed. These are the same rocks who don't flinch under cross examination by some hot-shot attorney. Often times these are the same guys or gals who have hundreds of interviews under their belts that they themselves have conducted. Get them in an IA interview, though, and they melt; they stutter; they bend the truth; they get diarrhea of the mouth. You as the union rep have certain responsibilities to protect the employee's interest here. No one else can or will do it.

At the very start of the interview, the interviewer will start the recorder (and you should start yours; make sure it is prominently displayed and placed in plain view) and note the date, the time, who is present in the room, and what the purpose of the interview is, such as: "This interview is being conducted in regard to Department investigation number 03-10." At this point, ensure the interviewer provides the employee with his *Garrity*[3] warning, that is an order to answer the questions. No *Garrity* warning? Red flag! An absence of a *Garrity* warning implies that this is a criminal investigation. Stop the interview right then and there and inform the interviewer that the employee has nothing to say to him without his attorney present. If there was no mention in the pre-interview meeting that *Garrity* wouldn't be given, then shame on you for not asking, and shame on the interviewer for not telling you.

A little background is in order at this point. In *Garrity v. New Jersey*, several cops were interviewed regarding their involvement in a ticket-fixing scheme. This was a criminal investigation, and the officers were ordered, on pain of discharge, to answer the questions posed by an interviewer. When the officers did so, their statements were used against them in the criminal proceeding. The Supreme Court held that police officers had the same constitutional rights as any other citizens, and that, under the Fifth Amendment, an individual is not only protected from testifying against himself in a criminal prosecution, but also gives the individual the right to not answer any questions in any other type of formal, informal, civil, or administrative proceeding, where the answers might incriminate him in a future criminal investigation. This sentiment was further fleshed out for our purposes in *Gardner v. Broderick*.[4]

In *Broderick*, a cop was being questioned about bribery and corruption, and he refused to sign a waiver of immunity, which would have allowed his statements to be used in a criminal prosecution. He was fired, and the U.S. Supreme Court reversed the discharge, saying that the discharge was the direct result of the officer refusing to waive a constitutional right.

So, what does this mix of *Garrity* and *Broderick* mean? Bottom line: A law enforcement agency can conduct an administrative investigation on an officer, but it can't, during the course of that investigation, compel the officer to waive his immunity granted under *Garrity*. If an employee lawfully invokes his Fifth Amendment rights, the employer cannot discipline the employee for refusing to answer questions unless it grants the employee immunity from his statements in a follow-up criminal investigation. This grant of immunity automatically flows from the employer's requirement that the employee answer the employer's questions. And when the employer conducts a disciplinary interview, the employer's questions must be, in the words of the Court, "specifically, narrowly, and directly relating to the performance of his official duties…"[5] That means that interviewer fishing expeditions are off limits.

Once the interviewer provides the employee with a *Garrity* admonition, the interview truly begins. Your main responsibilities are: (1) Make sure the employee

An absence of a Garrity warning implies that this is a criminal investigation. Stop the interview right then and there.

A law enforcement agency can conduct an administrative investigation on an officer, but it can't compel the officer to waive his immunity granted under Garrity.

tells the truth; (2) make sure the employee listens to the questions; and (3) make sure the employee answers only the questions that are asked.

Don't limit your representation to the accomplishment of *only* those three main responsibilities. As previously mentioned, you have to help the employee articulate what happened, and you have to make sure the interview stays properly focused. Don't hesitate to ask follow-up questions, and don't hesitate to do it immediately during the interview as opposed to waiting for its conclusion. Ask for clarification to questions that might be unclear or ambiguous. This is a good technique to ensure that the clarifications that you think are important are made in the immediate context of the employee's statement. If the interviewer insists on you not interrupting the flow of the interview, reserve the right to ask follow-up questions at the end to provide clarification for either questions asked or answers given. This, of course, could have (and should have) been worked out between you and the person conducting the interview at the pre-interview conference.

If necessary, take a break and counsel the employee in private. If a break is not possible, you may need to do something – clear your throat, interject an objection, stand up, whatever – that focuses your member back on the tasks at hand. Those tasks, of course, are to tell the truth and not unnecessarily volunteer information. While the interview is being conducted, you cannot be a disinterested "fly on the wall," you have to be an energetic "coach" with a vested interest in the outcome of the event.

Always keep this basic tenet in mind: You're the advocate for the employee. You're not the judge. Leave the judging to the employer and, if need be an arbitrator or civil service board.

AFTER THE INTERVIEW.

One or more of these four things will be clear when the interview has concluded: (1) The employee is toast; (2) the employee will be just fine; (3) the Internal Affairs folks need to do follow-up interviews; and/or (4) you need to run your own concurrent investigation.

Let's take the possibilities one at a time. As for the first, the only time you can be sure the employee's head is on the chopping block is if, during the interview, he lied or admitted to the terminable offense. If he lied after all your prep and warnings, well, there's not much more you can do for him. If, however, he openly and honestly admitted to a terminable offense, there is still the *Loudermill* or mitigation hearing. We will go into more detail regarding *Loudermill* hearings later in this chapter.

There is always the rewarding and reassuring result of the second outcome. Just as quickly as you will know whether or not someone is toast, you will be able to determine that he or she has nothing to worry about. This is rewarding because your efforts at helping the employee articulate his actions did nothing less than clear the employee of any wrongdoing, and it is reassuring because the investigative process was, hopefully, credible and complete. If the Internal Affairs investigators had been incompetent, be assured that there is no moral imperative for you to assist them in their efforts. Your role is to ensure that the union's duty of fair representation is appropriately carried out. Period.

Now it gets sticky as we address the final two potential results. If, at the end of the disciplinary interview, the interviewer turns off the tape and says words to the effect that "more questions have been raised" or "I need to do further research," you should, as the union representative, merely acknowledge the statement in the presence of the employee. Later, without the employee present, make a follow-up appointment with the interviewer and see if you can determine the direction that the investigation is going. Probe a bit. Some interviewers will come clean and tell you "your guy is okay, I just need to tighten a few things up," or "you know, he can still resign…" If it's the former, get your guy to keep a low profile and wait it out with him.

If it's the latter, see the fourth option. You need to consider conducting your own concurrent investigation. Speak to the key witnesses, follow investigatory leads, and do everything a thorough investigation into the incident would demand. As long as you're not interfering with the employer's own investigation, you have the right to do this sort of investigation. At a minimum, it forces management to conduct a fair and thorough internal investigation. This is why you are a Shop Steward.

Follow-up Interviews. If, as the result of that "informal" post-interview meeting with the person assigned to conduct the disciplinary investigation, you get a feeling that the concerns the interviewer has can be clarified with a follow-up interview, ask for it. But be sure it will benefit your employee. Don't ever put yourself in a position where you are gambling with your employee's job. You have to be sure that the follow-up interview will provide the investigator the information needed to close the investigation in your employee's favor. Remember, never give the interviewer an opportunity to salvage a bad interview if he isn't smart enough to know that it was a bad interview.

Don't ever put yourself in a position where you are gambling with your employee's job.

Write yourself a "memorandum to record" that details the request and the response. If the interviewer agrees, make the appointment then and there to get the interview done. Find your guy and prep him on how to best articulate what remains to be clarified. Then go back and prep him for the follow-up interview with the same ground rules as before.

If the interviewer is not prepared to grant a follow-up, make sure that is detailed in your memorandum to record. This might be an indicator that the interviewer thinks your employee has lied. This can be a valuable insight because, more often than not, unless you are already conducting your own concurrent investigation, the interviewer has more substantive evidence than you do.

What can you do next? As a shop steward, you can (and should) finish up that concurrent investigation. If you have to, be a better investigator than the guy doing the disciplinary investigation. In addition to pressuring the department administration for a fair and complete internal investigation, the results of your investigation will be used at a pre-disciplinary hearing, in arbitration, before an authoritative board empowered to make a decision regarding the issue, and sometimes in a court of law.

THE MITIGATION OR *LOUDERMILL* HEARING.

If the employee has some sort of guarantee of job security – for example, appeal rights through a collective bargaining agreement or civil service – an employer must give the employee notice of the intent to impose discipline, as well as provide, upon request, some kind of hearing prior to that discipline being imposed. These hearings are known as *Loudermill* hearings (or *Skelley* hearings if you are in California), and deal with the employee's basic right to procedural due process.[6] The essence of a *Loudermill* hearing is that the employee is afforded the opportunity to have his side of the story told to an unbiased person in a position of authority relative to the employee's discipline.

Notice Of The Hearing. Notice provided by an employer of alleged transgressions by the employee must include, at a minimum, the specific charges or rules violated. If, at a later time, new allegations arise, there is a new right to respond to any additional allegations. If an agency's own rules and regulations outline specific procedures for notice and a hearing, the employer must strictly adhere to those procedures.[7] In addition, a bill of rights can specify additional requirements for notice and a hearing, requirements beyond those required by *Loudermill*.

> Notice provided by an employer of alleged transgressions by the employee must include, at a minimum, the specific charges or rules violated.

The court decisions regarding the "opportunity to be heard" aspects of *Loudermill* are all over the map. Some give plenty of leeway for an employer to not hold an in-person hearing for minor discipline up to and including short suspensions,[8] while most reason that only an in-person hearing meets the intent of *Loudermill's* "opportunity to be heard" threshold.[9] From my perspective, in-person hearings are by far the most productive form of *Loudermill* hearing, allowing a back-and-forth exchange that often resolves a disciplinary issue.

In deciding how much your employee should speak at the *Loudermill* hearing, consider his/her personality. Face it, some of your employees may bring tears to the eyes of the most hardboiled captain, while others, perhaps more deserving of leniency but who happens to be less articulate or less "liked," will only succeed in alienating the decision maker. You, the union representative, have to be insightful enough regarding your employee to decide which method of exercising his "opportunity to be heard" will work best in any given situation.

Written Appeals. While the least used appeal mechanism, a written appeal can be effective if the employee that you are representing is one of those people whose mere presence creates a handicap, or if the employer's position is so set in stone that nothing said in a *Loudermill* hearing will matter. In these cases, it may be best to line out the employee's position in writing (so the employer cannot later claim it is surprised by any argument the union is making), and dispense with the in-person hearing.

The In-Person Hearing. Most courts would agree than an in-person appeal is a due process right when requested for cases of termination, demotion, and serious suspensions. Any time an in-person *Loudermill* hearing can be secured for lesser punishments, take advantage of the opportunity (except in the situations mentioned above). Think how easy it is to say no to someone over the phone, and how much more difficult it is to say no to the same thing when the person is standing in front of you. That same dynamic works during the well-structured *Loudermill* hearing.

If you are at an in-person hearing, chances are your member is being considered for some serious disciplinary action. That type of discipline will probably have long-term impacts on the employee's life in terms of finances, relationships, and sense of self. So, you have to give it your best shot. You must prepare to clarify facts, minimize negatives that can be minimized, and accentuate the positives once you identify them.

If you are at an in-person hearing, chances are your member is being considered for some serious disciplinary action.

It is your job to control the pace and structure of the *Loudermill* hearing. A good way to do this is to open with an overview of the reason that you and the employee are there. You will need to make the call as to when you want the employee to speak. Sometimes it's good to immediately allow the employee to make an appeal regarding why he did what he did, what he learned from the experience at this point. If the employee is articulate and you are convinced that a heartfelt appeal might be an appropriate way to wrap up the hearing, save the employee's remarks for last. The danger with this strategy is that the employee might make a statement or inference that you immediately recognize as in dire need of "clarification." Wrapping with the employee greatly limits your opportunity to clean up a major "punk attack." So, whether the employee on the hot seat is making his remarks at the opening or near the end of the hearing, make sure he has rehearsed his presentation with you before going into the hearing, and make sure the presentation is heartfelt and honest.

Now it's your turn. You start with a reiteration of the violation and an acknowledgement of the employee's acceptance of the appropriate level of responsibility (if any). Finally, and most importantly, whether you have collective bargaining rights or not, use the principles of just cause to frame your defense of the employee. Don't forget, this person or these people whom you are addressing are in a position of authority to impact the level of discipline administered.

Will Aitchison, in his book *The Rights of Law Enforcement Officers, Sixth Edition*, sets forth an itemized list of the twelve most common just cause defenses that can be raised by an employee facing discipline.[10] Before any *Loudermill* hearing, you should look through this list to see whether any of the defenses apply:

1. Have the charges been factually proven?

2. Was the punishment imposed by the employer disproportionately severe under all the circumstances?

3. Did the employer conduct a thorough investigation into the incident?

4. Were other employees who engaged in conduct similar or identical to that of the employee treated as harshly by the employer?

5. Was the employee misconduct the product of action or inaction by the employer?

6. Did the employer take into consideration the employee's good or exemplary work?

7. Did the employer take into consideration mitigating circumstances?

8. Was the employee subjected to progressive or corrective discipline?

9. Was the employer motivated by anti-union bias?

10. Are the employer's rules clear and understandable?

11. Is the employee likely to engage in similar misconduct in the future?

12. Was the employee accorded procedural due process in the disciplinary investigation?

Remember, if you can prepare and present a defense of the employee that raises serious questions regarding the motivations, considerations, and handling of the discipline, not only can you create a favorable atmosphere for reconsideration of the discipline by the employer, but you can lay a foundation that might cause a reviewing authority such as an arbitrator, civil service board, or a court to reverse or mitigate the punishment.

If you can obtain them, you should have handy letters from members of the employee's chain of command and the employee's co-workers. It is particularly effective if these well-respected role models, in addition to describing what a good employee the individual is, offer to assume responsibility to ensure the employee's remediation and to oversee the modification of the unacceptable behavior.

Often, there is a temptation by the employee or the union to have an attorney present and play an active role in the pre-disciplinary hearing. I'm a strong believer that you should not have an attorney present, no matter how complicated the issue might be. The presence of an attorney has an alienating impact on everyone else present, particularly those representing the employer, and the peer-to-peer type informalities that often work to the benefit of the employee are stifled. An attorney should be considered for advocating the employee's position only in the more formalized procedural forums such as arbitration and in court. The *Loudermill* hearing should be held among those of the same cloth, because there is a possibility that one or more of those presently sitting in judgment or review have found themselves in a like situation as the employee being disciplined. Let's face it, cops talk to cops, and firefighters talk to firefighters, more effectively than either talks to lawyers.

For example, I represented an employee at a pre-disciplinary hearing for excessive use of force. Having worked the street with the two captains and the one deputy chief who were tasked by the chief to conduct the hearing, I had first-hand knowledge of transgressions by each in the past 20 years that were arguably outside the parameters of the department's acceptable force guidelines. This gave me an opportunity to allude to how officers are forced to react in certain circumstances, seek empathy from the commanders present, and challenge them (respectfully) to empathize with the officer. Because the planets aligned favorably and I was present for each incident involving the commanders, I was able to cryptically quote or be specific enough so that each understood that I remembered their behaviors in the past. Outcome: minimal discipline with remediation in defensive tactics. It doesn't happen like that all the time, but helping it along by knowing who was going to be on the board and preparing for the appropriate audience made it a successful endeavor.

On a final note, the union rep should do a strategic assessment of the possibility or probability of the particular discipline going to arbitration. In most cases, an arbitration will be a thorough administrative hearing of the disciplinary issue. You are under no obligation to fully disclose the union's full case, or anything that would constitute discovery to the employer, during the pre-disciplinary hearing. As a matter of fact, there might not be time for the union to fully conduct its complete investigation prior to the mitigation hearing, and the employer is not compelled to provide the union with the full product of its investigation until discipline has been administered. Therefore, a conservative approach and a guarded discussion of the pertinent issues during the course of a mitigation hearing in complex cases where facts might be in dispute is recommended. This is a bit of a delicate dance, for you don't want to give rise to an arbitration argument by the employer to the effect of "why didn't they say that at the *Loudermill* hearing?" The solution often is to broadly allude to all of your essential points, but not go into great detail about them.

Second Mitigation Hearings. What happens if new evidence, or for that matter, new charges, are put forth after the mitigation hearing? The employee must be given the opportunity to respond, and if there is new evidence, the pre-disciplinary hearing board must receive it in the presence of the employee.

Finally, the employee can secure a second mitigation hearing if there is a specific right to appeal, review, or reconsideration before the imposition of discipline in the department's procedures or in the applicable Bill of Rights.

Once Discipline Is Imposed. If the result of the *Loudermill* hearing is discipline that your member wants to challenge, you've got one last obligation – make sure that the employee's appeal rights are protected. That means you should be familiar with the time limits in your contract's grievance procedure or any applicable civil service rules, and do everything you can to assist the employee is filing the appeal in a timely fashion.

> *The union rep should do a strategic assessment of the possibility or probability of the particular discipline going to arbitration.*

NOTES

[1] *National Labor Relations Board v. J. Weingarten*, 420 U.S. 251 (1975).

[2] http://www.mea.org/bfcl/index.html.

[3] *Garrity v. New Jersey*, 385 U.S. 493 (1967).

[4] *Gardner v. Broderick*, 392 U.S. 273 (1968).

[5] *Gardner v. Broderick*, 392 U.S. 273 (1968).

[6] *Cleveland Bd. of Ed. v. Loudermill*, 470 U.S. 532 (1985).

[7] Procedures, known as "process which is due" when a property right is involved, can be more stringent on the employer than any determined by *Loudermill*.

[8] *Gillard v. Norris*, 857 F.2d 1095 (6th Cir. 1988).

[9] *Click v. Board of Police Commissioners*, 609 F. Supp. 1199 (W.D. Mo. 1985).

[10] Will Aitchison, *The Rights of Law Enforcement Officers, Sixth Edition*, LRIS, (2009) pp.99-101.

CHAPTER 11

COLLECTIVE BARGAINING

Cops and firefighters have some of the most difficult working conditions in modern America. The place to have a substantial impact on those working conditions is the bargaining table. It is there that meaningful changes can be effected in areas such as hours of work, workplace safety, and compensation, changes that will have a substantial impact on the lives of your members.

There are things that we can do, and things that we should do better, in preparation before "going to the table." Some of the following suggestions might seem obvious, while others might convince you to change the way you presently prepare for your contract negotiations. While this chapter is intended to be a good overview, this should not be the only source for your prep work. Check out Appendix E, which has a pretty good list of on-line negotiations resources.

PREPARING FOR NEGOTIATIONS.

As with any project of value, preparations for contract negotiations will directly impact the quality and nature of the negotiations. A thorough game plan that addresses the manner in which "must haves" will be attained and "expendables" can be traded for the "like to haves" should be developed in order to get the most from and control the pace of the negotiations.

The Negotiations Binder. Arguably the single most important document that your union can have is the negotiations binder. "Binder" is a general term used here to describe the body of information collected since the last contract was signed. The binder should be the core document you present to your next negotiating team to assist in preparing for and conducting negotiations. It will also be invaluable to you in the day-to-day administration of the contract.

The binder may be a physical binder (or more likely, binders) holding papers. Even better, the "binder" should be an electronic database. The binder or database should contain all documents that are relevant to the negotiation and administration of the collective bargaining agreement.

Though I believe that the negotiations "binder" should be electronic, it is helpful to think of it as a standard three-ring binder. The binder should have three main sections. The first section should contain separate tabs for every article in the collective bargaining agreement. The second section should contain separate tabs for topics that potentially might be added to the collective bargaining agreement. The third section of the binder should contain separate tabs for general areas that are relevant to the collective bargaining process – areas such as memoranda of understanding or agreement, the employer's ability to pay, the cost of living, and the wages and benefits in comparable jurisdictions.

What goes in the binder? Every time a grievance is filed, a copy of the grievance should be placed in the binder under the tabs of all contract articles listed in the grievance. Every time a grievance is settled or an arbitrator's decision is received, or a memorandum of agreement or understanding is reached, a copy of the document should be placed in the appropriate sections of the binder.

> *Preparations for contract negotiations will directly impact the quality and nature of the negotiations.*

Correspondence about the contract should be placed in the binder, including e-mail, memoranda, and questions from constituents. If an employer's rules impact one or more contract sections, a copy of the rules should be placed into the binder. Notes taken during the collective bargaining process should be broken down by the contract article involved, then placed into the binder.

As cost of living information is received, the consumer price index data should be placed into the binder. Collective bargaining agreements from comparable jurisdictions, newspaper articles about wage settlements, information about the employer's budget, discussions of the general economic climate of the area, projections for key economic indicators, and articles about the members of the bargaining unit should all be placed in appropriate sections of the binder.

For example, assume that Article 43 in the collective bargaining agreement contains the contract's callback language. The negotiations binder might contain these things:

- The text of the contract language.

- Bargaining notes, organized by date.

- Copies of grievances dealing with Article 43.

- Copies of any memoranda of understanding resolving grievances or potential issues arising under Article 43.

- Arbitrator decisions interpreting Article 43.

- The text of contract articles on callback pay from comparable jurisdictions.

- Newspaper articles about the cost of overtime in the department.

As suggested in the preceding paragraphs, the best form for the negotiations binder is some sort of electronic database. The time has come when parties to the collective bargaining process should be operating on a largely paperless basis. With an electronic database, documents relevant to the bargaining process can be assigned a variety of "tags" which associate the documents with different contract articles and topics. For example, a memorandum of agreement resolving a grievance filed by John Smith on Article 43 of the collective bargaining agreement can be assigned the tags "memoranda of agreement," "Article 43," "callback," and "John Smith." If the databases is later queried for any of these tags, the memorandum of agreement will be immediately retrieved.

The flexibility of an electronic database makes it much more effective tool than a traditional paper negotiations binder.

An electronic database also allows for broad queries of the information in the database. Commands can be given, for example, to tell the system to retrieve all documents dealing with callback pay, or the employer's ability to pay, or detailing wage settlements in other jurisdictions over the last two years. The flexibility of an electronic database makes it much more effective tool than a traditional paper negotiations binder.

Membership Surveys. The benefit of membership surveys is that they will tell you what your members want. The drawback of membership surveys is that they will tell you what your members want. Here's what I mean.

If you craft the survey in such a manner as to ask open-ended questions regarding wages, hours, and working conditions, the data that you collect will be useless. For instance, if you ask a question such as "Do you think you are paid enough?" the guaranteed response will be an almost unanimous "No!" If, however, the question is posed in such a fashion as to give controlled parameters with a menu of answers, it can be much more beneficial. Consider this example:

"I expect the following appropriate wage increase for the next three years:

a) 3%, 3%, 3%

b) 5%, 3%, 3%

c) none (freeze)

d) other _____ "

Note that in the above example you can craft the available answers to reflect what your research shows as reasonable wage increases based on comparable jurisdictions, while not excluding an opportunity for a "write-in" response. Another reason for posing questions in this manner is that you may have generated other information in the same survey regarding the bargaining priorities that your union has. For instance, a question that asks the membership to prioritize bargaining issues might very well reflect the priorities to be health care, wages, leave, and shift start times. Knowing that health care trumps wages as a priority, and using the data gained regarding the spectrum of wage increase expectations, you can look for opportunities in bargaining that might trade off wage increases for improved or maintenance of health care benefits while still attaining a wage increase within the expectation of a majority of your members.

Any survey is only as good as the questions asked, particularly how those questions are asked. The need to develop a credible and useful survey is something that your union leadership will need to assess in terms of importance to the bargaining preparation process. The cost of having the survey professionally prepared, administered, and assessed should be weighed against the potential cost of not having the information that appropriately reflects the priorities of your bargaining unit.

There is another benefit to conducting a membership bargaining survey. When all is said and done and the contract is put to bed, either by negotiations, arbitration, or court order, it is always useful to refer back to the survey results as the union leadership briefs the general membership on the language of the new contract. There is a benefit to explain how the survey served as a guide to the negotiating team as the contract was hammered out, and the survey can be a telling document by which to measure the union's bargaining successes and failures by comparing the resulting contract to the priorities articulated by the member-

The need to develop a credible and useful survey is something that your union leadership will need to assess in terms of importance to the bargaining preparation process.

ship in the bargaining survey. This also tempers any "Johnny-come-lately" accusations about what the bargaining team should have done.

A consideration that always comes up in any discussion of membership surveys is the advisability of integrating questions regarding morale and the performance of elected officials, appointed officials and chain of command in the survey. Remember, the membership survey in preparation for negotiations is not something that should be shared with the public, and therefore, any survey that addresses morale, the performance of public figures and public safety administrators within the context of bargaining priorities is not appropriate. However, a separate survey specifically addressing these subjects might be beneficial if appropriately timed and utilized.[1]

TRYING YOUR ARBITRATION CASE (EVEN IF YOU DON'T HAVE ARBITRATION).

Before You Begin Negotiations. More than half the states with collective bargaining for public safety employees have binding interest arbitration as the last step in the bargaining process. In interest arbitration, three areas are the most important: What is the total compensation paid in comparable jurisdictions, what is the cost of living, and what is the employer's ability to pay? In preparing for bargaining, a bargaining team should be collecting and analyzing information in each of these areas. Arbitration is a fairly predictable process, and knowing how an arbitrator might rule is invaluable in crafting proposals.

Even if binding arbitration isn't the last step in the bargaining process in your jurisdiction, you should still include in your bargaining preparations the gathering of information in these areas.

Even if binding arbitration isn't the last step in the bargaining process in your jurisdiction, you should still include in your bargaining preparations the gathering of information in these areas. Comparable wages, the cost of living, and the employer's ability to pay are all factors that are debated at any negotiations table, binding arbitration or not. Since the information in these areas can influence the overall result in bargaining, or can shape arguments for or against a particular position, a union's bargaining team should know the information before bargaining starts.

Comparable Jurisdictions. The first step in the process is to select your comparable jurisdictions. Usually, there will be historically agreed-upon comparable jurisdictions, and there will be little need to go through the process of selecting new jurisdictions. However, conditions do change, and it is necessary from time to time to reassess which jurisdictions are truly comparable. Usually, demographic characteristics such as population, assessed valuation, median family income, and crime rates are used to select comparable jurisdictions.

Total Compensation. The next step is to construct a comparison of total compensation. Some unions send total compensation surveys to their comparator jurisdictions (and unions).[2] As information becomes more and more available, unions have found that most of the information necessary for a total compensation comparison is easily available on line. For example, many employers and labor organizations post on their web pages the collective bargaining agreements to which they are a party.

Cost of Living. Knowing the cost of living is also important to bargaining preparations, though its relative importance tends to wane in difficult economic times. Thankfully, calculating the impact of the cost of living on wages has never been easier. The Bureau of Labor Statistics, the arm of the federal Department of Labor that publishes the Consumer Price Index, has a user-friendly web page that allows you to look at historical cost of living information.[3] There are any number of web pages that allow you to use CPI numbers to calculate inflation-adjusted wages so you can see if a catch-up raise is appropriate.[4]

Projections for inflation in upcoming years are also readily available on the Internet. Perhaps the most reliable of these are the projections used by the Congressional Budget Office.[5]

Ability to Pay. Obtaining budget information from the employer is basic to any negotiation preparation. Members on your negotiating team should become as familiar with your Department's budget, as well as that of your city or county. Make sure you secure at least the past three years of approved budgets, and the latest version of any projected budget. The ability to master the employer's budgets will provide a terrific foundation to your preparation for an "inability to pay" argument that might be put forth by a cash-strapped public sector employer.

The most valuable financial document goes by the unwieldy name of Consolidated Annual Financial Report, or CAFR. Where budgets look forward to expenditures and revenue in an upcoming year, CAFRs look backwards to the audited results of prior budgets. CAFRs, which are usually downloadable from the employer's web page, allow a union to identify patterns of expenses and income that can be revealing.

Ultimately, the essence to any negotiations preparations can be encapsulated in the following:

(a) Start gathering information immediately, preferably right after the last contract has been signed. Use source documents whenever possible and never rely on hearsay. Constantly challenge or "truth check" the information you are collecting. Don't discard any information that can possibly be of value.

(b) Prepare for negotiations with the intensity that you were preparing for fact finding or arbitration. Such preparation and mind-set from the beginning will prove valuable should negotiations break down and you find your union on the road to arbitration.

(c) Know your opponent. Find out who is likely to be on the employer's negotiating team and plan to defend against their strengths and capitalize on their weaknesses. Just as important, select your own team with the care and planning to capitalize on your strengths and defend your weaknesses.

Selecting The Negotiating Team.

The selection of the negotiating team is so important that the burden of this selection should not be borne by one person. Any president about to lead his union into contract negotiations had better be prepared to ensure that the negotiating team he selects will be committed to seeing the negotiating process through until the end, committed to working hard with little or no recognition or compensation, and reflective enough of a cross-section of the bargaining unit to give the team the necessary credibility to sell a deal, or, if necessary, hold the employer at bay until the bargaining process is completed. With such a mandate for the team, the president should seek help from those who have participated in previous negotiations and possibly well-grounded Executive Board members who have no desire to be on the team, but who have insights pertaining to the characters that do.

The fresh perspective brought to bargaining by rank-and-file members is a precious and necessary contribution to the team.

Try to avoid a bargaining team that is made up strictly of Executive Board members. Like any organization, even your Executive Board can be unaware of festering issues among the rank and file. The fresh perspective brought to bargaining by rank-and-file members is a precious and necessary contribution to the team.

The president's role on the team should be one of coordination, conciliation within the team, and ultimate executive decision making regarding policy. A smart president will constantly assess the team's input on bargaining issues, orchestrate sub-committee assignments, act as sheriff during the course of raucous caucus sessions, and prepare and deliver any updates on negotiations to the general membership and the press. The president can function as the chief spokesperson during negotiations, though many will opt to have that role filled by a professional.

Work Areas. The team must represent a good cross-section of your association. It is impossible to have a member of each particular job classification on the team; it is, however, possible to ensure that each work area or division is appropriately represented. For example, if you are a police union, you would do well to include a member from patrol, detectives, dispatch, records, forensics, and any other entity that could not fall under a more generalized category. Also, if you have the type of association that includes non-sworn personnel, be sure that their interests are represented. The same considerations for a fire union might be to include an engine company representative, someone from the paramedic unit, and a dispatcher, if appropriate.

Personality, Race, and Gender. Like it or not, personality is a key consideration when assembling the team. The reality of a prolonged caucus with team members who can't get along diminishes the effectiveness of the team. The caucus room is no place for petty squabbling among those who allow personal chemistry to interfere with the team's ability to discuss and evaluate an issue. So, if a candidate for your negotiating team has a history of disruptive behavior or a reputation for causing friction among co-workers, exclude that person from the team.

Consider the level of credibility that the negotiating team must maintain with the general membership and with the other side of the table. Any time a member who is well respected by the employer can be engaged in the negotiation process, that inevitably adds as much credence to a position as someone who is not respected and predictably resentful can take away from it. Remember, if and when it comes to playing hardball with your employer, your most respected negotiating team member is often your best pitcher. Also, consider the faces in your bargaining unit. Seek out capable negotiating team members who reflect the cultural and gender diversity of your union.

Experience. Team members need not necessarily have experience at negotiating, especially if you are using a professional as the chief spokesperson. However, once again getting to the credibility issue, your team members must be experienced in their job functions and have a history with the Department. They will be relied upon to be content experts on how the job is actually performed, not how the employer envisions it will be performed. It is that same experience that will provide the team the needed credibility to sell a negotiated deal to the general membership.

Skills. Efforts to create a diversified negotiating team that reflects the workforce cannot ignore the need to match team members with important tasks that take advantage of specific skills. There might be a fraud detective in your union who has a penchant for running spreadsheets and seeking out hidden pots of money. At the same time, that dispatcher who types so fast while answering 911 might be the perfect note taker for the bargaining sessions. So canvass your union for talented individuals, and don't hesitate to identify those folks who, while not interested in a full-time commitment to the negotiating team, might be willing to bring a specific skill to the team at a specific time regarding a specific article or section. Utilize them in selected caucuses if possible.

Ground Rules For Negotiations.

The first step in the actual bargaining process is the setting of ground rules for bargaining sessions. A good starting place is the ground rules from previous contract negotiations, since they were once acceptable to both parties. Ground rules usually cover at least the following matters:

Where To Hold Negotiations. The physical location of bargaining sessions is a serious consideration. The descending order of preference is first, at your own union hall; second, at a neutral place such as a hotel or rented business suite; and last, at your Department or City Hall. There is a psychological consideration to having the other party outside their comfort zone.

Wherever negotiations are held, there should be at least two private rooms available for caucusing. These rooms should have ready access to Internet connections, a printer/scanner, and a copier. The room in which the negotiations take place should be large enough to comfortably seat both negotiating teams as well as any observers. Ideally, the room would have an LCD projector and a telephone with speakerphone capabilities. The location itself must be easy for both parties to reach, yet provide the level of privacy necessary to ensure focused and uninterrupted negotiations.

Seek out capable negotiating team members who reflect the cultural and gender diversity of your union.

The first step in the actual bargaining process is the setting of ground rules for bargaining sessions.

It is customary for formal negotiations to begin at least 120 days out from the expiration of the present contract.

When, How Often, And How Long. The time to start negotiations is usually articulated in statute or ordinance. It is customary for formal negotiations to begin at least 120 days out from the expiration of the present contract. Ideally, negotiations would being at least 90 days before the employer normally adopts its budget. It is not uncommon for informal "feelers" from both sides to precede the start of the negotiations. These "feelers" will often provide insight to both parties as to where the "deal" might be, or, in the worst of cases, underscore that your union's disciplined preparations since the signing of the last contract will be put to good use.

How often you hold negotiation sessions is directly proportional to the sense of progress those sessions impart to your team. It is not unusual to meet once a week at the beginning of bargaining so that each side can familiarize themselves with the proposals put on the table. The sessions should eventually become more regular. As the possibility of a deal or impasse gets closer, the meeting pace can become feverish, with sessions lasting for as long as that elusive sense of progress is maintained.

The Role Of The Chief Spokesperson. The message across the table from your team to the employer's team must be well prepared, on point, and spoken with one voice. There is no room in a formal bargaining session for the unchoreographed dissenting voice that the free-wheeling environment of the team caucus can provide. That is not to say, however, that well-choreographed passion from members of the team who know their limits is not an effective tactic.

It is ultimately up to the chief spokesperson to determine what will be said, how it will be said, and who will say it. Consider the chief spokesperson as a front man for a rock band; that is, he is usually the soloist, backed by varying degrees of harmony and music. He sometimes shares his solo duties with other members of the band. Sometimes those solos are musical, sometimes they are singing, but they are all done to showcase the strengths of the band members as they strive to put forth the band's musical message. That, in essence, is how a negotiating team works.

Who should be the chief spokesperson? This role is best filled by a knowledgeable, credible, and articulate debater. The person must be knowledgeable of the collective bargaining agreement and articulate in the reasons for modifying it. The person must be well respected by both the union's negotiating team and the employer's team. Many unions opt to have their attorney as the chief spokesperson for these reasons. Remember, the chief spokesperson is not the final decision maker. This individual is the messenger for the team, and with the team's approval, he can have the flexibility to establish a one-on-one relationship with the employer's chief spokesperson. This is an important dynamic when the potential for sidebar meetings as a tool to enhance and expedite the process becomes timely.

Sidebar Meetings. A sidebar meeting is an off the record, issue-oriented conversation that usually takes place between the two chief spokespersons out of earshot of the two negotiating teams. Many times, the chief spokespersons are accompanied by the primary decision makers for each side, usually the union president and his counterpart in the employer's administration. Sidebars cannot take place without a high level of trust among the negotiating team members that no deals will be cut without an assessment by the entire team. Successful sidebars result in either a distilling of complicated issues of contention, or the floating of an offer for consideration by a respective team prior to returning to the formal bargaining session and hopefully, a tentative agreement on a specific article or contract issue.

Tentative Agreements. When agreement is reached on bargaining issues, they are usually removed from the table as "tentative agreements." Tentative agreements are usually initialed by the chief spokesperson for each side, and are considered "off the table" and are not again brought up in the context of negotiations short of impasse.

THE NEED FOR AN INTEGRATED APPROACH TO NEGOTIATIONS.

Negotiating a contract is much more comprehensive than the give and take that takes place at the bargaining table. As a union leader, you have to remember that communication with your membership, communication with elected officials, and communication with the public are all part of the synergy that makes up the whole of the negotiating process.

Communication With Members. As a broad proposition, it's a good idea to give your membership general, and not specific, updates on how bargaining is going. Too much information can actually be harmful, as your membership might react disproportionately to individual tentative agreements without considering the entire package. Ground rules may even preclude an update regarding the specifics of the tentative agreements and the positions taken by the opposing side.

It's a good idea to give your membership general, and not specific, updates on how bargaining is going.

All that said, it is important that your communications with the membership accurately reflect the amount of progress that has been made as well as the negotiating team's level of optimism or pessimism that the contract will be settled in the near future.

Communication With Elected Officials. As a general rule, once negotiations have commenced, there should be no communication with elected officials (unless they are at the table) regarding issues discussed at bargaining. That said, there are times when a one-on-one conversation with a "trusted" individual might be the only way to jump start good faith negotiations or to actually bring home the deal. But be wise if you implement this strategy. "Trusted" is a relative term when dealing with politicians. Tempting as it might be to try to pit elected officials against one another (or their staffs, in some cases) you run the risk of accusations of bad faith bargaining and potential of leaks to the media. Don't forget, as hard as a politician tries to establish good relationships with cops and firefighters, they try harder with the media.

I was always of the mind that politicians can be useful prior to negotiations, not trustful during them, and while they might be more prone to be sympathetic to a public safety union than some other labor entity, they are still generally inappropriate audiences for the discussion of confidential information. It is very much a high risk-high reward assessment and decision you will have to make. Remember, though, the person you "trusted" might someday be across the table from you in a future contract negotiation – how will they view you then?

Communication With The Public. Usually there is mutual agreement that ongoing negotiations will remain closed to public scrutiny. Such a ground rule is beneficial because it provides flexibility for the give and take inherent to the process; that is, it keeps the parties from playing to the cameras, reporters, and audience that might be present to monitor the bargaining. The high profile and newsworthiness that often accompanies public safety contract negotiations provides a challenge to the union to show its members to be responsible public safety partners within the community while maintaining the pressure on elected officials and bureaucrats to provide an acceptable agreement for the bargaining unit.

KEEPING RECORDS OF NEGOTIATIONS.

Keeping good records of the negotiating sessions is an important piece of the bargaining process. Years later, bargaining notes can make or break an important grievance. I can speak from personal experience on this one.

Anchorage elected a new mayor in the early 1990s. He decided that if he changed patrol officers from a 4/10 to a 5/8 shift, it would be the equivalent of adding 52 new officers. As he "reasoned," the schedule change meant officers would be working one extra day a week for 52 weeks; hence, 52 more officers. You can go figure on the math. At any rate, three years after the change, we won an arbitration challenging the change to 5/8s, with patrol officers awarded millions of dollars in back overtime. The key evidence in the arbitration hearing? Negotiations notes taken 20 years before on the meaning of the "work schedule" language in the contract. Even though the note takers were long gone from the department, and in some cases deceased, the notes they took in bargaining swayed an arbitrator to the correct interpretation of the contract.

Your bargaining team should have at least two note takers assigned specifically to that task. NO ONE will initially volunteer to do it, and all things considered, can you blame them? The note takers must be sensitive to statements that reflect not only directly on the mechanics of the contract, but they must be able to pick up on (and make note of) the kinds of statements made that show intent or mindset of the employer's representatives. It only takes one time for an employer's chief spokesperson to speak or misspeak beneficially to the union on an issue, and the benefit of having the noted record available to clarify intent or hold the employer's "feet to the fire" becomes clear.

Training the note takers is valuable if the time is available and the persons are open-minded to it. Two skills to be honed are the speed at which the notes are actually taken and the ability to separate the wheat from the chaff; that is, to be able to identify the important statements and papers that are exchanged across the table. If there are already members on your team who are proficient at shorthand, these would be likely candidates for note takers.

Taking notes on a laptop is a great idea, but do it quietly! Having three or four people typing away while you are trying to negotiate a deal is sufficiently irritating. All notes should be circulated to union bargaining team members for review prior to the next bargaining session, and should be maintained on a permanent basis by the union.

Recording Negotiations. This is an easy one: Don't! While note taking really does nothing to diminish the free flowing discussion necessitated in a good bargaining session, nothing stifles the give and take like the presence of a tape recorder. While I never hesitated to use an appropriate expletive to make necessary and timely points – though rarely in negotiations, sometimes in a sidebar, and regularly in caucus – there were, in retrospect, points made that would have lost their necessary punch had I been concerned that my color commentary was being memorialized on tape.

THE USE OF PROFESSIONALS DURING NEGOTIATIONS.

I've already talked about the use of a professional negotiator. If you can afford one, do it. The relative additional value that a professional negotiator brings to the team more than offsets the cost of the negotiator's time.

When making decisions on whether to hire a professional negotiator or another expert, keep in mind marginal costs and benefits. Let's say you have a 200-person bargaining unit, and the average total compensation is $75,000. That means that a 1.0% increase in wages will be worth $150,000 (200 x $75,000 x 1.0%). And that's just in the first year. All future year increases will "roll up" on the higher base, with the result being that a 1.0% marginal difference in the result can quickly mean millions of dollars to your bargaining unit over time. It's math like that you have to consider in deciding whether to retain experts in bargaining.

Economists. Economists are a dime a dozen, but a good economist is worth his weight in gold. At risk of employing yet another example of tired phraseology, I can tell you unequivocally that you get what you pay for. Find out, either through your local university or your contacts in the chamber of commerce, who the well-respected economists are in your area. Be careful not to hire a testimony whore – you know, the type of "professional" who all too often shows up in court to testify as an expert for the side who offers the most attractive stipend the soonest. And don't discount strategies such as hiring someone with the intent that they would be conflicted out if you were to engage them before the employer is able to contract with them.

Why would you hire an economist? For two reasons. Obtaining good projections of the local economy can be invaluable in deciding on whether you want a short-term or long-term contract. In addition, an economist with the right sort of experience can dissect your employer's budget, challenge the underlying assumptions upon which the budget it based, and help you figure out if there's discretionary money in the budget.

Insurance Analysts. Over the years, health care has become one of the two or three most important issues in public safety bargaining, reaching a point of importance where it occasionally plays a larger role in negotiations than wages. Nothing cuts so quickly into a wage increase than increased premium co-payment costs and higher deductibles, particularly with the medical cost of living increasing at a rate multiples of times higher than the Consumer Price Index. As long as health and welfare issues remain subject to collective bargaining, accessibility to information, plan design, flexibility, and the true cost of coverage must be addressed.

No cop or firefighter is expected to have the skills or time to provide your bargaining team with the information necessary to determine an appropriate bargaining posture on these issues. Long before bargaining begins, it is in your best interest to cozy up with a trusted insurance analyst, gather the appropriate information, and have your team or Executive Board address the health care priorities for your union.

Obtaining Information For Professional Evaluation. Remember that part of the obligation to collectively bargain in good faith is the obligation to share information relevant to the bargaining process. That means that mounds of data possessed by the employer must be disclosed to you if you ask for it. The type of data commonly exchanged in bargaining includes employer budgets and CAFRs (or Consolidated Audited Financial Reports), workload and productivity data, and health insurance utilization information.

Part of the obligation to collectively bargain in good faith is the obligation to share information relevant to the bargaining process.

THE PROCESS OF CONTRACT RATIFICATION.

Once you reach a negotiated deal, educating and marketing the agreement to the general membership is the next challenge. Any agreement brought back to the general membership without the full support of your negotiating team is almost surely destined to fail to gain the needed votes for ratification. For purposes of our discussion, let's assume that early on in the process you chose your team wisely and each member is a reasonable and responsible individual. Let's also assume that, as a team, you became educated through your work with the professionals that you hired regarding the economic and political impacts of your deal and its realistic relationship to what could possibly have been achieved. Let's also assume that your team would not consider putting before your membership a deal that was not the best possible under the present financial and political conditions. Let's finally assume that each member of your team is willing to stand up, take ownership of the deal, and personally sell the deal to the general membership as a good contract for your union. If those assumptions can't be made, you need to get yourself back to the table or call impasse and move on to the next phase of your bargaining process.

It goes without saying that no negotiated deal will please everyone, and the job of the bargaining team and the union leadership is to ensure that the naysayers are in the minority when it comes time to vote. It also goes without saying that if the team did its best and is returning to the members with a solid and fair deal, those naysayers will be the same members who were too busy to be a part of the bargaining team or who have other agendas in regard to the union or the union's leadership. But if the deal is falling flat amongst the most intelligent and reasonable of your membership, prepare to take a licking and re-evaluate what you are presenting.

How To Educate The Membership. The best way to educate the membership is through informational meetings. Make sure that the informational meetings are completed at least a week before the ratification vote to allow for personal lobbying and educating by the negotiating team and Executive Board members. A time delay like this also helps to mitigate any emotional reactions that, over time, will most likely be replaced with more rational perspectives.

The best way to educate the membership is through informational meetings.

Make sure that all of your members are aware of the informational meetings. Post flyers, use snail mail, e-mail, and social networks (if you use them) to get the word out, and have people sign in at the meetings to memorialize who was present when the deal was discussed. Have at least three meetings, at different times on different days, and once again, make sure the meetings are scheduled, noticed, and held within the parameters of your union's bylaws.

A good way to introduce the deal is to place it in the context of the negotiations survey of the general membership that was conducted in preparation for bargaining. Since the result of this survey provided your bargaining team with a guide as to the priorities of the general membership, the bargaining team should feel comfortable placing the survey results side by side with the parameters of the tentative deal. If the team did its job, the comparison should reflect very closely what the membership had told you they wanted, and what you have brought back to them for ratification. Use the information and perspectives of your hired professionals, who should be present at the meetings, to explain why some of the bargaining priorities might not have been achieved. Don't hesitate to also discuss the projected outcomes should those issues be pushed toward fact finding and arbitration.

How Much Information Should Be Put Out To The Membership During The Ratification Process? Never keep substantive information from your general membership. Never patronize them. Never lie to them. Make sure the presentation provides all of the information about the tentative deal that they need to make an informed decision about the contract. Highlight the differences between the present contract and the new deal. Craft what your team perceives to be potentially important questions that might be asked into an informational handout in question and answer format. Be professional and prepare a PowerPoint presentation. Memorialize all handouts and PowerPoint slides and place them into the negotiations record for your union's use later should there be disenfranchised members alleging that they were misled.

Never keep substantive information from your general membership.

Remember, there are no secrets. As soon as a tentative agreement is struck, put the wheels in motion for a full and thorough briefing to the general membership. Your team has no control over the members of the employer's team, and it is

As soon as a tentative agreement is struck, put the wheels in motion for a full and thorough briefing to the general membership.

not unusual for word of a pending settlement to "leak out." The worst thing that can happen is to have your Executive Board and general membership read about the tentative agreement in the morning paper or to see a story about it on the Internet. Don't forget, on any given news day, police and fire stories are usually the leads, and on a slow news day, bet on it.

Involve The Executive Board. Before there is any attempt to educate the general membership about the tentative agreement, efforts should be made by the negotiating team to secure support from the union's Executive Board. Support from the Executive Board is paramount in the strategy to sell the deal to the general membership. While the negotiating team was most likely selected by the union leadership, the Executive Board was probably elected at large from the general membership, and the benefit of harnessing that inherent credibility in support of a negotiated deal is immeasurable.

While much has been said about selling the agreement, there is another benefit to running the tentative contract past the Executive Board. For the bargaining team caught up in the emotionally draining exercise of negotiations, there is a potential to be "too close" to the merits of a tentative agreement. It is only human nature to revel in the fruits of your labor. An Executive Board that is savvy to the needs and expectations of the general membership can provide a "truth check" to the negotiating team before members of the team put their credibility on the line.

How To Hold Your Vote On The Contract. Your union's bylaws will likely articulate how a contract ratification vote will be conducted. I'm not a fan of mail-in votes. This helps to preclude the "ignorance" factor; that is, the tendency for those least informed to cast a ballot. At least by having to make the effort to get to a designated place to vote, the odds are that those willing to make the effort to travel to vote are the same members who have put forth some effort to learn about what they are voting for – and because you believe in the contract you have negotiated, that is a good thing.

Of course the employer has a ratification process, too. This usually consists of a vote by the city council to accept the negotiated agreement. It is always in everyone's best interest for the police or fire union to have already voted on an agreement and accepted it, thereby putting the pressure on the city council to articulate why what is good enough for the employer and the union is not good enough for them. There will always be the usual pontificating on the part of the politicians, but if the union and the administration presently in office can speak as one voice pertaining to the contract, there is virtually no chance that a legislative body will block the contract's approval.

NOTES

[1] Such a "Morale Survey" can be a two-edged sword. If the timing is right, it can be a strong message of no confidence to politicians and administrators that will echo, but never foster, public sentiment. If such a survey is publicized, you had better be sure of the outcome. There is nothing so embarrassing or potentially devastating to a politician than a survey of public safety employees who have no faith in the chain of command; at the same time, there is nothing so embarrassing or potentially devastating to a public safety union if they misread the public and their own members, and the union leadership comes across as self-interested whiners with no credibility. Never publicize the results of a morale survey to coincide with pending contract negotiations. The transparency of such a stunt diminishes any good will with the public that might have been established over time.

[2] *See* Appendix F, "The Total Compensation Survey."

[3] *See* http://www.bls.gov/cpi/.

[4] http://data.bls.gov/cgi-bin/cpicalc.pl.

[5] http://www.cbo.gov/ftpdocs/99xx/doc9957/01-07-Outlook.pdf.

CHAPTER 12

FINANCES AND FUNDRAISERS

Public safety employees have good reason to believe they are underpaid, and the last thing they want to do is pay more than they think they should in union dues. There's a funny thing, though, about public safety folks. As a rule, they are pretty savvy as to where their bread is buttered, and they are willing to invest in a union that provides them the kind of representation that has the potential to improve their lot in life. Make the case, the esprit and loyalty to the union grows exponentially. Screw it up, and the sense of distrust, cynicism regarding the quality of their representation, and overall dissatisfaction that leads to disenfranchised groups of members starts to snowball.

INCOME TO THE ORGANIZATION.

Modern public safety labor organizations usually have more than one form of revenue. Here are some of the issues that can come up with the most common forms of revenue.

Dues. The first question any union leader should ask when it comes to the question of dues is "What is fair?" Simple enough, right? The main thing here is that a fair level of dues is easily explainable if the union leadership can justify it in terms of services versus costs, and the long-term financial needs of the organization.

The first question any union should ask about its finances is, "Do we have enough money to fight the good fight?" What's that amount? I think a public safety union should have no less than $2,000 in liquid or semi-liquid assets for each member. That means a 200-member organization should have $400,000 in cash or cash-like investments. Obviously, as organizations get very, very large or are small, the $2,000 per member number can vary, but for most public safety unions, it's a good guideline.

The next question you should ask is where you want the organization to be in five years. Do you want to buy a building? Do you anticipate a huge public relations campaign to stave off layoffs or sway the public on a privatization issue? What can you reasonably project about the growth or shrinkage of your membership? Factor all of these sorts of considerations into the equation, and adjust your aims accordingly.

Once the union has a handle on how much income is needed to function in the best interest and to the realistic expectations of its members, the determination must be made as to how dues should be collected. You start with two choices: Either by a percentage of wages or a fixed-dues amount.[1] The lower-paid members will almost always opt for the percentage, while the higher-paid members will feel that they should not have to subsidize their brothers and sisters for the same level of services that all receive. When the dues are figured on a percentage basis, the organization always has access to an almost painless and understandable methodology for adjusting the actual amount of dues collected. For example, if the bargaining unit were to negotiate a three-year contract in which wages increased by 3% the first year, were frozen the second year, and increased by 3% the third year, union dues would respectively increase by 3% the first year, freeze the second year, and increase by 3% the third year.

Above all, it should be the general membership and not the Executive Board that sets dues. Should an Executive Board succumb to the siren song of expediency promulgated by Board-set dues, Board members will soon find they are expendable. Ultimately, the method used to set and adjust dues must be fair, predictable, and legitimized by the general membership.

Dues Increase And Dues Reduction. Nothing generates as much organizational pain, anguish, divisiveness, and discontent as a discussion about raising dues. It's funny, though, how a discussion regarding dues reduction, while having just as much potential impact on the financial health of the bargaining unit, suddenly creates an aura of goodwill and satisfaction, without regard to the potential risk.

No matter how justifiable a dues increase is, cops and firefighters will scrutinize, challenge, and question every cent above what they have been used to paying. Only when you have been matter-of-factly grilled by a very competent and experienced white-collar crime detective in a packed general membership meeting regarding pro-forma budgets can you fully appreciate the value of having worked through and prepared in detail every possible justification for the dues increase. That is why I am partial to having dues set on a percentage basis where the amount of dues will increase with bargaining unit wages.

If your organization chooses a fixed-dues amount rather than a percentage, you must prepare yourself for a helluva ride through the fickle landscape of member whims and economic uncertainty. While your union might thrive on a renewed debate about dues levels, it is no fun for union leadership. It is time consuming, and often highlights the potential divisiveness between relative "haves" and "have-nots." Don't forget, we're talking police and fire here, so even if there are no nonsworn employees in your union, you will soon see the self-proclaimed "have nots" come out of the woodwork, particularly if anything in your collective bargaining agreement is tiered or grandfathered.

And, if your economic forecast provides you the opportunity to lower dues, pay bills, and provide the expected member services…great! For a while, that is. It only takes one time to decide that dues will be lowered to set up the organization for the inevitable and always difficult day when you must face an angry and demanding general membership that must be convinced of the need to raise their dues. Some firehouse philosopher might tell you such discussions are healthy for the organization and engender awareness of how the union's monies are being spent. Nonsense. They are not standing up there trying to convince folks who usually pay no attention to what their union is doing unless they are in trouble or it impacts their paycheck about the organization's upcoming budgetary needs.

An alternative to dues reductions – and one I like – is to keep dues at the same level but give the Executive Board the opportunity at the end of the year to authorize a partial dues rebate. Here's how a rebate system would work. Say your dues are $100 a month, you've hit your goal of liquid assets of $2,000 per member, and your anticipated expenses are only $80 per month. Instead of lowering dues to $80, keep them at $100, and at the end of the year the Executive Board will have the latitude to authorize a dues rebate of $100, $200, or whatever amount is fiscally prudent. The union then writes checks to each member in the amount of the dues rebate. Not only does a rebate system avoid the more constricting result of a dues decrease, it provides members with a year-end check that is much appreciated.

The Deductibility Of Union Dues From Federal Income Taxes. Your union dues can be deducted from your federal income tax, but only to the extent that your union dues together with all your miscellaneous itemized deductions exceeds two percent of your adjusted gross income. Check out IRS Publication 529, "Miscellaneous Deductions" for more detailed information.

Assessments. Dues assessments are troublesome (and sometimes avoidable) beasts that are a function of poor planning, unforeseen and unavoidable events, or a strategy to get the attention of the employer, politicians, and/or the public. Basically, an assessment is a one time, issue-oriented fee paid by all members. Usually, union leadership will go hat in hand to members for a specific amount or percentage added to dues that will be earmarked to be spent on that one issue that forced the leadership into the lion's den. Let's lay it on the line: It better be worth it, and there better be sunset provisions for the assessment.

An assessment is a one time, issue-oriented fee paid by all members.

Excluding the need to assess as a reaction to poor fiscal planning, assessments can be useful tools to garner quick action or attention. Say your union wants to buy a building that would be perfect for your organization, but there is tight market and you need influx of cash to make the deal work. You can set up a building fund and assess the general membership an appropriate rate for a specific period of time to help buy the building. Perhaps you're locked into difficult bargaining, or need to establish a war chest for arbitration. Once again, an assessment may be the answer.

Some labor organizations have even sought assessments they haven't really wanted, simply as a way to communicate a message to the employer and the public. For example, let's say you anticipate that you're facing what portends to be quarrelsome and contentious contract negotiations. An assessment, particularly a carefully publicized one, sends a message that your membership is willing to expend whatever resources are necessary to prevail. There may be a certain transparency to such an action, but if you control the message and stay on point with the fact that assessments are reserved only for the "gravest and most serious circumstances," the tactic is a very effective way to gain media and political attention.

Dues From Associate Members. Dues from associate members are typically quite modest – $5 or $10 per month. Once again, if you choose to have associate members, you should make sure your bylaws specify what rights they have and, more importantly, the rights they do not have.

Initiation Fees. Initiation fees are paid by new members when they hire on with the employer. Initiation fees are largely a vestige of days past, when private sector unions such as the Teamsters began to represent public sector employees. Some would argue that there should be no initiation fee, but should a new employee utilize union services and then abruptly terminate his employment, the initiation fee allows the organization to recoup some of the potential expenses. Initiation fees also have their place as a tool to engender a sense of commitment to the union right from the get-go. The initiation fee usually causes new members to pay attention to what their money is being spent on, to ask questions, and to thereby familiarize themselves with the benefits (and responsibilities) of union membership. A good formula for figuring an initiation fee is 10% of the initial wage for the employee's first month of service.

FUNDRAISERS.

Public safety unions have the kind of leverage in fundraising that other labor organizations can only envy. The goodwill that public safety employees generally enjoy with businesses and private citizens often manifests itself in dollars. But along with that incredible standing in the community comes a responsibility, particularly if the police or fire union intends to nurture annual fundraising events with a potential to grow.

There are all kinds of fundraising events, each of which has pros and cons associated with it. Some examples are appreciation nights, circuses, variety acts, concerts, celebrity sports events, raffles, lotteries, magazine and newspaper sales, and simply asking for money. Before deciding on the type of event your organization wishes to sponsor, take a good look at the purpose of the event and how much money is intended to be raised. While this might seem simplistic, it is a very important first step. For instance, there is a huge difference between a fundraising event sponsored by a police union where all the proceeds are earmarked for a charity, as opposed to the same union sponsoring an event where all the proceeds go to the operation and fiscal well-being of the union itself. While either purpose is valid, the marketing and public relations strategies are different.

Appreciation Nights. The best kind of fundraiser is an appreciation night. Typically, an appreciation night is a way for the community to express its thanks to public safety employees. They may involve honors given to employees who have gone "above and beyond" in the public's interest.

Appreciation nights usually involve two types of income. Attendees purchase seats at a table, or entire tables, with the ticket price set high enough to produce decent income after expenses. Income is also often produced at appreciation nights through silent and oral auctions, with the items put up for bid having been donated by local businesses. A good master of ceremonies can keep an appreciation night lively and interesting, and a good auctioneer can encourage the free flow of contributions.

If you go this route – and some of the most successful public safety union fundraisers in the country are appreciation nights – make sure you start the process by contracting with an event planner. A good event planner can provide you with "cradle to grave" service, starting with the development of the budget for the event, negotiating with the event site, lining up potential donors, and even picking the menu for dinner.

Performances. Circuses, variety acts, concerts, and celebrity sports events are all effective, though sometimes frustrating, avenues for fundraising. The problem common to all of these types of fundraising events are you are never really sure of what you are getting until the event gets underway. Usually you are working with a promoter (the virtues of which will be discussed below) and each of the events usually has a level of risk involved. While you might have an airtight contract with the promoter as to the split on profits, did you expect the low-keyed yet very organized PETA (People for the Ethical Treatment of Animals) branch in your city to picket the circus that you have based your entire fundraising strategy around? Did you ever consider that the popular rock band you booked for the police union's concert is made up of replacements or aged has-beens? And as for celebrity athletic events, before any deal is inked, make sure there is quality control language in the contract with the promoter. Insist on a binding roster of "stars" by a certain date to ensure no last minute surprises.

Whenever possible, scout the gig. Use the strengths and weaknesses of the act as bargaining tools when dealing with the promoter. Be realistic. Really big acts usually don't play high school gyms or small town halls. Retired athletes who are willing to travel for "donkey" basketball games or who willingly play the Police and Fire All-Stars are usually not Hall of Famers.

Raffles. If the thought of putting your organization's reputation and financial future in the hands of geriatric rockers or donkey basketball makes your Executive Board nervous, consider the possibility of a raffle or a lottery. Most states require a permit or a license to hold either of these types of fundraising events, so be sure to check your state statutes, speak with organizations that have done a raffle or a lottery before, and seek legal counsel to ensure the "big draw" doesn't result in a "big fine." If your union has its ducks in a row, a raffle or a lottery can generate significant revenue.

What types of items are raffled? Up in Anchorage, we raffled a four-wheeler. A quick Internet search shows that public safety unions are currently raffling things like a cord of wood, a Harley-Davidson, a Corvette, and cruises.

Magazine and Newspaper Sales. Some larger public safety unions publish magazines or newspapers, and use the ad sales for the publications to generate revenue for the union. The ad sales are really nothing more than another form of telemarketing, with the advertisement being the "product" that is sold. Individuals purchasing ads usually have simple listings of their names; businesses tend to have larger, more elaborate, and more expensive display ads. The union's percentage of the total revenue is usually the same as with other telemarketing efforts, around 20%.

Perhaps the most recent form of fundraiser is a direct solicitation for donations. This form of solicitation usually involves a mass mailing to the public. The mailing briefly describes the aim of the union, and asks for a donation. The request can be coupled with an offer that if the donation is at a particular level, say $50, the person will become an "honorary" or "associate" member of the organization. Some public safety unions even set up a PayPal link on their web pages for direct donations.[2] The disadvantages of approaches like this are that the public may think they are "owed" something for their donations or honorary membership, and that there is something a bit distasteful about just asking for money. The advantages are that telemarketing is not involved, and unions typically keep a much larger percentage of the proceeds (70% v. 20%) that are collected. An additional advantage is that the union is able to build a mailing list of supporters, a list that can be used in times of political difficulty.

> **Whatever your organization does to generate revenue involving interaction with the public or with businesses must be honest, straightforward, and beyond reproach.**

Whatever your organization does to generate revenue involving interaction with the public or with businesses must be honest, straightforward, and beyond reproach. In some jurisdictions, the benefits leveraged by the very nature of being connected with public safety, particularly law enforcement, can diminish or even disappear. A case out of Maine, *Auburn Police Union v. Carpenter,* upheld the state's position that solicitation by the police union was inherently coercive because at least the appearance of coercion inheres in every solicitation on behalf of law enforcement.[3] Bummer. Maybe the guys in Maine should try donkey basketball with celebrity judges.

FUNDRAISERS AND PROMOTERS.

There are only two rules to remember when dealing with professional fundraisers and promoters. Rule 1: They are all sleazy. Rule 2: Don't ever forget Rule 1.

I know from experience that the first time you deal with a fundraiser or a promoter, you are apt to be taken to the cleaners when it comes to the percentage of gross. For hard-charging, hard-bargaining labor unions, our track record in holding the line with fundraisers and promoters make us look wimpy. They know that, and can usually get away with an initial multi-year contract until we open our eyes and see the amount of money that comes in as a result of the goodwill and leverage that police and fire organizations wield. The fundraisers and promoters are generally more aware of that than union leaders, and initially enjoy the benefits of our ignorance and our hard-earned goodwill in the community.

With that said, let's look at ways to maintain quality control on the use of your organization's name by fundraisers and maximize the financial relationship.

How To Research The Background Of A Fundraiser Or Promoter. Do your homework. Cops and firefighters have as good a statewide and national network as any other profession. Numerous seminars and conferences are held annually that afford plenty of opportunities to ask others about their successes and failures with fundraisers and promoters. Each state keeps a list of firms and individuals that have registered as professional fundraisers. These lists can be obtained through the Department of Justice or from the Attorney General of each state. A good example is the comprehensive report posted by California at http://www.ag.ca.gov/charities/publications/cfrreport.pdf.

Get a list of recent references. If there is a mutually satisfactory experience between your organization and a specific fundraiser or a promoter, there is a good chance that you will be used as a reference by them as they try to drum up new clientele. Expect to be contacted by prospective clients in regard to your level of satisfaction with the person or persons dropping your name or that of your organization. After all, they are only doing what you should be doing before you engage in any business agreements with any fundraiser or promoter. You do the same.

Don't just rely on the references listed by the promoter. Find other organizations the promoter has worked for. You can track these down through Internet searches, by asking other labor organizations, and the attorney general listings discussed above are an invaluable source of this information.

The Contract. Do not use the form contract provided by these folks. Above all, don't take the initial split offered on any boilerplate contract, and be wary of any promises not made in writing. Once again, our good friends in California have come up with a solid model to use when crafting your contract with a fundraiser or a promoter. It can be found at http://ag.ca.gov/charities/publications/modelcontract.pdf. While your specific event might not require the comprehensive language that a much larger function would demand, there are certain "take-aways" that are applicable to the crafting of all of these contracts.

Depending on the type of event, two or three clear, concise pages will usually suffice.

Be sure to specifically articulate in the contract how all expenses are to be divided, and how all revenues are to be dispersed. These contracts do not have to be 100-page tomes; in fact, depending on the type of event, two or three clear, concise pages will usually suffice.

As a minimum, the contract should cover:

1. The date the deal was struck.

2. The specific fundraising event's name, place, and time.

3. Clarification as to which party is responsible for securing the appropriate permits necessary to conduct the event.

4. Clarification as to which party is responsible for securing the appropriate permits necessary to conduct advance ticket sales, if appropriate. This is usually done by the promoter, as is the contracting for a sales force to conduct advance ticket sales.

5. Clarification as to who will provide the office space and telephones to conduct advance ticket sales. This is usually done by the promoter, since few unions have halls and phone banks set up already.[4]

6. Clarification as to the method in which all monies collected by advance ticket sales will be deposited and withdrawn. The best system is for all receipts to be deposited in the union's account, though you often see contracts calling for receipts to be deposited into a joint bank account of the promoter and union.

7. A clause listing the typical production costs of the event, and specifying that the promoter will pay those costs. Typical costs include:

   • Rent of location, including custodial services. Be aware of any hidden costs that might result from requirements by local unions, such as additional stagehands and electricians, in addition to those carried by a show or event;

   • Liability and property damage insurance;

   • Advertising for radio, television, newspapers, and posters;

   • Telephones and office space as mentioned above;

   • Licenses, permits and clearances as mentioned above;

   • Tickets for advance sales;

   • Anything else that might be mutually agreed upon as expenses.

8. A clause that specifically states that the promoter will underwrite all expenses and assures that there will be no possible loss to the union. This sort of clause should also require the promoter to defend and indemnify the union against any claims resulting from the event.

9. A clause that states that final settlement and division of funds shall be made on site, immediately following the completion of the event.

10. A guarantee of a certain percentage of gross sales going to the union. In no case should this percentage be less than 20%.

11. A clause that refers to authorized signatures necessary to validate any agreements.

Don't sign any contract until it has been reviewed, revised, and rewritten by your union's attorney.

Finally, don't sign any contract until it has been reviewed, revised, and rewritten by your union's attorney. I once took a promoter's proposed contract to our union lawyer; what came back from him was a completely changed document.

WHAT CAN GO WRONG AND HOW TO PREVENT IT.

Your fundraiser or promoter might hire employees to promote the event and generate advance sales. I guarantee you that your cops might see some familiar faces among the newly-hired help. These outfits may well pay minimum wage and their screening criteria are based on expediency, not quality. The potential for misrepresentations to the public, complaints from the public, and problems with tracking cash receipts are all very possible.

Probably the easiest way to alleviate potential problems is to establish a liaison to the fundraiser or promoter. Not only will this person function as the clearing-house, this representative of your organization can monitor all ongoing activities with the fundraiser or promoter, to include ensuring compliance with any charitable solicitations laws, relationships with the State Attorney General's office or the appropriate office responsible for monitoring charitable solicitations, and ensuring prompt payment of the various expenses incurred by the fundraiser or promoter.

It is best that the person who acts as the liaison to the fundraiser or promoter provide a regular update to the Executive Board, Audit Committee or a subcommittee tasked with fundraiser or event oversight. Such a report should ensure that mechanisms are in place to truth check the entire enterprise to which you have attached your organization's name, goodwill, and financial interest.

BANKING AND INVESTMENTS.

Your union should establish a relationship with a banking institution, and should consider the role investments might play in the growth or stabilization of your organization. Keep two things in mind: (1) A strategic plan, or at a minimum, a sense of near-term and long-term goals for your union, will provide valuable guidelines and planning tools as you deal with incoming revenues; and (2) you are cops and firefighters…not bankers and financial consultants. Planning and the use of professional assistance will always pay big dividends in the long run.

How To Select A Bank. Ogden Nash once said, "Bankers are just like everyone else, except richer." The selection of a reputable financial institution to handle your union's money is a decision that should not be taken lightly. You should understand the services offered by commercial banks, how to use those services in the best interest of your organization, and what those services cost. Any commercial bank should be willing to supply you with the American Association of Banker's booklet, *Using Banking Services.*

The selection of a bank should be based on five criteria:

1. **Your money must be safe.** Have your Executive Board review the financial statement of all of the banks that you are considering, and make a judgment as to the bank's financial health.

2. **Convenience of doing business with the bank.** Years ago, proximity was a major consideration for a successful relationship with your union's bank. That is not the case these days when banking is done online and through the mail. Remember, the bank that provides you the most service at the least cost might be hundreds of miles from your union offices, police department, or fire station.

3. **Service.** Quality service and efficient management are huge considerations when your union develops a relationship with a commercial financial institution. Some banks actually specialize in small businesses and labor organizations. Consider the speed at which your deposits are acknowledged, the ease with which loans might be

obtained, and the efficiency with which any unusual problems are handled. Competition among banks generally keeps service quality high, but if the time comes when a bank and its management are not viewed as a supportive partner by your Executive Board, then start shopping for an institution that will provide the services required by the organization and the professional customer service that will preclude daily business transaction angst.

4. **Cost concerns.** Barring any qualitative differences, this should drive the selection of the bank for your union. If all the banks under consideration are judged the same in regards to safety, convenience and efficiency, then base your decision on cost. If there are noticeable differences in the services provided, then your organization should assign a value to each of those services and factor those considerations in accordingly. Bottom line, if the least-cost bank provides your union with everything it needs to function and grow, then the choice is obvious.

5. **Politics.** You're a political organization, or you should be. Why not choose a bank based on political concerns? Perhaps you should stay away from a multi-national bank in favor of a local bank, the president of which is prominent in local politics. I can't emphasize enough that public safety unions must constantly think in terms of the political implications of their actions. Choosing a bank is one of those many decisions that can have future political ramifications.

Choosing a bank is one of those many decisions that can have future political ramifications.

Establishing More Than One Bank Account. It is important to have a general operating account from which the daily business of your union can be accomplished. Any account that exceeds the FDIC insured ceiling of $250,000 should be split, with a separate account established at a different bank. Establishing an activities account, as previously discussed when dealing with a fundraiser or promoter, is always a good idea, and is sometimes demanded by state law. Any time you want to track or itemize a historical record of a specific fund or event, consider establishing a separate account.

Investments. This issue of investments for a police or fire labor union is one that breeds contention, yet investments can be the best way for your organization to financially provide your union the tools it needs to better represent the membership. Remember, activism costs money. Status in the community is often a function of financial capability. A union that uses up its financial resources every month to meet the operating needs of the present is not planning for the future. Even if the membership does not grow in numbers from year to year, there is no reason for the financial identity of the organization to stagnate too. Growth is not merely a function of the size of the membership, it is a measurement of all that is important to the organization in terms of influence, real property, and financial health.

The goals of the organization will help to determine an investment strategy that is right for your union. Research and hire a financial consultant, who should not be the recently-retired firefighter or cop looking to make a second career out of investment advice. Remember, not every broker is capable of offering a smorgasbord of investment options, so it is important that the broker you choose provides what your union truly wants to invest in. This leads to another consideration, comparing broker fees and services. A little effort on the telephone and on the Internet will result in a pretty good comparison of commissions and fees.

Make your broker an integral part of your organization. Expose him or her to Executive Board meetings and, every once in a while, to the general membership. Educate your membership in the types of investments available, and assess your organization's risk tolerance as you strive to grow your union financially.

Some investment options to consider:

1. Securities backed by the full faith and credit of the U.S. Government. Let's start with the simplest – Savings Bonds. Savings bonds are debt securities issued by the U.S. Department of the Treasury to pay for the U.S. government's borrowing needs. Saving bonds are considered one of the safest investments because they are backed by the full faith and credit of the U.S. government. There are several types of U.S. savings bonds:

> Series EE Bonds. These savings bonds replaced the Series E bonds. They are purchased at a discount of half their face value. You cannot buy more than $5,000 (face value) during any calendar year. EE bonds increase in value as the interest accrues or accumulates and pay interest for 30 years. When EE bonds "mature," or come due, you are paid your original investment plus all of the interest.

> Series HH Bonds. You can purchase Series HH bonds, but only in exchange for Series EE or E bonds and Savings Notes, or with the proceeds from a matured Series HH bond. Unlike EE bonds, Series HH bonds are purchased at their face amount in $500 to $10,000 denominations, but there is no limit on the amount you can purchase. These bonds don't increase in value and have a maturity of 20 years.

> Series I Bonds. These bonds are sold at face value and grow with inflation-indexed earnings for up to 30 years. You can buy up to $5,000 in any calendar year.

Treasury bills, notes and governmental bonds are also generally backed by the full faith and credit of either the U.S. Government or a state or local governmental body. These investments necessitate a larger amount of cash at time of purchase. Treasury bills are sold at a discount and redeemed at full value. Treasury notes are registered or can be redeemed from one to seven years, and treasury bonds are like notes but mature over a period greater than seven years.

There are other bonds that are issued by governmental entities, but not backed by the full faith and credit of the U.S. Government. It is unlikely that the government would allow such bonds to fail since, at the federal level, they are established by Congress and the government is a part owner. These bonds generally pay a higher yield than Treasury bonds. Examples of these bonds are those issued by the Government National Mortgage Association (GNMA), the Federal National Mortgage Association (FNMA), and Federal Land Banks. Other types of bonds, such as municipal bonds, are also available and provide generally low risk investment opportunities for your union. Be aware, however, that the recent recession has brought more scrutiny to the operations of GNMA and FNMA, and allegations regarding the role of both entities in the crash of the housing market will surely test the government's future commitment to their overall health.

2. **Mutual Funds.** Mutual funds were devised by investment companies to address the common problems for small investors relating to time, technology, money, and risk. If you view your union as a single small investor, mutual funds offer options that provide opportunities to invest monies into a diversified, professionally managed pool of investments that would otherwise be a time consuming, riskier, and relatively expensive way to invest. The popularity of mutual funds for small institutional investors like a public safety union has resulted in a tremendous amount of information regarding available programs and options. Like anything else pertaining to your union's money...Do your homework!

3. **Common Stock.** Common stocks are the riskiest form of equities your union should consider, if you should consider them at all. The time, technology, money, and risk considerations that make mutual funds so attractive to a union might prove too unwieldy for common stock investments. Someone in a position of responsibility for your union must develop a relationship with a broker and be willing to monitor the stocks' performance and make recommendations to the union's leadership.

Common stocks are the riskiest form of equities your union should consider.

While common stocks are subject to wider variation and can offer higher possible returns, there is also the danger of not recouping anything should liquidation occur in the company in which your union has invested. Common stock investments can also result in cash dividends or extra shares of stock. Investment in common stock should be viewed very warily by your union as it seeks a diversified, balanced, and manageable investment portfolio.

Monitoring The Broker's Activities. Financial advisers, including stockbrokers, must follow certain rules imposed by the National Association of Securities Dealers and the New York Stock Exchange. Monitoring a broker's activities might become an afterthought since the investment world is complicated and intimidating to those who would rather leave the intricacies of finance to those best suited to manage it. However, you don't have to be a Wall Street guru to assess your organization's broker. Think in terms of these basic concepts that describe the critical functions of a broker:

1. Did the broker provide an investment strategy suitable for your organization?

2. Does the broker routinely suggest to your union which securities to acquire, liquidate, or hold?

3. Does the broker explain how news about a stock issuer's financial outlook might affect the performance of the stock?

4. Does the broker provide relevant information and answer specific questions that your organization's members might have about your union's investments?

5. Does the broker keep your union informed about your organization's investments?

6. Does it seem like the broker is making investments in the best interests of your organization, or instead is more interested in the commissions that changing investments can produce?

If a person or group of people in your union (possibly an investment committee of your Executive Board) takes the time and places the demand on the organization's selected broker to meet the above expectations, the organization will gain education and sophistication as its investment strategy becomes an integral part of the overall growth strategy for your organization.

I feel strongly that your bylaws should contain investment guidelines. Those guidelines should set the maximum percentages of the union's assets that can be placed in only one form of investment. For example, your guidelines might require that no more than 10% of assets be in common stock, 20% in mutual funds, and 35% in Treasury Bills. There are some who would argue that having investment guidelines built into bylaws deprives a union of the flexibility it needs to move money around in different forms of investments. To which I say that's just the point. This isn't your money you're investing, it's your members' money. You should be especially prudent and conservative in the way you approach the union's investments. If you're into an investment that requires "market timing," you're into an investment that's unsuitable for a union.

Your bylaws should contain investment guidelines.

The Actual Making Of Investments. The Executive Board should set the investment strategy for the union. The actual making of the investments should be delegated to a team or committee, which should brief the Executive Board at regular intervals regarding investment performance. Appropriate internal controls, such as countersignatures on investments, should be guided by the organization's bylaws and a clear written understanding with the broker.

FINANCIAL REPORTING TO THE EXECUTIVE BOARD AND GENERAL MEMBERSHIP.

A financial status report should be presented at each general and Executive Board meeting. Here's what should be included in the status report:

A financial status report should be presented at each general and Executive Board meeting.

- A category-by-category listing of all budget categories and the original budgeted amounts, together with a listing of year-to-date expenditures and income in each category.

- A balance sheet showing the organization's net worth, and the change in net worth from the prior reporting period.

- Any unusual expenditures that warrant particular attention by the Executive Board or general membership.

Access By Members To Financial Information. Dues-paying members have the right and should be granted access to the financial information of your union. However, there should be strict adherence to protocols regarding the viewing of this information and the security of the documentation. Never let any financial records be viewed singularly by a member. Always have at least the organization's treasurer present for any review of the organization's finances.

Do members have the right to copies of the union's financial records? The lawyers say that the issue is unsettled, but why be the test case? I see no harm in providing any member who requests them with copies of financial records. After all, they have the right to inspect the records and hand-copy whatever they want.

What To Watch In Expenditure Patterns In A Labor Organization. It always seems that "red flags" are often best seen in retrospect than when they are flapping wildly to get your attention. Let me tell you a quick "war story."

When I was vice-president of our police union back in 1988, we stocked and maintained the pop vending machines in our headquarters building. It was a pain for the guy on our Executive Board who single-handedly shopped for the pop, stocked the machines, and collected the change from the boxes. Since our union did this more as a service to the employees than a revenue generating mechanism, no one really paid any attention. We just gave him a check when he needed to go shopping to fill the machines. And for years, the machines were always full. Well...

We decided, as an Executive Board, to conduct an audit of our Association's finances. This had never been done before, and with an annual budget of only $230,000 there had been no previous financial imperatives to do so. But in 1988, it became clear that our union was not only entering contract negotiations with a mayor who was determined to make the City's unions the scapegoats for all the existing financial woes, but that the police union had been singled out as the initial target in a wholesale attack on the local collective bargaining ordinance and a court challenge to the constitutionality of binding arbitration.[5] It was this atmosphere of uncertainty that precipitated a motion to bring a vote for the establishment of a "war chest." That meant, in plain English, the doubling of dues for the general membership. The Executive Board recognized at the time that if we were going to request that the dues be doubled, we would have to account for all the monies collected by and expended by the union. Hence, the audit.

We all knew that the fellow who had been collecting checks from the union to buy the soda for the pop machines was also collecting the cash from the machines, sorting the change, and allegedly depositing what was collected – when he got around to it. Problem was, he sometimes hadn't gotten around to it for quite a while, and because no one else wanted to do it, the fact that he had bags of change in his garage became sort of an ongoing departmental joke. In fact, he was known to carry bags of change in his trunk during the winter for traction on the snow and ice. During the course of the Executive Board's discussion regarding the audit, he was in Disney World with his family.

When the audit was concluded, not only had it been discovered that over $30,000 was "borrowed" from the police union over time, but it turned out that the recent family trip to Disney World had been financed by a whole lot of quarters from the pop machines. Our hardworking Executive Board member was left with a felony conviction, and those of us on the Executive Board were left with red faces and a hard lesson learned: Always account for all revenues, all expenditures, all deposits, and ensure the treasurer keeps up on a monthly "budget to actual" report to the Executive Board. Look for aberrations in spending, missed deadlines for deposits, unusual transfers of funds. By the way, stay out of the vending business.

Credit Cards. Credit cards are a fact of life, and essential to doing business. If you read the news articles on union officials stealing from their unions, you'll learn that credit cards are also one of the "flash points" where theft is most common. Here are some news stories from just the last couple of years:

- "Charges were filed today against the former president of County Sheriff's Officers' Policemen's Benevolent Association and a former state delegate for the union, who were both accused of using union credit cards to make unauthorized purchases."

- "The Police Department's Internal Affairs Division opened an investigation after Chase Bank noticed in 2009 that [the police union official] had deposited tens of thousands of dollars into a personal account from a union credit card account."

- "The president of an Orange County firefighters' union has resigned in the middle of an investigation Friday. Credit card statements revealed three union leaders spent some of the organization's money at strip clubs and restaurants."

- "A former Police Department lieutenant was indicted Thursday on charges related to theft of money and misuse of credit cards from the Police Officers Association."

- "Ex-Cop Thought Union Credit Card Was For His Own Use."

- "A former town firefighter was arrested Tuesday and charged with second-degree larceny and illegal use of a credit card for allegedly using a firefighters' union credit card to purchase several thousand dollars in goods for personal use."

- "According to documents filed in court, [the corrections union president] admitted that she charged personal expenses to the Union's

American Express credit card, paid her government issued credit card with Union funds, and wrote numerous checks from the Union's checking account to herself."

- "According to the 37-count indictment, [the police officer] served as executive director of the police association from 1986 to 2004. Between October 2000 and February 2004, he defrauded the association by charging personal expenses of $8,879 on association credit cards issued to him and then disguising them as association expenses by cutting the tops and bottoms off the receipts."

How can you minimize the risk that your organization will show up in a headline like this? I'd recommend you follow at least these rules with respect to credit cards:

1. **Limit who receives credit cards.** I recommend issuing as few credit cards as you can to get the business of the union done. Your president and treasurer will likely need a credit card, but do members of the Executive Board really need one? Make the assessment on a position-by-position basis.

2. **Establish credit limits, and consider different credit limits for different officers.** Your president may need a limit of $5,000 on his credit card, but individual Executive Board officers, if they are to be issued a credit card at all, may only need a credit limit of $250 or $500.

3. **Safeguard your PINs.** Your policy should require that each credit card user report his or her Personal Identification Number to the union's treasurer and president, and the treasurer should maintain a record of all PINs in a confidential file.

4. **Specify the expenses that can be charged to the credit card.** Your policy should limit the types of expenses your union officials can charge on credit cards. Can travel, transportation, and meals be charged to the card, and if so, under what circumstances? Itemize these things in your policy.

5. **Forbid use of the card for personal purposes.** Based on first-hand experience, I recommend that the policy specifically forbid even the briefest use of the union credit card for non-union expenses lest you encounter a situation where a union official says something like, "Yes, I used the card to buy airplane tickets for my family, but I paid the union back before the bill came." I'd call that theft.

6. **Prohibit ATM withdrawals.** Make sure your policy prohibits ATM withdrawals, cash back at point of purchase, or other access to cash. Better yet, if you can get credit cards without the ability to make ATM withdrawals and engage in other cash transactions, do it.

7. **Require documentation of every charge.** Your policy should require credit card holders to submit receipts and/or invoices and, if you wish, an expense voucher for every credit card use. The treasurer and president should independently review all credit card expenses, and do so on no less frequently than a monthly basis.

Policies like these won't prevent credit card theft. However, they may well deter most of it, and most certainly will limit the losses to the union should theft occur.

BUDGETS.

You cannot run a dues-collecting labor organization without having a budget that provides those in leadership positions with a method for accountability and fiduciary discipline. A budget for a public safety union is also a planning tool necessary to efficiently prioritize to get anything accomplished. Budgets force those who are collecting the monies to account for the spending of those monies. More likely than not, an organization's budget affords those who are paying dues an opportunity to demand explanations as to how the monies are or will be spent, and holds the decision makers to a level of discipline that reflects the organization's priorities. There is nothing as formidable as a general membership that is sensitive to its financial resources and has a sense of the union's priorities.

You cannot run a dues-collecting labor organization without having a budget.

How To Construct A Budget. Constructing a budget for your organization is simple in method, though it takes some thought in regard to its substantive content. There are computer programs available today, such as QuickBooks, that take the mystery out of setting up budgets. But these programs are only as good as the data that is provided.

To begin, project your union's income. The largest portion of your income is likely dues revenue, but you likely have a variety of different revenue streams. I recommend you use these assumptions in budgeting.

Dues. If your dues are a fixed-dollar amount, budgeting involves nothing more than multiplying the amount of your dues by the number of expected members. Percentage-based dues are a bit more work to budget in that they require taking into account not just the expected membership, but also any anticipated adjustments in wages over the course of the next year.

Investments. Be conservative when you're budgeting for investment income. Look at the rate of return on your investments over a lengthy period of time – at least five years – as the starting point for budgeting investment income. Then, adjust that starting point by current market conditions, consulting your investment advisor before settling on a final number.

Other Income. Your union may have a variety of other income streams, from fundraisers to rental income. Once again, your mission should be to use reasonably conservative numbers in projecting income. Much better to have money left over at the end of next year than to find that aggressive budgeting of income has left you with inadequate funds.

Next, looking at last year's expenditures, anticipate what expenses will be in the upcoming year, building in a reasonable estimate for changes in the cost of living. Try to identify any unusual expenses that will be coming up in the following year. Is next year a bargaining year? If so, you might anticipate expenses for consultant fees that you might not ordinarily incur. Do you have a high number of pending grievances? If so, next year's attorney fees or arbitration costs might be higher than usual.

Once you have constructed your organization's budget and have attempted to adhere to it over a period of time, there will be an opportunity to identify faults in the way your union spends money. Do the expenditures reflect the union's priorities? Is the organization realizing its optimum allocation of the income generated? These are the questions that must be asked as your union's budget is reviewed and discussed and decisions are made regarding reallocation of income. This re-evaluation of priorities should be done at least once each year after truth-checking your organization's priorities and long range goals. It is this process of re-evaluation and reallocation that provides the information necessary to maximize financial discipline and accountability.

The Process Of Approving A Budget. The process for approving a budget should be in your union's bylaws. It is a good idea to require the treasurer to submit to the Executive Board a draft budget no later than three months before the start of the next fiscal year. Depending upon your organization, the treasurer might be assisted by a Budget Committee in the process of drafting the budget. The Executive Board should consider the budget for a minimum of one month before voting on it. Most public safety unions will leave approval of the budget within the purview of the Executive Board and not require approval by the general membership. A sample budget is attached as Appendix G to this book.

The process for approving a budget should be in your union's bylaws.

FINANCIAL SECURITY OF THE ORGANIZATION.

The financial security of your organization is reflective of the leadership's planning and organizational skills, ethical and operational priorities, and fiduciary responsibility. All of these considerations can be measured in light of the financial security of your organization.

Fiduciary Responsibilities. All members of a union's Executive Board owe a fiduciary duty to the organization. Exactly what the term "fiduciary duty" means varies somewhat from state to state. In general, though, it involves these obligations:

- **A duty of loyalty.** The fiduciary duty requires Executive Board members to have primary loyalty to the union. This means (among other things) that Board members should not provide assistance to those suing the union nor should they try to assist competing labor organizations.

- **A duty of to act reasonably with respect to the organization's assets.** Executive Board members must act with reasonable care as custodians of the union's assets. That means they should read financial reports, ask questions about budgets, make sure the union is following its strategic plan with respect to financial matters, and participate meaningfully in discussions about income and expenditures.

- **A duty to avoid self-dealing.** Members of an Executive Board must scrupulously avoid any business dealings with the union where they or members of their families will benefit from the dealings. Let me reemphasize that, avoid any business dealings with the union, even where the arrangements might be approved by the Executive Board. Among dozens of stories I could tell, one of the more vivid was learning that a police union had hired the president's wife as its office assistant. What could possibly go wrong, I thought? Well, divorce and theft could, and did, happen.

Bonding Of Officers. "Bonding" is a special type of insurance that covers losses owing to theft by employees or others with access to an organization's funds. It is a good idea for a union to purchase bonding insurance for every member of the Executive Board with any access to union funds.

Various Types Of Insurance. There are two types of insurance that public safety labor unions should not be without: Errors and omissions insurance and duty of fair representation insurance.

Errors and omissions, or more appropriately professional liability insurance, is foundational coverage for any union. Face it, mistakes happen. If well-intended employee representatives or Executive Board members make a mistake, and as a result you find your organization is sued, errors and omissions insurance will cover your organization up to the policy limits and generally will include any judgments against your union and court costs.

Duty of fair representation insurance covers a union's actions in regard to specific incidents when dealing with a member with whom the union has a duty of fair representation, as discussed in Chapter 8. Suffice it to say that this insurance is expensive, and until recently, extremely difficult to obtain. It is well worth the cost, even with the high deductibles that generally come with the insurance. It has been my experience that the court costs and attorney's fees incurred while defending against the most baseless of allegations can run into the tens of thousands of dollars, and the benefit for your organization knowing that there is a ceiling on your union's liability makes this insurance worth every penny.

The "Risk Conference" – Something No Union Should Be Without. Once a year, every year, your union should arrange for a meeting between the union's president, treasurer, attorney, and insurance broker. There should be one topic for the meeting – is the union covered for every reasonably anticipatable risk. During the conference, the participants should ask questions about possible liability, and should get answers from the insurance broker as to whether coverage exists for the risk. Among the questions that can be asked are these:

- What happens if the union is sued when the president, in his personal vehicle and on the way from one union meeting to the next, misses a red light and is involved in an intersection collision? Does it matter if the president is on duty or off duty?

- If a union member has too many beers at the union picnic and is involved in an automobile collision, is the union covered if it is sued?

- Is there coverage if a member slips and falls in the union's offices? Does it matter if the offices are owned or leased?

Based upon the results of the "risk conference," your organization may decide that it needs to beef up its insurance coverage or possibly look for other carriers who offer different insurance packages.

Auditing The Books. Now we get into a quick discussion about "terms of art." Bottom line, you get what you pay for, and if you don't know what you really want, you really pay a bunch. So, let's talk about what you really need when it comes to having your union's finances reviewed, not what you think you need because you are familiar with a certain term. A good way to get into this discussion is to talk about what an audit is, and what other (read cheaper) options exist that might get your organization the information that it needs regarding the organization's financial well-being.

An audit is the highest level of financial examination that can be provided by a disinterested and objective professional entity. An audit is designed to reach a certain conclusion or provide an opinion about what was audited. An audit provides your union with an official, professional examination and verification, according to generally accepted auditing standards, of your organization's financial statements and accounting documents. So, if your union requested an audit, you would receive a meticulous, methodical, and objective examination of all accounts and items that support the financial statements of your union, down to the last receipt.

An audit is appropriate if there is a change in leadership or there are reasons to believe that financial improprieties might have occurred.

Audits typically cost around $8,000 to $10,000, and sometimes the expense of the audit exceeds the benefits derived. An audit is appropriate if there is a change in leadership, to include the treasurer, or there are reasons to believe that financial improprieties might have occurred. I recommend that an audit is appropriate and cost effective every three to five years, and a review is the process that should be conducted annually.

A review is a financial assessment that will result in limited assurances regarding the financial health and management of your organization. The review is based on analytical procedures and inquiries to your union management. Usually, a review will result in the professional entity (usually a certified public accountant) reporting that there is conformance with Generally Accepted Accounting Principles and there is no apparent need to modify any financial statements.

This conclusion must be based on sufficient inquiry and procedures taken by the accountant during the course of the review. Such a review is usually done on an annual basis to provide the organization the limited assurances not provided by the least expensive of all financial services, the compilation.

A compilation is a service in which an accountant prepares or helps to prepare the financial statements of the union. There is no assertion that the statements are accurate, complete, or are in conformance with Generally Accepted Accounting Principles. The compilation is based solely on information given to the accountant by the union's officers, and there is no opinion, assurances, or conclusion expressed by the accountant. A compilation is usually done for a specific period of time or in order to assist a new treasurer and the Executive Board to compile and interpret financial statements for planning and budgeting purposes.

Creating An Accounting Manual. There is great potential benefit to your union to prepare, or pay to have prepared, a manual or set of SOPs that provides guidance to your treasurer on how to account for the finances of your union. Such a manual should include a philosophical foundation for the use and tracking of the union's finances, a clear explanation of fiduciary responsibilities and potential liabilities, and the nitty-gritty methodology by which your organization expects certain reports to be formatted and presented. Such an accounting manual should conform to your bylaws, be updated and reviewed regularly by your professionally-contracted accounting firm, and approved and accepted by the Executive Board.

> *There is great potential benefit to your union to prepare a manual that provides guidance to your treasurer on how to account for the finances of your union.*

OWNING REAL ESTATE.

To own or rent? Ah, the perennial and almost uniquely American family quandary now comes home to roost in your organizational family. Buckle up, it'll be a rough debate.

For a public safety union, the decision to own property should not be made lightly. Real estate is expensive, and the issue of not using a building for which a large mortgage is being paid, or owning a building that is not in some manner generating revenue or cost savings to your organization, is certain to be a topic of discussion whenever the issue of dues or the general financial health of your organization is discussed. What I can say is that every union rep I've spoken to whose union has purchased real estate has said the purchase was the single best financial decision the organization ever made.

Consider the purposes for which the property will be used. Any real estate purchase by your union should be driven by your organization's needs and investment philosophy, not merely its size. Generally, an organization of about 50 dues-paying members can sustain the payment schedule and get good use of the property.

Why do some organizations choose to buy or develop real estate? There are actually three reasons, all of which are implied above. The first is your union's investment philosophy. While your organization might choose to invest in stock or bond markets, the potential benefit of a certain percentage of assets being invested in real estate provides a certain level of cushion should the securities market not meet your union's expectations. The second is that a union building can provide positive cash flow, and increase the net worth of the organization. Third, having "a place of your own" provides certain benefits that might never reflect on a balance sheet. The ability to hold Executive Board and general membership meetings and social and political functions in your own building carries with it opportunities to generate a sense of ownership and pride on the part of your members (which in turn generates strength within your organization) and prestige and status in the community (which in turn generates accessibility to politicians and community leaders).

Should your union have the inclination to buy a building large enough for you to become a landlord, by all means explore the possibilities. Oftentimes, leasing commercial space to other businesses or stable non-profits will provide enough income to make the monthly payment on the building, and if your organization uses a portion of the building, the monthly leases from your tenants should cover the revenue lost from leasing to yourself and still provide the benefits discussed above. And don't forget about the benefits derived from depreciating the rental property! A comprehensive cost-benefit analysis and a pro-forma budget workup should be completed before any purchase is made.

Don't forget that you are a public safety union. The type of tenants who run businesses in your building will be linked with your organization. For instance, when I was union president for the Anchorage Police Department Employees Association, we rented to the American Lung Association and Habitat For Humanity. Both were well respected and financially stable non-profits. The sign outside was a backlit attention grabber that proclaimed "Anchorage Police Department Employees Association Professional Building" and beneath the heading was listed each tenant. When "Habitat" got too big for the space we were able to provide, we had no problem immediately leasing the soon to be vacated space.

Being a landlord has its drawbacks. One of the good things we did as landlords was to hire a property management company. As cops, clerks and dispatchers, we learned early on that we were not plumbers, electricians, and roofers. Suffice it to say that the monthly fee for coordinating the building maintenance and overseeing the interaction with our renters was well worth it.

However, we did learn that it is effective to show up personally every so often to say hello to your renters and let them know that you care about their needs. Visiting the folks leasing office space from you is also a great quality control technique regarding the monitoring of and the satisfaction of your renters with the property management company and spot checking that the property management is to your expectations.

NOTES

[1] Remember to put the manner in which the amount of dues is assessed in the constitution and bylaws to avoid regularly revisiting this usually divisive issue. Once the battle is fought (and there will be a battle) ensure that a process for change is deliberate, well reasoned, and demands that the change be sold to a majority (or supermajority) of the members. One way to avoid periodic dues debates is to enshrine the methodology in the constitution and bylaws tying the dues to wage increases (or decreases).

[2] http://www.lbpoa.org/lbpoa-honorary-dues.htm.

[3] *See Auburn Police Union v. Carpenter,* 8 F.3d 886 (1st Cir. 1993).

[4] There is an inherent danger if your fundraiser or promoter is concurrently working with another organization and is tapping into the same potential market for attendance or ticket sales at your event. If the customer pool is diluted by concurrent events or the same market being farmed by the same fundraiser or promoter, it is obviously harmful to your organization and potentially lucrative and efficient for the fundraiser or promoter. Be wary of this angle and ensure there is exclusive language in your contract that would forbid such a situation.

[5] The police union became aware of the constitutional challenge to binding arbitration when, after a particularly contentious bargaining session, we exited the building and read the headline in the evening paper.

CHAPTER 13

POLITICAL ACTIVITY AND USING THE MEDIA

Nothing is so distasteful to a cop or firefighter than becoming involved in politics. Nothing is so important to a cop or firefighter than becoming involved in politics. Okay, I said it. You have to believe it.

We've seen in recent years that politicians can be the greatest threat to a fair organizing and bargaining process. In particular, we've seen events that one might have thought impossible. Who could have imagined, for example, that a Republican takeover of the legislature and governor's office in Ohio would have resulted in a statute that essentially eliminated the ability of police and fire unions to negotiate (thankfully, the voters overturned the statute in an extremely expensive referendum election). Who would have thought that 2010 would see the simultaneous introduction into state legislatures across the country of bills that would eliminate payroll dues deduction, that would declare topics like health insurance or vacations to be off limits for bargaining, or that would flatly declare public safety unionism illegal?

Your union needs to heed that wakeup call. You need to educate your members about the need for political activity, get those members involved in your political efforts, and establish your union as a political force to be reckoned with. This chapter will provide you with a roadmap for those efforts.

By the very nature of your job responsibilities, you have all the necessary tools to make your union a political force, one that politicians will readily recognize as a valuable ally or a formidable foe. Face it: You are the heroes in today's society, and rightly so. The uniforms, sense of professionalism, and the nature of the jobs done by your rank and file establish a level of inherent credibility with the public that no modern politician could ever aspire to.

The Importance Of Your Union Having A Relationship With The Public.

The starting point for political power is a good relationship with the public. This is a relationship that has to be constantly nurtured and expanded, and never ignored.

The starting point for political power is a good relationship with the public.

Let's start with the low-hanging fruit. Consider how many working families there are in your local area. Find out which labor unions represent the workers in those families. Take the lead in reaching out to those other unions and, if one is not yet in existence, form a coalition based on your common community of interests. Recognize that the other unions will immediately see the benefit to coat-tailing on the goodwill generated by public safety, and this can be leveraged to the benefit of the police and fire unions. Suddenly, you will realize that cops and firefighters can be key players in the labor community.

Next, build avenues of communication and, when appropriate, join with community activists. These are the folks who can be as formidable as foes as they can be supportive as allies. The energy, passion, and organizational skills that most community activists bring to various issues can shame any police or fire union that has to beg members to volunteer or even take an interest in the union's activities. So get to know these people. Arrange with your departments to have them ride along with cops or have fire safety demonstrations. Engage in conversations, and even if you disagree with the views you hear espoused, disagree respectfully and continue to search for issues on which you can agree. If, through education and mutual respect, you form personal relationships that transcend the stereotypical polarization between these people and your members, you have laid the foundation for true grass roots community support when you need it.

Your third step in building a relationship with the public is to Do Good Things. Encourage your membership to engage in volunteer activities. The possibilities are almost endless. Have a "firefighter day" at the local food bank, with off-duty firefighters wearing union t-shirts providing the labor. Have off-duty police volunteer in a high school, or staff child-identification events. Buy seats at tables for charity fundraisers and auctions, put on CPR demonstrations at community centers, and make modest donations to local non-profits. Whenever you do these things, you're building positive relationships, and those relationships may later be important when your union is under siege.

Building bridges with anyone who has political power is as complicated as it is effective. Political power refers not only to the positional authority possessed by those in elected office, but also the power of influence wielded by our favorite community activists, sometimes skittish yet trusted political appointees, entrenched bureaucrats, our friends in the media, and our brothers and sisters in the labor community.

The fourth step is to seek out the unelected opinion shapers in your community. Think for a moment. To whom do elected officials turn for guidance, advice, or approval on various issues? You can see their faces as you read this. Business owners, church leaders, neighborhood association members, and community activists all have a huge impact on the formulation of a policy or a political stance. You get the picture. If you build relationships with these people, they may one day become your champions.

As cops and firefighters, there are so many tools at your disposal to seed, nurture and cultivate relationships. Everyone loves a ride-along with a patrol officer. And who wouldn't want to bring their kids to a fire house and have them meet real firemen and maybe ride on a fire truck? When it's a slow news day, it's pretty much a guarantee that a police or fire story will be the lead story. How hard is it to generate a human interest story for the local paper and then start a relationship with the reporter who has just been assigned to the local police and fire beat? You get the picture.

Ultimately, the goal is to get the public on your side. We used to think that public support was automatic for public safety employees. The last few years have taught us that we have to earn and maintain that support. It's even important to reach out to your critics. Establishing and nurturing relationships with those most likely to be critical of organized labor, yet supportive of public safety, can only result in less criticism of the former and increased support of the latter.

A Public Safety Union's Relationship With Politicians.

Cops and firefighters live in a political environment. Elected city council and county board of commission members set the bargaining agenda for the employer, and vote on whether to accept a proposed contract. In difficult economic times, these same politicians make the decisions whether layoffs occur and, if so, how many and for how long. City councils hire and fire the police and fire chief, and hugely influence the enforcement, staffing, and policy decisions of public safety agencies.

These are the cold, hard facts. And those facts mean one thing – if you're going to be as successful as possible, you're going to need to engage in politics. That may mean making endorsements, it may mean making contributions, and it may mean going door-to-door to make sure your mayor is reelected. It will also mean that you need to work on your political relationships on a 24/7 basis. Don't just be there at election time. You need to constantly engage the politicians who set your employer's labor relations policies.

You need to constantly engage the politicians who set your employer's labor relations policies.

This isn't just a one-way street. As cops and firefighters, true heroes in the public's eyes, you can provide a politician with the kind of good will and public safety credibility that he or she could only otherwise wish for. Just as importantly, politicians live for and survive on campaign contributions. Politicians need you just as much as you need them.

I'll predict that your biggest hurdle is not engaging in the political system. Instead, the problem is in convincing your members that you need to engage in the political system. Public safety employees like to believe their jobs are above politics, and that getting involved in the process somehow sullies them. Sometimes, your members will chafe at your endorsements, not wanting to align their union with a politician who truly understands labor issues, but who might be on a different page on "social issues."

It's easy advice to give that you should say to your objectors, "Get over it." More helpfully, you can point to the events around the country in the years that followed the 2008 economic downturn. Police and firefighters were laid off across the country. Pension plans were slashed, health benefits reduced, and in a development none of us have seen in our lives, police and fire wages were actually cut. If you look at the "winners" and "losers" among public safety unions, you'll see a consistent trend. Those that did well were likely those who had engaged the political system, and had done so effectively. Those who did poorly were likely those in an antagonistic relationship with elected officials or, almost as bad, had no relationship at all with them.

What should you be doing? I think of these as the minimum steps any public safety union should take, regardless of the size of the union:

1. **Form a PAC.** Forming a political action committee is simple; just about any accountant or lawyer can take care of the necessary paperwork for you, as well as the documents you need to file on an annual basis to comply with any local laws. Your PAC will exist as a

separate legal entity from your union, a degree of separation that might ease your members' angst. You'll need to make sure that your dues deduction system can direct member contributions to the PAC.

2. **Interview Candidates.** You'll need a committee to interview every candidate for the governing body of your employer (e.g., city council, board, etc.). I meant to use the word "every." Sometimes there will be candidates you might overlook, thinking they have no chance to get elected, and then you end up with an election-night response. Develop a short, no more than ten-item, questionnaire that you'll ask the candidates to fill out in advance. Needless to say, the questionnaire should be stuffed with questions about attitudes towards collective bargaining, staffing, and other issues important to your organization.

> *Develop a short, no more than ten-item, questionnaire that you'll ask the candidates to fill out in advance.*

When the interviews occur, try to round up as many members as you can to be present. The stronger the showing, the better. Some public safety unions make video recordings of PAC interviews; I'll confess I'm not enamored of this, preferring the more informal give-and-take that occurs without a camera operating. You'll need to train your members to remain absolutely and completely professional, no matter if the candidate is espousing mainstream views or seems to have just arrived from the planet Venus.

3. **Pick Winners.** Boy, if it were only that easy. It's not, of course. It's rare that public polls are done in municipal and country races, and your guess as to who will win the election won't be any better than the next person's. On other occasions, your endorsement will be dictated by other factors such as loyalty (see No. 4, below) or the fact that the likely winner is implacably hostile to your position. All these things aside, try your best to pick the candidates who will win their elections. There will be times you need to recognize political reality and make an endorsement while figuratively holding your nose. If a candidate is an overwhelming favorite, you should consider endorsing him or her even if you feel he or she will vote against you 75% of the time. With your endorsement, you may gain the access that will either whittle that 75% down to 50% or may temper the other votes in a way that will hurt you less.

4. **Be Loyal.** If an incumbent has been on your side in past battles, stick with him no matter if he's got only a 10% chance of winning. Not only do you owe it to the incumbent, but even politicians on the other side will completely understand your loyalty.

5. **You Don't Have To Make Contributions** (but it helps). It's been said that the "mother's milk of politics is money." I'm not sure that's true with public safety unions. Politicians treasure your endorsement more than your money. Gaining the support of cops and firefighters wins

them far more votes than the $100 or $1,000 you might contribute to their campaigns. Of course, if you've got the resources, contributions are always appreciated, particularly given the ever-escalating cost of even local political campaigns.

6. **Don't Let The Relationship End With Election Day.** All too often, public safety unions think their relationship with a politician begins and ends with an endorsement, perhaps a contribution, and an election-night party. The election cycle should begin, not end, your relationship with the politician. Once a month, you should be taking each city council or county board member out for coffee or lunch. You don't need to talk about bargaining issues; in fact, it's probably better if you don't. Talk about crime or the latest fire. Talk about some of the community events in which your organization has been participating. Talk about one of your members who's done something special, or who has overcome adversity. Ask the politician how his family is doing, talk about sports, build a relationship. You can leave the more direct discussions for the politician's office; what's important is that the politician comes to know you and can humanize the members of your organization.

You've got other things to offer, of course. Facilitate a visit to the fire station, or arrange a ride-along with a stand-up officer. You'd be surprised how much mileage you can get out of a ball cap or a sweatshirt with your logo. Make sure the politician subscribes to your Twitter feed or is your Facebook friend, and that you reciprocate.

7. **Do You Need To Be In This Race?** I'm not a friend of spreading yourself too thin politically. Consider the races that are really important to you, and those that aren't. Are you a union representing firefighters in a city department? If so, you definitely need to be engaged in your city council and mayoral races. But do you really need to be weighing in on who should be elected to your state's court of appeals, or who will be the tax assessor? Candidates for those offices will want your endorsement, of course, but where's the value of your getting involved in the race? I much prefer concentrating time, resources, and effort on the political campaigns that really matter.

Don't get me wrong. You will not always agree with all of the positions the candidates you endorse might take. Actually, that's healthy. Few politicians want to be identified too closely with any union, because such identification creates polarization in the electorate. So expect some bumps from even your closest political allies. After all, they need to get re-elected.

But remember that as unhealthy as it is for a politician to be too closely identified with a union, it is just as healthy for a politician to be identified with public safety. If you are doing your job, chances are the public will see the police union as police officers and the fire union as firefighters. Period. They won't usually take the time or have the insight to differentiate between the union and the department. How many times have you heard the media refer to "the police officers" or the "fire department personnel" when covering a public safety labor issue, and if you weren't a union representative, you would have no idea that they were talking about the respective unions? Politicians know it is good to be supportive of public safety, and as union leaders you have to identify your union as true public safety entities. Speak out on public safety issues in your community with the authority of the content experts that you are. Gain the trust and goodwill of the public, and the support of the politicians will not be far behind.

WHERE IS YOUR UNION ON THE POWER GRID?

Ask yourself a question. If you're at impasse with your employer during a contentious contract negotiation, does your union have the political juice to bring the dispute to a successful resolution? If you can't fairly answer that question "yes," then you've got work to do.

It all comes down to relationships. As I've just said, you need relationships with your elected officials. Good relationships hopefully, but at least respectful relationships. However, getting yourself on the power grid involves much more than relationships with politicians.

You need to involve yourself in your community. A simple step is to join the Chamber of Commerce, even though the anti-union philosophies of the Chamber will no doubt grate on you. Go to their monthly meetings, and make a point of talking to the business leaders in attendance. Stress public safety in your conversations, not labor issues.

You need to involve yourself in your community.

Beyond the Chamber of Commerce, get yourself involved with non-profit corporations in your community. Encourage your members to get involved in a Habitat for Humanity building project. Attend charity auctions until you've eaten enough banquet food for a couple of lifetimes. When your union makes a substantial charitable donation, deliver the check in person and take the time to talk with the charity's executive director for ten minutes or so. These aren't just good things to do, they're valuable to your organization. You're all about building relationships that someday, in a time of contentious negotiations, might bear some fruit.

Make sure your organization has an ongoing presence in your community. If you're half-decent at it, make the occasional appearance on radio talk shows to discuss public safety issues. Work up a "sign campaign" that results in hundreds of yard signs around the community saying things such as "We support our firefighters" or "Protected by the XXX police department." Engage in community outreach efforts, whether it be teaching fire safety, running a "Kinderprint" program, or putting on CPR classes. What's important is that you become a constant presence in your community. If you are – if the community and the politicians can "put a face on you" – you'll weather storms all the better.

Finally, in assessing where your union is as a power player in local politics, you need to do an honest evaluation of your strengths and weaknesses. Those evaluations can be had for the asking – I'd even suggest you make them part of your PAC interviews. Also invaluable in this regard are public opinion polls that test not only views about the union but also how various messages can alter those views.

While polls are only as good as questions posed to the sample of voters who are asked, in times of duress they are a tremendous tool to give a snapshot into the thinking of those who are likely to influence either directly or through elected officials the outcome of your particular issue. They can help craft strategy for priorities and target audiences as you assess the impact and effectiveness of your message. Polls are not cheap. Prices are driven by the number of questions asked and the size of the sample contacted. There are other considerations in regard to interpreting the numbers generated by any given poll, and oftentimes the tabs attached to the poll by the firm hired to conduct it can tell an in-depth story that the responses to the direct questions cannot address. Often, the baseline questions regarding race, age, and political party affiliation give a more complete picture than the mere statistics provided by the answered questions. Just remember to engage a reputable polling agency and have a strategy regarding how you plan to use the poll results. In a city of substantial size, expect to pay at least $5,000 for a usable poll. There are, however, technologies now available, such as Pollster ™, that afford opportunities to run opinion polls for a fraction of the traditional cost.

A bit of advice: Always keep the poll and the polling results secret until you are ready to use the results. If a poll is taken early enough, the results can help you plan adjustments to your strategy, and a later poll can provide a mechanism to measure the results of your efforts. But be aware that poll results not favorable to your position on a particular issue, once made public, can cascade and impact public opinion.

Developing A Media Strategy.

Modern society is information driven, with most of that information provided by television, radio, the Internet, and to an increasingly lesser degree, newspapers. A foundation to your media strategy should be based on establishing good relationships with those who report the news. Reporters (or TV commentators, or radio hosts, or bloggers) are not only potential carriers of your message, they also put the emphasis and spin on that message, often outside any control that you might think you have retained. That is why developing personal and professional relationships with reporters is so important. Like politicians, reporters like to be on the "inside." As a public safety union leader, you have to convince a reporter that your message is not only newsworthy, but that you can become a constant, consistent, and credible source of both public safety and labor perspectives. They will see you as a "two-fer" and you will find yourself quoted regularly on public safety and

A foundation to your media strategy should be based on establishing good relationships with those who report the news.

labor issues in your community. This is good. It builds up your union's credibility and keeps your organization out front in the public's eye.

Can you trust reporters? Yes, some reporters, some of the time. You need to know who and when. A good way to develop and ultimately gauge a relationship with a reporter is to take a chance, albeit one that cannot damage your organization. Provide the reporter an opinion, color commentary or background information that would be considered newsworthy and convince the reporter that you do not want it disclosed. Advise the reporter that this is "off the record" information. See what the reporter does with the information. If he or she lives up to your expectations, start to feed the reporter information beneficial to your union or comments on appropriate public safety issues in which your union holds a vested interest. Such a reciprocal and eventually trusting professional relationship will serve you well in those times when your union is at the heart of a controversial story such as contract impasse. The credibility you have cultivated in public safety oriented issues will serve you well as you forward your labor agenda.

The union's relationship with editorial boards, either those of print, television, or radio, is also an important component of your media strategy. The opportunity to sit and talk with those people who make decisions on storyline, placement, and opinion page comments is extremely beneficial. If your organization has the news-making potential regarding public safety and labor issues, you will most likely be granted at least an initial consultation with the board of the chosen media outlet. Reinforce the concept to the board that your union is not only a labor entity, but a credible and articulate source of insights regarding public safety issues.

> **The union's relationship with editorial boards, either those of print, television, or radio, is also an important component of your media strategy.**

The use of the media should be an ongoing component of your long-term strategy in educating and eventually winning the public over as valuable allies. Recognize that there will be times when one medium is better utilized than another. For example, if you decide that a paid advertising campaign is the best way to get your message out, then assess the most effective media venue based on time considerations, how complicated the message is, and of course, budget. Usually, editorial op-ed pieces in a newspaper only reach an audience that is inclined to read the editorial page of the newspaper (these days, that's less than 10% of the public). Drive time radio ads bring a kind of "guerrilla" mentality to the media campaign in that they can strike hard and quick and, if appropriately planned, seem to be all over the dial. The most expensive will be television ads. They are most effective in prime time and on prime channels. Figuring out just what those times and channels are can be a science in itself, best left to the pros that you might hire as advisors.

No matter what form of media you choose to utilize, your message must transcend the usually self-interested perspective of your members' narrow economic interests. Sharpen your message so that it resonates with the folks in the community that you are trying to reach – the same folks who vote for the politicians, the same folks who will determine your union's status in the community, and the same folks who *"will depend on (police or fire) to make things right for them at the worst moments of their lives..."* Hey! Try that line and see if it gets their attention!

If you follow these steps, you won't fall into the trap of having a crisis be your first contact with the media. Always define issues on your own terms, but give reporters the information that they need to tell the story correctly. Always try to have experts who are sympathetic to your side of the issue lined up and willing to talk to reporters. After all, they have air time and print space that needs filling. Why not fill it with your side imbedded in a serious news story?

FREE AND PAID MEDIA.

Never lose sight of the fact that the people you want to reach are the voting public. You already know that the perspective that most voting citizens gain on a police or fire department is formulated by either a relatively rare personal experience or stories in the newspaper, on television news, or more recently, through unvetted and usually biased online blogs. A poll my union conducted a few years ago showed that only 13% of the 800 voters sampled differentiated between the police department and the police union. So keep in mind that it is probable that most of the voting citizens in your area do not differentiate between the specific public safety department and its respective union; cops are cops, firefighters are firefighters.

Free media consists of the traditional newspaper and television news stories that have been the bread and butter of image making for cops and firefighters. While the nature of our jobs pretty much ensures that we will be a party to the lead story on most evenings on most local media outlets, it is important to take advantage of that free exposure with individuals who are professional and articulate representatives of our organizations, both department and union. Remember that tendency toward lack of differentiation that the voting public is prone to? What better way to take advantage of such a win-win opportunity. And even if it's a slow news day, your union should be capitalizing on those relationships you have already established with local media reporters to have some human interest stories ready to go that reflect your employees' professionalism and commitment to the community. The media hates slow news days, and they are always looking to fill air time and content space.

The editorial pages of newspapers and online magazines and news entities often afford readers opportunities to voice opinions, either through letters to the editor or as guest columnists. Also, it is not uncommon for local radio stations to have call-in talk shows or to invite in-studio guests to address topics of local interest. It is not a bad strategy to have a team of potential callers favorable to your position standing by to flesh out points and to create an atmosphere of support for your specific position.

Paid media is advertising, plain and simple. Paid media might involve print or electronic advertisements, or an Internet campaign. Paid media might also include the production of infomercials if the organization's budget allows it and its strategic goals demand it. The operative word in paid media is paid; make no mistake, it is expensive and fleeting. Paid media is most effective when targeted and timely.

Before venturing into this potential money pit, it is best to research and hire a professional firm to assist you in getting your message out. Crafting the message in such a manner that it will resonate in the very short and expensive time allotted is best handled by the pros doing it for a living. You can reach the most people; that is, the most voters, with a well designed and effective media campaign.

IN A CRISIS? SOME THOUGHTS ON EXTREME ACTIONS.

Votes Of Confidence. Votes of confidence, or as they are sometimes called, votes of no confidence, are risky and not often successful undertakings. What seems like a life and death issue to your union can seem meaningless, or worse, totally out of synch with the view of a public that you might not have done a very good job educating over the years. If your union becomes so myopic that it sees a vote of confidence in an elected official, or more often, in the chief, as the only way to resolve an issue, then I'd suggest that the union leadership slow down, take a deep breath, and start polling immediately.

While I'm not a fan of no-confidence votes, I can suggest a few parameters if you decide to go down that road. Never take a vote of confidence if you are unsure of the outcome. A union that is not unified on such an important and eventually public issue will make no points with the community or the membership. Your union can come out looking divided and petty if you have not laid the groundwork to ensure the outcome. You also need to make sure that the vast, vast majority of your members cast ballots in the confidence vote. Nothing looks as weak as a no confidence vote in which only 55% of your members have even bothered to cast a ballot.

A prelude to a no-confidence vote should be a low-key yet internally-aggressive referendum on the individual or individuals. Consider the following example: Your chief has lost credibility with your workforce. Grievance after grievance has piled up, and your union's leadership is under pressure to do something about it. After exhausting all other options, your Executive Board determines the time is right for a vote of no confidence. But the issues that are driving the distrust and dissatisfaction are too particular to the internal business of the organization and have no appeal to the general public.

Recognizing this, the Board determines that the best course of action is to hold a secret, yet well-attended ballot regarding employee confidence in the chief. Once the results are known to the Board, the president makes an appointment with the mayor to secretly share the results, giving the mayor the opportunity to "fix the problem." Sharing information in this way can bring about the change you want without the results of the vote ever becoming public, and you will have earned the thanks of the mayor.

Strikes And Job Actions. These types of actions as they pertain to public safety employees are prohibited by law in most jurisdictions. Informal job actions, such as a "blue flu" or, heaven forbid, "ticket speedups," rarely resonate positively with the public and should be avoided at all costs.

Informational Picketing. Though some public safety unions set up the occasional informational picket line, I'm not at all sure that informational picketing works. Maybe, just maybe, if you could get enough of your members to show up for an informational picket, and if you could get the right professionally-designed signs made up, and if your members behaved appropriately during the event, you might sway the hearts and minds of those who happened to see the picketing. More likely, though, is that the public will find the picketing more an annoyance than educational, and the 30 seconds of publicity you get on the nightly news won't begin to tell the story you're looking for. In an electronic age, you need to focus on electronic communications, not picket signs.

Pulling Out All The Stops. Inevitably, there will come a time when a blitz to win over the public is the only option available to ensure the survival of your union as a viable entity or the perception of your organization as a credible provider of public service. Those are the occasions when there is a high profile arrest of one of your members, a shooting that, by all accounts, might be "iffy" or racially charged, impending mass public safety lay-offs or possibly a wholesale attack on collective bargaining.

In 2010, the Stockton, California police union's officers paid for billboards that advised the citizens of the city that massive layoffs of police officers would lead to higher crime rates in an already violent city. The police were able to take the issue of lay-offs, which would initially be categorized as a pure labor issue, and transcend it into a public safety issue that asked how they were to fight crime with 58 less officers in what was already California's second-most dangerous city. The billboards included the telephone number of the City Manager.

Seeking Professional Help. Sometimes, we as union leaders can get too close to a particular situation that our sense of righteous outrage does not afford us the clear and rational thought process necessary to weather the storm. In this case, dial up a Public Relations Consultant.

Hear me out on this one. PR consultants can help you fashion your message and target the folks who will matter in the formulation of a strategy that turns public opinion into either public support or public outcry, that then turns into political and decision-making leverage. A good PR person will keep his fingers on the pulse of the public's reaction to what might very well be that "watershed moment" for your union and coordinate the response in the most effective manner possible. They will orchestrate press conferences and, more often than not, come from a media background and have maintained media connections that cannot hurt your cause. The value of having a dispassionate professional working closely with your union in times of crisis cannot be understated. The value of a Public Relations professional for strategic public relations is further discussed in

Strikes and job actions as they pertain to public safety employees are prohibited by law in most jurisdictions.

The value of having a dispassionate professional working closely with your union in times of crisis cannot be understated.

Chapter 16, but the value of immediate professional guidance in times of crisis should never be underestimated.

CHAPTER 14

RESPONSES TO CRITICAL INCIDENTS

The Importance Of A Prepared Response To Critical Incidents.

You can't overstate the importance of a prepared response to critical incidents. We are not talking a tactical response here; well, not in the sense of what we as public safety professionals might be inclined to categorize as a tactical response. Here's the union perspective: When an incident culminates in the use of some level of response to resistance (I like that terminology better than "use of force"),[1] an in-custody death, an accidental death, an automobile or apparatus accident, or any other type of incident when we respond within the scope of our duties and it results in an injury or death, we will be second-guessed for doing what we did. We will be second guessed in the media, in a criminal investigation, in a civil lawsuit, and in a disciplinary investigation. Union leaders must be prepared for these incidents, but the reality is that a response on the part of the union, and an expectation by management as to what that response will be, is often ad hoc and "off the cuff."

> You can't overstate the importance of a prepared response to critical incidents.

Right now you firefighters out there might be thinking "this is more for the cops, not me." Wrong. Is there a chance you will run someone down while responding to a five-alarm or en route to a Hazmat scene? That you may be accused of theft by a homeowner? What if you, as a medic, were called by police to respond to a "cold" scene that unexpectedly turned "hot" and you were ducking bullets? Any chance you or someone you know is a paramedic attached to a SWAT team and has an active role during or immediately following entries? How many scenarios can you put yourself in where a split second decision under a set of extremely stressful circumstances could make you the subject of an investigation?

So before we actually start fleshing out what the protocols should be, let's do a quick review of the rights afforded the involved employee that are pertinent to a union's response to a critical incident. Some of what follows has already been discussed in detail in Chapter 10 of this book.

The Origins Of The Right To Respond To An Incident.

Let's start with two basic propositions:

- Police officers and firefighters have the same constitutional rights as all other citizens.

- A critical incident involves conduct that is at least potentially, if not inevitably, the subject of criminal and disciplinary investigations.

You might think, "Tell me something I don't already know!" Okay. Well, what if I were to tell you that more often than not, a police officer who is involved in an on-duty fatal shooting is almost immediately asked questions by investigators, *Miranda* notwithstanding, even though the officer is, in essence, the suspect in a homicide investigation? What if I were to tell you that most officers feel duty-bound, *Garrity* notwithstanding, to volunteer to answer any questions that internal affairs investigators might be asking shortly after or at the same time the detectives finish their questioning on the shooting? Anyone see a problem here? It gets dangerously complicated. That's why you as the union representative have the responsibility to slow things down after a critical incident to ensure your member's rights are preserved.

Whether the employee acted within or outside of policy, constitutional rights and due process must be respected, department procedures must be adhered to, and contract language must be understood and followed.

Bottom line: Whether the employee acted within or outside of policy, constitutional rights and due process must be respected, department procedures must be adhered to, and contract language must be understood and followed. Your members should understand that, after a critical incident, they need not and should not discuss the incident with anyone until their attorney arrives. Your member is a homicide suspect, and the subject of the most serious of criminal investigations. There is no reason why your members should not avail themselves of the full extent of their right to representation.

The *Weingarten* Rule – The Right To Representation By A Union. In Chapter 10 we discussed the right to representation under the *Weingarten* Rule. Don't forget that the *Weingarten* rule allows representation where the employee specifically requests representation in an interview about a matter which he reasonably believes could result in discipline. Certainly the specter of potential discipline is present in a critical incident. The key here is the member has to request the representation.

Educate your membership to request union representation immediately after a critical incident. Make sure one side of those "Advice of Rights" cards you should be distributing to all members is captioned, "What To Do After A Critical Incident," and make sure the first heading after the caption is "Request Your Union Representative." Teach your members that any represented employee with knowledge that a critical incident has occurred should immediately contact a union representative.

The *Garrity* Rule. As mentioned in Chapter 10, *Garrity v. New Jersey* prohibits the use of compelled statements in a subsequent criminal prosecution of the employee. If a department is investigating a critical incident, it will most assuredly handle it as a criminal investigation, and will likely not compel the employee to give a statement. Since *Garrity* only protects the employee against the subsequent use of compelled statements, it is the union rep's job at the scene of a critical incident to (1) try to ensure that the employee is compelled (as a condition of employment) to make a statement, and, failing that, (2) advise the employee that a voluntary statement could be used to prosecute the employee and that the employee should wait to speak to counsel before answering any questions.

PREPARING FOR THE RESPONSE.

Preparing for a critical incident response starts long before the critical incident itself. There are three key elements to that preparation: (1) Agreement on the procedures to be used after critical incidents; (2) selecting the attorneys who will be responding to critical incidents; and (3) training everyone who will be involved in the response, and then training them again.

Agreeing On Critical Incident Procedures. Critical incident investigations involve five key players: The union, the district attorney, department management, the detectives investigating the incident, and the involved employee. Each has a vested interest in adopting critical incident procedures that result in credible and expeditious investigations that are respectful of due process and constitutional rights. What is difficult about getting critical incident procedures in place is that not all of these five players always recognize the legitimate interests of other players.

From the union's perspective, the main concern is the preservation of members' constitutional and contractual rights. The district attorney's office will ultimately be concerned about the need to prosecute (or not) as a result of the investigation, and will be pressured by the media for quick public statements about the incident and the prosecution decision. Police management will be concerned about the credibility of any investigation regarding the actions taken by the member and the expected media fallout that usually accompanies a critical incident. Investigators will have a mixture of motivations, including the desire to complete the investigation in a timely fashion, and a fervent wish to avoid pressure from above. These folks are usually extremely professional and constantly aware of the potential scrutiny of their role in the investigation. As a result, they might also be a bit impatient and at times pushy regarding the scheduling of interviews. Finally, there is the member, who wants the investigation over now so he can get back to his real life, but at the same time is in the wake of what is likely the most traumatic event of his lifetime.

Unions should take the initiative to engage the various stakeholders in discussions of critical incident procedures. Far better that those procedures be discussed in a series of afternoon meetings around a conference table than at an emotionally-charged crime scene at 3:00 a.m. Unions should be ready to propose the procedures they want used in critical incident inquiries. The proposed protocols should be built from procedures already in use in the agency, and should consider successful procedures that are in place in neighboring agencies. At a minimum, the protocols should include clearly-stated guidance regarding the immediate notification of a union officer, the accessibility of an attorney and the accessibility of union representation to the scene.

Union representatives must recognize the clear lines between the Department's responsibility to investigate a crime scene and the union's responsibility to facilitate effective representation for the employee. All is well with the world when these two objectives can be achieved cooperatively and collaboratively; however, the world is not often well during the course of crime scene reconstruction and attempts to interview distraught and often self-serving witnesses. Consider the following points as you work through this with your Department's management.

Inclusion Of The Union On The Dispatch Notification List. Ultimately, whether to adopt many proposed critical incident procedures may well be a prerog-

Union representatives must recognize the clear lines between the Department's responsibility to investigate a crime scene and the union's responsibility to facilitate effective representation for the employee.

ative of management. Even if their proposals are rejected by an employer, unions should be prepared to act as if their proposals are in place, and to do everything they can to ensure that the legal rights of their members are respected after a critical incident. Step One in this process is to ensure that the union is immediately notified whenever a critical incident occurs, and is placed on the critical incident notification list used by the employer's dispatch agency.

Critical Incident Attorneys. No question, a timely response by a trained and prepared attorney is the most important thing a union can do to preserve the employee's constitutional rights. The first step in that planning is the selection of the attorneys who will be on the critical incident call-out list. In some cases, it will be the unions selecting the attorneys. In other cases, it will be a legal defense fund doing the selection and compensating the attorneys. In both instances, the same considerations apply:

> *A timely response by a trained and prepared attorney is the most important thing a union can do to preserve the employee's constitutional rights.*

- Critical incident lawyers should have criminal law backgrounds, and ideally should have handled homicide cases. After all, a critical incident is usually a homicide case. If possible, you should try to retain lawyers who have recently moved up the ladder from day-to-day state court criminal cases to handling federal court cases. That also minimizes the chance that a lawyer needed for a call-out will have an active non-police case ongoing with your agency.

  Sometimes, though, you'll be in the position where the best critical incident lawyers have active state criminal defense practices. Some of your members, particularly detectives, may grumble about the union using a criminal defense attorney for critical incidents, particularly if it's an attorney who has recently grilled them on the witness stand in a criminal case. You need to ask these members a simple question: If you were involved in a critical incident and were the subject of the most serious of criminal investigations, who would you want to represent you, a criminal defense attorney or a divorce attorney?

- If possible, the lawyers should have decent relationships with the district attorney's office, as well as police management and investigators. A good relationship means more communication, and more communication means a lower likelihood of misunderstandings and surprise.

- The lawyers should not have conflicts of interest, either ethical or emotional. You should also make sure that the lawyers have no qualms about representing police officers and other public safety employees. This usually isn't a problem – experience has taught that top-flight criminal defense lawyers jump at the chance to get on a critical incident call-out list.

- The lawyers need to agree to provide all of their phone numbers, and to be prepared to respond on a 24/7 basis. Critical incidents usually occur between 9 p.m. and 6 a.m. The lawyers on a call-out list need to understand this, and should provide you with the phone numbers for their residence or their cell phones.

Training. The next step is training. Training in critical incidents is a two-way street. The union should train attorneys selected for the list in what will be expected of them. Part of that training should be a refresher course in *Garrity* and *Weingarten*, since most critical incident lawyers rarely encounter these principles in their normal practices. Once critical incident lawyers are experienced, they can in turn become the trainers, conducting annual classes for your union representatives.

WHEN THE INCIDENT HAPPENS.

The union should always have an on-call point of contact, and a backup if that person cannot be reached. It is not uncommon for the union contact's phone to start ringing off the hook prior to formal notification because a well-trained general membership will be contacting that person moments after the incident occurs. In some jurisdictions, the union's point of contact even gets a call from the shift or watch commander before a formal notification by dispatch or an informal "heads-up" call from a union member. That's when you know that your union and your administration are communicating! The point of contact – usually, the union president or another union executive officer – should have all of the contact numbers for the attorneys on the call-out list.

The first thing the union should do is determine how many employees will need representation by an attorney. Often, this can be figured out immediately from the first telephone calls received by the union. On other occasions, the union executive will not have the necessary information until after responding to the scene. Once the union executive gets a good handle on how many lawyers will be required, the representative should start down the call-out list, getting the requisite number of attorneys to respond.

The attorney and the union executive should respond to wherever the involved employee is awaiting the reassuring presence of the union representative and the attorney. Typically, that will be at the scene of the incident. However, if a scene is stabilized, it is not uncommon for a union representative or supervisor to drive the involved employee to the department headquarters.

The Role Of The Attorney At The Scene. The primary role for the responding attorney is to SLOW THINGS DOWN! The attorney should take the employee aside and immediately establish an attorney-client relationship with the employee. Before getting the employee's account of what happened, the attorney should explain in deliberate terms what the employer's procedure is for handling similar incidents. The attorney should explain what steps will be followed in the investigation, and what the likely time frames are. The attorney should make sure the employee's creature comforts are met (food, water, restroom stop), and that the employee has spoken with his or her spouse or significant other.

Only then should the attorney ask the employee what happened. This deliberate approach is, well, deliberate. The whole idea is for the attorney to start the process of calming the employee down, and building a supportive relationship with the employee. "There's no rush here" should be the message that comes through all of the attorney's actions.

Once the employee has gone through the account, the attorney should pause, discuss something else for five minutes, and then ask the employee to tell the story once more. To the unschooled, it would be amazing how different, and likely more expansive, the employee's second account will be compared to the first. The employee isn't making things up. What's happening is that the influence of a stress reaction is beginning to dissipate, and the clouds of memory impairment are beginning to lift. There is now growing recognition regarding the physical and psychological effects of involvement in a critical incident, including the perceptual distortions and memory problems that may have a direct impact on any statements given shortly after the incident.[2]

Your union can help the responding attorney by having a flash drive ready to hand to the attorney when he or she appears at the scene. The flash drive should contain your union contract, the department's policies on the use of force and deadly force, any SOPs that detectives will follow in investigating the incident, state statutes on the use of deadly force, and material you may add to the flash drive at the scene. What could you add? You could download a map of the area, for example, or do a computer search of public records to obtain the criminal record of the suspect, or even take some photographs of the scene (from a permitted area, of course) and store them on the flash drive.

The Role Of The Union Representative At The Scene. It often occurs that a union representative responds to a critical incident scene before the attorney. The union representative's primary function should be to make sure that the involved employee is separated from others, and that the employee is giving no substantive statements about what occurred.

It used to be that a well-intended supervisor or co-worker would take the involved employee for a cup of coffee to "settle down" and "depressurize" by talking about the incident. STOP! Don't allow this to happen in your jurisdiction, and particularly not with one of your members! Remember, anything that the employee "vents" to anyone else can (and probably will) be used against them during any phase of the investigation, criminal assessment and adjudication, and civil proceedings. You should tell your member that an attorney is on the way, and that any statements can wait until the attorney arrives.

Don't forget that critical incident investigations are criminal investigations. If the district attorney demands disclosure by a union representative of what the involved member said in the wake of a critical incident, the representative's options would be few and just about untenable. There is no union official/union member privilege, or at least none that can resist a district attorney's subpoena. That is why all of your union's representatives who might be responding to a critical incident should be schooled in the dangers of allowing an involved employee to tell

Critical incident investigations are criminal investigations.

them anything about the incident. They should avoid any conversation regarding thoughts, motivations, and actions about the incident.

Once the attorney arrives, the union representative assumes three different roles. The first is to act as an intermediary between the attorney and the employer's investigators and supervisors. Typically, it will be the union representative who will relay requests by investigators for things such as photographs, and messages from the attorney to investigators.

The second role assumed by the union representative is to gather as much information as possible about what occurred during the critical incident, and relay as much of that information as possible to the attorney. The third role of the union representative should be to deal with other union members on the scene, and the 101 things that should be tended to in the wake of a critical incident. Are there witness employees who will need representation during interviews? Has pizza been ordered so that the employees spending long hours at the scene will be fed? Do investigators want a "walk-through," and, if so, have they selected the employee they would like to use for the walk-through? Have other union representatives been notified? Are there media issues to deal with? All of these, and more, will become the tasks for the union representative as the investigation begins to gather steam.

Many agencies have specially trained Crisis Intervention Stress Debriefing Teams. These groups of professionals and fellow employees are valuable assets in the assessment stage of the response, and they give those employees who are directly or indirectly involved in the incident tools to deal with the psychological and emotional ramifications of the incident. Your union attorney should advise you on whether statements made by members to debriefing teams are privileged. Some states have enacted statutes that extend testimonial privileges to debriefing teams, though how these statutes would apply in federal (as opposed to state) court is untested; other states have not even attempted to create any debriefing team privilege. Your union attorney should give you the lay of the land in terms of a debriefing team privilege in your state.

Your attorney's advice will guide your union's approach to debriefing teams. Is your state one without a debriefing team privilege? Then it's your job to make sure your members discuss nothing substantive with members of the debriefing team. I'd even go so far as to suggest that you speak with the members of the debriefing team in advance, and ask them not to elicit substantive information in any critical incidents. What if your state does have a debriefing team privilege? I'd still be wary. The potential for information cogent to the incident being transmitted, misunderstood, or misinterpreted looms large whenever there is uncontrolled, yet well-intended, access to the principals involved.

Your attorney's advice will guide your union's approach to debriefing teams.

Remember: No call-out will be efficiently initiated unless the call-out list is updated regularly. This should include home phone numbers, cell phone numbers, and pager numbers. Hopefully, your coordination meetings with your administration previous to the critical incident will have ensured that the union representatives are called out along with the investigative response teams.

Spousal Notification. After a traumatic incident, the involved employee will most likely want his or her spouse to know that they are all right. This should be done as expeditiously (and as carefully) as possible. For instance, how do you think the spouse of a police officer would feel if he or she saw an officer or two pull up into the driveway, looking quite somber and concerned? Here is a better way: Have the officer (in the presence of a union rep and investigator, if necessary) call his spouse and tell her that he was just involved in an incident, he is okay, and so-and-so can be on the way over to bring her to the station if she needs to come by (and child care has already been taken care of). Usually, the spouse will see no reason to come to the station and appreciates hearing in the involved employee's own voice that he or she is okay. Some might want to, and your organization's culture should accept that as normal and appropriate. Even though spousal information is privileged, it is still best that the employee not start to go into details about actions taken at the event.

Crime Scene Preservation. Many of you might not like the term "crime scene," but by its very nature, a critical incident takes place at what becomes a crime scene. While responsibility for the preservation of the scene belongs to the agency and its investigators, never do anything or allow the involved employee to do anything that would compromise the scene. Period.

Never do anything or allow the involved employee to do anything that would compromise the scene.

Because it is a crime scene, the uniforms and equipment of the primary players will be considered evidence. Of course investigators will ensure that appropriate photographs of the employee's physical condition and the state of his equipment are taken. The most common occurrence is the securing of a police officer's uniform and weapon as evidence. You should tell members involved in critical incidents that this may happen, and describe the process as simple routine.

A good way to deal with this aspect of post critical incident protocols is to ensure that everyone has at least one serviceable uniform in his or her locker. When the uniform is turned over to investigators, a fresh uniform can then be put on. Never send an officer home without a weapon, unless it is a rare case where the officer is immediately arrested. Always arrange to have an accessible replacement weapon available, and issue it as your specific department procedures dictate. Many times a vehicle is a part of the scene, so take the initiative to make arrangements for your employees to be driven home, and be sure a serviceable vehicle is available for their use when they return to work.

Speaking With Witness Employees. It has always been (and always will be) a sticky situation regarding the preservation of the rights of witnesses and the need to elicit timely information from them regarding an incident. The union should push for protocols that provide that, prior to any interviews with employees who are witnesses, the following should occur:

1. The witness should be advised as to the criminal nature of the investigation;

2. It should be made clear to the witness employee that he or she is a witness and not a suspect; and

3. The witness should be informed of and afforded the right to union representation.

In a dynamic situation, timely witness information can impact the outcome of the incident. By securing prior agreements with your department's administration and implementing employee training and discussions oriented toward expectations of witnesses, concerns regarding the content and context of questions that will likely be posed at the time will likely ameliorate concerns on the part of employees.

A CHECKLIST.

Summing everything up, here is a checklist for the use of union representatives responding to a critical incident:

CRITICAL INCIDENT CHECKLIST

- Make sure the employee is not giving substantive statements.

- Assess the situation, and decide how many attorneys should respond.

- Call out additional union representatives as needed.

- Gather as much information as possible about what occurred.

- Act as a liaison between the attorneys and the department.

- Arrange for interviews with and representation for witness employees.

- If the employee's weapon is taken, make sure a substitute is provided.

- Try to have input into the information being given to the media.

- Make sure involved members have spoken with their significant others.

- If the scene takes time to process, make sure union members are fed.

FINAL CONSIDERATIONS.

A critical incident can result in a department's finest hour or it can be an example of ineptness fostering tragedy. No matter how the department comes out at the end, the individuals involved will have their own perceptions, needs, and memories.

Consistency is an important consideration when dealing with involved employees. It is important for your union to work with your department in the development of a policy that treats all employees involved in a critical incident in a manner that does not encourage presumption of guilt or incompetence. For instance, psychological aftercare for all involved personnel is recommended; that is, as a matter of course and not as a function of subjective assessment on the part of the union, the chain of command, or the individual. Write it in your policy that all employees who are primary players in a critical incident will receive a confidential psychological consultation.

Another consideration for the union is to ensure that the employee and his or her family are supported throughout the grand jury, inquest, or, if necessary, trial process. The stress of a high profile incident combined with that imposed by the disinterested procedures of the justice system can take a toll in personal and professional relationships.

Finally, what happens if support for the individual involved in the critical incident is not popular with your membership? Suppose it is, by all accounts, a "bad shooting" that has captured headlines and not only puts your department in a bad public light because of present policy or training deficiencies, but also places the union under scrutiny because of its insistence that constitutional rights, due process rights, and bargaining rights are respected? Well, all that means is that the union has been doing its job. The hell with those who would react emotionally or with a special interest in seeing your department and employees discredited. Union representatives must be aggressive yet professional commentators on process and investigative protocols, recognizing that the audience is not only the public, but your own membership. In dealing with your members, appeal to their own sense of "There but for the grace of God go I" perspective. Reinforce to them that a thorough and honest investigation conducted within the parameters of the law, and not under the emotional and sensationalist perspective of the media, is what the union, the Department, and the responsible members of society are demanding.

> *It is important for your union to work with your department in the development of a policy that treats all employees involved in a critical incident in a manner that does not encourage presumption of guilt or incompetence.*

NOTES

[1] *Use of Force* implies a proactive implementation of some level of force within your department's Force Continuum. It is in the employee's and the department's best interest to rename and refocus your Use of Force policy to a Response to Resistance policy. Such terminology implies that the level of force used was in response to the level of resistance encountered, and puts the employee in much better stead by sending a different and more desirable message to the public and to juries. Consider discussing this with your administration.

[2] While the body of work in this area continues to grow, an excellent examination specific to officer involved shootings is by Alexis Artwohl, *Perceptual and Memory Distortions in Officer Involved Shootings. FBI Law Enforcement Bulletin*, October 2002, Volume 158, N10, 18-24. Most certainly the publications and training of the Force Science Institute in Minnesota are the most state-of-the-art on the subject of critical incidents.

CHAPTER 15

ESTABLISHING A HEALTH AND WELFARE TRUST

A health and welfare trust[1] is a vehicle for financing employee health costs. Consider this quote from a recent study on health care costs that was a cooperative effort by the Center for Studying Health Care Change and Milliman, Incorporated: "…the most important driver of health care spending – advances in medical technology and its ready acceptance into mainstream medical practice – shows no sign of slowing. Indeed, a 'magic bullet' to contain costs continues to elude us."[2]

Maybe your union members have no health and welfare component included in their pension plans, or if there is a medical component for actives or retirees or both in your collective bargaining agreement, the time might be right to remove the language from your contract and consider establishing a health and welfare trust. If you have a membership of 200 or greater, or for that matter, you can combine with another union or unions with the same community of interests to get to 200, read on.

ADVANTAGES OF A HEALTH AND WELFARE TRUST.

The benefits of establishing a health and welfare trust are:

Lower costs. Though there are no national studies published on the issue, any number of local studies confirms that public safety officers use health care at a rate substantially lower – 20% lower – than general city or county employees. There have been several reasons advanced for this lower utilization, including:

- Thanks to lower retirement ages, public safety employees are relatively younger than general employees. In general, younger individuals use health care at a lower rate than older individuals.

- Public safety employees include relatively more males than general employees. At the age levels for active employees, males use health care less than females.

- Public safety employees are the beneficiary of presumptive causation workers' compensation laws, which presume that conditions such as heart and lung problems are caused by the job. That means the cost of health care for these conditions is borne by the workers' compensation or pension system, not the employer's health plan.

- Public safety employees are in relatively better physical condition than general employees. I know what you're thinking right now, or rather, I know who you're thinking about right now. I'm not saying that every cop or firefighter is in great shape. I'm just saying that on the average, they're in better shape than general employees, and that means lower health care usage.

Lower utilization rates translate into lower health care costs. As a result, if you are successful in breaking out into your own trust, you will be able to buy more

Lower utilization rates translate into lower health care costs.

health care coverage for the same premium dollars. That also means, of course, that the employer will be reluctant to let you go off on your own. After all, your presence in the employer-wide group actually subsidizes employees who use health care more often than your members.

Increased control. Establishing a trust puts control of plan design, funding and claims decisions in the hands of your own Board of Trustees.

Accessibility to information. For purposes of making informed decisions, all financial information associated with the plan is readily available in detail to the Board of Trustees. Such information enables the Board to make informed decisions regarding plan changes and funding requirements.

Plan design options. Plan design managed by the Board of Trustees accommodates the unique and special requirements of your members.

Leveraging opportunities. Your union should be substantial enough on its own to achieve the economies of size in administering a health and welfare plan. Just how "substantial" should your union be? Remember, economies of size are not a direct function of the number of covered employees. As a rule of thumb, a group of 200 to 1,000 employees can achieve most of the efficiencies of groups two or three times larger. In addition to the economies of size, a group of employees allows for special underwriting consideration and plan design, and opportunities to explore alternate funding arrangements such as minimum premium or partial self-funding.

Flexibility. If your union has control of its entire health and welfare plan, flexibility exists for an elected Board of Trustees regarding plan design, funding, and reactive adjustments necessitated by localized economic or political climates and collective bargaining considerations.

True cost transparency. The accessibility of the information mentioned above provides the data necessary to manage the trust and collectively bargain trust benefits when the employer is a contributing entity. This information is first hand and not subjected to the potential manipulations and interpretations of data requested from the employer.

DISADVANTAGES OF A HEALTH AND WELFARE TRUST.

While the advantages to your union of establishing a health and welfare trust are truly tempting, the disadvantages of such a venture can be truly intimidating:

1. Time and liability commitments. Okay, just how easy is it for you to get folks in your union to volunteer? And how often do your initial volunteers hang around to do it again? And what about your chances of finding members of your union who are willing to launch into the rewarding world of heath care cost management? And how many of them are willing to assume a fiduciary responsibility at the same time? Now you see one reason you'll need at least 200 members to get started…you will need a relatively large membership pool so you can have enough volunteers to make up your Board of Trustees! Bottom line, trustees must devote sufficient time to deal with the management of all trust matters and assume fiduciary responsibility for their actions and decisions that affect the financial status of the trust.

2. Initial operating expenses. The operating expenses associated with establishing a trust, such as drafting the trust document, production and mailing of announcement packages, and consulting fees, may be higher the first two years because of one-time costs associated with establishing the trust.

3. Claims appeals. When you operate your own health and welfare trust, your Board of Trustees will be responsible for dealing with claim disputes and appeals. While this can be viewed as a benefit, the "hands on" nature of your Board will also provide a level of exposure and time commitment that might very well be underestimated.

When you operate your own health and welfare trust, your Board of Trustees will be responsible for dealing with claim disputes and appeals.

ESTABLISHMENT OF THE TRUST.

Establishing a health and welfare trust begins with collective bargaining. Through negotiations with your employer, your contract should be amended to establish a health and welfare trust for your particular bargaining unit (or group of bargaining units). The contract must include the employer contribution rate that is to be paid monthly on a dollars per eligible member rate, and specific language that requires the monthly payments be made directly to the trust.

Board of Trustees. Immediately after ratification of the contract amendment, if not sooner, the union must designate a Board of Trustees. The Board of Trustees is the policy-making group for all aspects of the trust, separate from the union's Executive Board. The Board of Trustees is responsible for determining plan design and eligibility, arranging for and providing direction to an administrative staff for day-to-day administration and operation of the trust, purchasing required professional services and insurance, authorizing expenses for newsletters and other communication to the membership, and (our favorite) presiding over claims appeals. A good working number is four or five elected trustees. One individual must assume the dubious honor of Chairperson, while another must be willing to be elected to or designated as secretary. The Chairperson will, of course, preside at the Board of Trustees meetings, while the secretary assumes responsibility for the recording of the proceedings at the meetings, and the issuance of meeting minutes when deemed necessary.

Service providers. The initial duties of the Board of Trustees will be the selection of professional service providers such as trust counsel, trust auditor, employee benefits consultant, third-party administrator, bank or trust company, insurance company, and an investment manager.

The *trust counsel or attorney* should draft the trust document. This document effectively establishes the trust as a legal entity. This document details the purpose of the trust, designates the methods used to appoint and remove members of the Board of Trustees, explains the method of voting by trustees on issues before the Board, articulates the authority of the trustees, and establishes the rules and parameters of future trustee behavior.

The *trust auditor* conducts annual audits and issues financial statements. The responsibility of preparing and filing any federally-required forms, such as Form 5500, belongs to the trust auditor.

The *employee benefits consultant* advises the Board of Trustees on all aspects of the trust's operations and the renewal of health and welfare benefits, including the negotiation of insurance company renewals on the trust's behalf, drafting communication to the membership, advising on projected income and expense levels, designing a plan or combination of plans of benefits that can be funded by the employer contribution rate, assisting in the selection of an insurance carrier, and assisting in the selection of a third-party administrator or arranging for in-house administration.

The *insurance company* bears the financial risk of any claims exceeding pre-planned levels, and if the plan is conventionally insured or on a minimum premium basis, the insurance company provides all administrative forms, claim payment, plan booklets that summarize the plan description, monthly paid claim reports, utilization reports, and contracts and amendments. The insurance company will usually provide claim cost containment and utilization review, such as hospital pre-certification, and access to preferred provider networks.

An *investment manager* is a fiduciary appointed by the Board of Trustees to provide professional investment advice and, in general, is charged with the responsibility of maximizing investment returns on plan assets. If your trust fund is relatively small, this is usually done by the trust company or bank, while for larger trust funds, independent firms are often hired to manage the trust's investments.

The *third-party trust administrator* is responsible for the day-to-day operation of the trust and its accompanying health plan. This position is key to the successful and efficient performance of the trust. The administrator's duties include reviewing the eligibility information on a monthly basis from the employer. This information must be reviewed for accuracy and adjusted accordingly. Other responsibilities should be the calculation and payment of insurance premiums to the carrier; the payment of fiduciary liability and bonding insurance premiums; the calculation and transfer of trust assets to a claim deposit account representing the monthly claim liability if the plan is a minimum premium or partially self-funded program; answering questions on eligibility, claims, and benefits; preparing and mailing summary plan descriptions and identification cards; assisting the trust consultant in compilation of eligibility and other plan statistics; assisting the trust auditor in preparing the annual audit; maintaining the official trust records; the administration of COBRA; and advising the trustees on ways to improve the trust's efficiencies.

Administration of the trust can be provided by a third-party contract administrator or an in-house administrator. While in-house administration provides greater flexibility and complete control of the entire administrative process, your union must assess its ability to administer the trust in-house by ensuring that there are available data processing facilities; existing staff; available personnel with the skills, professional expertise and experience to administer a health trust; and consider the relative cost of providing the service in-house as opposed to hiring a third-party contract administrator.

No matter which way your union chooses to administer the trust, be sure to do your homework. You must craft a request for proposal and aggressively market (or have someone market) the administrative services you need. Draft a specific job description so that you can evaluate all potential in-house administrators. Be prepared to train anyone hired as in-house administrator in the specific demands of your particular trust to meet the expectations of the trustees.

The role of the bank or trust company. The role of the bank or trust company depends largely on the plan's funding arrangement. If the plan was conventionally insured, the bank or trust company would collect and hold contributions from the participating employer in the trust account, provide check writing and reconciliation for payment of premiums and trust operating expenses as directed by the trustees or the administrator, and provide monthly statements on all trust accounts.

If the plan is on a minimum premium or a partially self-funded basis, the trust company would be responsible for providing an account to hold funds for claim payment, and to wire transfer funds to the insurance company for the minimum premium or pay claim drafts written on the account if your trust is partially self-funded.

PLAN DESIGN CONSIDERATIONS.

An issue of high importance is establishing the level of benefits to be provided. Coverage afforded under the trust fund should be equal to or better than the coverage currently provided by your present employer-sponsored plan. Your plan design should be based on a feasibility study that should be conducted prior to, or if you are a group of masochists, during collective bargaining.

Coverage afforded under the trust fund should be equal to or better than the coverage currently provided by your present employer-sponsored plan.

Feasibility study. The feasibility study is exactly what it implies, a comprehensive assessment that will tell your union if the establishment of a health and welfare trust is a viable and worthwhile endeavor that will provide equal or better benefits than those currently provided by the employer. To begin assessing the feasibility of a potential trust, you must obtain the eligibility and experience information for the group that will be insured over a minimum of 24 months. The information should be reviewed by an actuary to determine if the employer contribution rate is sufficient to fund the current plan of benefits, trust administration expenses, trust start-up expenses, and necessary trust reserves.

While a prudent fiscal policy for the trust is important during the first years of its existence, setting aside trust reserves to meet unexpected contingencies is necessary. These reserves should not be confused with those you have set aside to deal with incurred but unreported claims.

Budgeting. Establishing an initial budget is critical to ensuring the solvency of the trust during the first two or three years and an important part of the trust's fiscal management into the future. Remember, first-year operating expenses are usually higher than what can be expected in following years because of start-up costs such as the drafting of trust documents and the production and mailing of announcement packages. Ongoing operating expenses to be considered are the administration, printing and postage, legal advice, consulting fees, audit fees, meeting expenses, bank agency fees, costs of an ERISA fidelity bond, appropriate fiduciary liability coverage, and conference and convention costs.

Health Care Trends. It is generally accepted that changes to providing health care coverage are attributed to two factors, inflation and utilization. Usually measured on an annual basis, inflation is the factor representing the increase in the cost of providing a particular unit of health care service. Examples are the increase in the cost of prescription drugs, hospital stays, or a visit to the doctor. The rate of inflation of costs of health and medical services is almost always higher than that of other sectors, so do not depend on cost of living analysis, unless they are specifically medical cost of living analysis, to plan cost projections for your trust.

Utilization measures the change in the number of health care services used or purchased from one year to another. Obviously, utilization rates can be either positive or negative, impacting the effects of inflation. An increase in the number of covered participants will generally result in a decrease in utilization, while a decrease in the number of covered participants will result in increased utilization. Changes in utilization as the result of fluctuating eligibility tend to be short term in nature and occur several months after the change in eligibility.

GETTING THE WORD OUT.

Once it has been determined by the union leadership that the trust should be established, communication with your members is critical. Of course, if you had been doing your job, the possibility of the formation of a health and welfare trust should come as no surprise to your general membership. So while most members will know that a trust is in the offing, the first formal communication from your previously-elected Board of Trustees to them will be the announcement package.

This announcement package should be a clear and understandable explanation of the trust that covers all aspects of the pending change in health and welfare coverage, to include:

1. The reasons for establishing the trust.

2. How the trust will benefit the membership.

3. What employees should anticipate during the transition to the trust.

4. A description of the benefits level.

5. How to file claims under the new plan.

6. Required materials such as identification cards, claim forms, enrollment forms, pre-addressed envelopes for submitting claims, and

pre-addressed envelopes for returning enrollment forms.

Follow-up announcements reflecting such issues as a result of the rates relative to anticipated plan costs should be updated and shared annually with members.

SUMMARY.

Before undertaking the establishment of a health and welfare trust, there should be at least 200 covered employees to provide a large enough user base and the predictability of costs to achieve economic stability, economies of size, underwriting flexibility in plan design and funding alternatives, and the establishment of trust reserves. Getting a health and welfare trust off the ground is a challenging and sometimes intimidating undertaking for union leaders. But you know that there is nothing in the present labor environment that has garnered the attention of union members like the future of their medical coverage. Remember that the benefits realized from the establishment of a value added trust fund will help you control accurate information and allow timely communication to members regarding true plan costs, remove the health and welfare plan design and benefits level issues from the collective bargaining process, meet specific member needs through flexibility in plan design, and allow you to react on a timely basis to health care and economic issues.

NOTES

[1] Some of the foundational information in this chapter is based on interviews and source material provided by Mr. Ed Burgan, retired pension plan expert and trust fund consultant from Johnson and Higgins/Brady Company, Anchorage, Alaska.

[2] B.C. Strunk, P.B. Ginsberg, and John Cookson, "Tracking Health Care Costs: Declining Growth Trend Pauses in 2004," *Health Affairs*, 21 June 2005 http://content.healthaffairs.org/cgi/content/abstract/hlthaff.w5.286.short (21 June 2005) and T. Gilmer and R. Kronick, "It's The Premiums, Stupid: Projections of the Uninsured Through 2013," *Health Affairs*, 5 April 2005, http://content.healthaffairs.org/cgi/content/abstract/hlthaff.w5.143 (20 April 2005).

CHAPTER 16

USING PROFESSIONAL STAFF

A common theme throughout this book has been that cops and firefighters are very good at what they do when it comes to their jobs, but not necessarily good at some of the other stuff that they have to do during the course of running a union. Not to mention the fact that for medium and small unions, the organization's leadership often does union work on a "catch as catch can" basis at worst, and at best during on-duty time when they are not shagging calls. Anyone who has tried to wear both hats when both jobs demand so much will attest to the fact that neither job gets done to the level of efficiency and effectiveness that both jobs deserve.

Whether you can retain professional staff, and to what extent, will depend first on the size of your union and then on the nature of your collective bargaining agreement. For example, if your contract includes such far-reaching responsibilities for your organization as a health and welfare trust, it becomes intuitively obvious that engaging a medical insurance carrier to administrate the distribution of benefits and tracking of co-payments will be necessary.

Let's take a look at the different types of professional staff to consider.

KEEP THE PHONE LINES OPEN: RECEPTIONISTS AND ANSWERING SERVICES.

I realize that cell phones are ubiquitous. However, you've got both a full-time job and a life beyond the job, and you may well want someone to screen phone calls or simply want to have a human being on the end of the line when someone calls you. Answering services are relatively inexpensive, and can give you 24/7 coverage. A receptionist, even one working part-time, can handle filing and do administrative chores in addition to answering the phone. If you go either of these routes, make sure the person representing your organization does so in the manner you want. Never put the receptionist or answering service into a position in which they are making a policy decision. Provide whoever is answering your phones with a specific script and specific time parameters for forwarding messages and getting in touch with you if a phone call presents a time-sensitive matter.

If your union has offices with a reception area, ensure that someone is always present to greet guests. This sounds basic, but there is nothing more unprofessional or unproductive than to have a union member, elected official, or member of the public come to do business with what they perceive as a professional organization only to leave with the sense that your outfit doesn't have its act together.

KEEP THE BOOKS STRAIGHT: BOOKKEEPERS, ACCOUNTANTS, AND TAX PLANNERS.

The responsibilities of the treasurer should be focused primarily from the perspective of a watch dog and policy advisor regarding the union's fiscal health and long-term direction. If you can afford it, hire a bookkeeper to handle the day-to-day, often mundane and time consuming tasks of handling the bookkeeping for the organization. If possible, your organization should engage a full-service firm in which the bookkeeping, accounting, and tax preparation can be provided at reasonable cost. Remember, though, that when the time comes for an audit or an annual review, you must engage another firm to ensure a credible and honest process.

Bookkeeper. What exactly should a bookkeeper do in the context of a police or fire union? Basically you hire a bookkeeper to enter transactions in a journal (or on a computer), make adjustments, and prepare reports such as budgets and balance sheets. Since bookkeeping is a relatively mechanical and regimented process that occurs within predictable time parameters (usually a monthly cycle), you may only need to retain a bookkeeper for a few hours one day a month. A full-charge bookkeeper does it all, from the data entry to the preparation of financial statements.

You might argue that a bookkeeper is not necessary with the new software that now exists that is specifically designed to run a small business. If your organization is a small and relatively straightforward operation, you might be right. But who will do the data entry? Who will track the transactions? Who will ensure that all is done according to generally accepted accounting principles? All in all, whoever is engaged to accept this responsibility must work closely with your treasurer and be accountable to your organization. One other word of warning: Part-time bookkeepers who are full-time public safety employees are generally only good at one or the other, rarely at both.

Accountant. Should your union have an accountant? And what is the difference between an accountant and a bookkeeper? The answer to the first question is "yes," unless you're the smallest of unions and can't afford a few hours a year of an accountant's time. As to the second question, probably the easiest way to differentiate between a bookkeeper and an accountant is to think of the accountant as the person who interprets and monitors what the bookkeeper does. Accounting is a much more subjective process than bookkeeping and has value at various levels. An accountant can design a bookkeeping system and budget categories that will help your union gather the information necessary for decision making without making the system too burdensome for your bookkeeper.

Accountants will work as much or as little as you want. For some unions, all you may need is an hour or three of the accountant's time once a year, to review your bookkeeping and, if necessary, file tax forms. For larger organizations, you may want your accountant to provide monthly updates to your union regarding the organization's financial health.

Your accountant must be familiar with the non-profit corporation rules and charitable solicitation laws. Some of the rules are awfully arcane. For example, did you know that revenues from advertising sales in a union newspaper might be treated as taxable "unrelated business income" even though the union is otherwise a tax exempt organization? Having an accountant in your corner can help you avoid potential tax pitfalls like this.

Keep It Legal, Timely, And Efficient: Hire A Good Labor Attorney.

Your union needs an attorney. It's that simple. Labor relations is just too complicated today. A given factual situation may involve the intersection of your collective bargaining agreement, state bargaining laws, federal statutes such as the FLSA, the ADA, or the FMLA, different state statutes, and even court-made rules like the duty of fair representation. Good attorneys can sort through these sorts of issues and give you advice on how best to present your arguments. The best attorneys have a knack not just for advising you of the law, but helping you devise effective long-term strategies that will help your union. The good attorneys are not just effective litigators, they're not just "book lawyers" who know the law, they are advisors in the best and most complete use of the word.

Sometimes an attorney is even more valuable for the fight he might prevent than for the actual legal labor shootout he might become a party to. Everyone, including employers, knows how expensive a good attorney can be. The fact that your organization is serious enough about an issue to employ an attorney generally speaks volumes as to your intentions regarding that issue. If the attorney is one with the reputation and credentials that spur the other side towards resolution of your differences, then who can question the value of the money invested?

The fact that your organization is serious enough about an issue to employ an attorney generally speaks volumes as to your intentions regarding that issue.

Finding a good attorney can be difficult. If possible, you want an attorney firmly grounded in labor law. If that's not possible because of your location, you want an attorney who is willing to learn, someone who will grow with your organization over a lengthy period of time. A good starting point is to learn who the attorneys are who are representing other public safety unions in your state. If there aren't many (or any), then track down the attorneys who represent private-sector unions with locals in your state, unions such as the Teamsters, the Service Employees International Union, or any of the trade unions. Interview the lawyers and speak to their clients about their capabilities. If you've got a decent relationship with some arbitrators in the area, ask them for their off-the-record and hopefully candid assessment of the lawyer.

Let me tell you how my union found our lawyer. Anchorage had just elected a new mayor, one who ran on the platform that police officers were overpaid. Some of us involved in the union saw the potential for a huge fight, and worried about whether our local lawyer was up to handling a protracted battle. Anchorage is fairly isolated, and there aren't many union lawyers in town. We decided to investigate lawyers outside of Alaska, and if they were good enough, consider hiring them.

We went to a multi-day conference put on in Las Vegas by the National Association of Police Organizations. Most of the speakers were public safety union lawyers. We focused on one of them, Will Aitchison. We asked around the room, and learned he was generally well-regarded. We talked to him over a break and, long story made short, hired him. The mayor made good on his threats, and we found ourselves in a massive arbitration over our contract, with 101 issues on the table, most of them take-back proposals made by the employer. Twenty-one days of trial later, we received an arbitrator's decision ruling in our favor on 98 out of the 101 issues. More than 25 years later, Aitchison is still the union's lawyer.

In the best of all cases, your organization can retain a trusted attorney who is willing to stay with your union over time and provide quality representation in everything from grievance resolution to contract negotiations. It is possible for your attorney to become trusted by your membership, become a consigliore to your union's leadership, and even earn the respect of the employer as a source of honest and credible legal perspective. Such an attorney can even provide additional services to members such as "will kits" for estate planning, reduced cost representation in divorces for the occasional police officer or firefighter divorce, and specially-tailored training to union members and union leadership.

In terms of fees, I like a retainer agreement instead of a flat fee arrangement. With an attorney charging you by the hour, you can encounter wildly fluctuating legal fees depending upon the case load of the moment. Retainer agreements, where the attorney is paid a flat sum per month regardless of how much or little work he or she performs, allows both the union and the attorney to "smooth" and plan for legal costs.

You may want to have more than one labor attorney at your union's disposal. There are some cases that demand a particular personality, something your normal attorney might not bring to the table. Having a "junk yard dog" handle a case for you from time to time can be helpful.

Keep The Issues Packaged And Spun: Lobbyists And Public Relations Specialists.

If the last few years have taught us anything, it's that a public safety organization needs an integrated approach in order to be effective. You have to be at the bargaining table, of course, but you also have to package your message to the public, politicians, and opinion shapers as effectively as you can. That means you may need at least the occasional help of a lobbyist or public relations firm.

Lobbyists. Most cops and firefighters will cringe when discussing the merits of hiring a lobbyist almost as much as they do when assessing the need for an attorney. As has been previously discussed in Chapter 13, when it comes to accessing politicians for public safety issues, you will generally find the doors wide open. Unfortunately, the very same lawmakers who embrace you as uniformed cops and firefighters seem not to see you when you are dressed in civilian clothes pushing for the types of wages and benefits that are fair. A lobbyist can help you span that breach.

Even more importantly, the last few years have seen a coordinated nationwide effort to weaken public safety collective bargaining laws. Governor Scott Walker in Wisconsin, Ohio's Senate Bill 5 that would have practically eliminated bargaining for police and fire, and bills introduced in legislatures around the country that would convert states to right-to-work laws or outright declare collective bargaining to be illegal. Some point to the American Legislative Exchange Council, funded by powerful and wealthy corporations, that puts on seminars that "train" state legislators in how to attack unions and drafts model statutes that will accomplish that goal.

Without regard to who is behind the movement to attack bargaining rights, the attack is real, and you need to counter it. You can't sit back and count on the public to make phone calls and send emails to legislators trying to convince them not to pass this sort of legislation. You need to become active on the legislative front, and that means a lobbyist.

For many public safety labor organizations, hiring a lobbyist is as simple as joining an organization with an established presence in your capitol. Most firefighters belong to the International Association of Fire Fighters and automatically become part of state firefighter councils who already have a lobbying presence on hand. Law enforcement officers tend to be more independent, and may need to seek out a state law enforcement group to join.

If you're big enough, consider retaining a lobbyist. Most lobbyists work on a retainer basis, and even a small labor organization might be able to retain a lobbyist for a manageable fee. All lobbyists bring with them political baggage. They get labeled as Democrats, Republicans, industry or labor due to the nature of the majority of the causes and clients that they serve. This "side of the aisle" problem might initially polarize support for a bill because of who is shopping it around, so be aware that the lobbyist can only do so much. If you are working on the cheap and use your lobbyist to do nothing else but get you into a politician's office so that you can do the talking, that may be a plus. Once in, you can re-establish those strong ties that make you a cop or a firefighter in the politician's eyes, sometimes tempering the potential anti-labor sentiment that your particular issue might engender.

What to pay a lobbyist is a direct function of the lobbyist's position in the hierarchy of influence peddlers that roam the halls of legislatures everywhere. Expect to pay a reputable lobbyist on par with any other professional service, such as an attorney. Not surprisingly, many lobbyists are attorneys or former attorneys who find satisfaction in practicing the art of persuasion in the less formalized and more intimate bar where liquor and political discourse flow freely and where complicated deals can be cut outside the court of public scrutiny. A high powered lobbyist has a record of victories that indicates effectiveness, and he or she exercises a network of contacts that creates political leverage that can only be developed over time.

Just remember that lobbyists do not create the issue or the piece of litigation. They are like the car salesman who must sell someone else's product. You have to establish your legislative priorities. You need to train your lobbyist in what to look for in legislation introduced from other fronts, and to be ready to warn you when a piece of attack legislation comes down the pike.

Make sure your lobbyist regularly reports to your Executive Board or Political Action Committee. Just as importantly, try to hire a lobbyist who participates in an on-line service to which you'll have access, a service that will allow you to read the full text of bills and track their progress as they wend their way through your legislature. Like an attorney, your lobbyist should be able to provide an itemized record of actions taken on your union's behalf since the last update. You need to know if your particular issue or piece of legislation has been appropriately shepherded through the right committees, and you need to know what kind of help your sponsor needs to succeed.

What about potential problems if your lobbyist is identified with only one flavor of political party, or if your lobbyist is one who is specifically considered a labor lobbyist? Probably the best way to answer those concerns is to recognize them as valid, and it's up to you to determine if you're willing to bank on the party in power always being user-friendly toward your union. I wouldn't. Try to find a lobbyist who can work both sides of the aisle and who is welcomed into anyone's office. These folks are certainly in the minority, but when found, they are truly worthy of efforts toward the development of a long-term relationship.

A danger in dealing with lobbyists is their propensity to have a conflict of interest. This becomes more of an issue when a lobbyist has a large client base and is engaged in a host of issues. Openness and transparency are all key elements to cultivating a relationship with a lobbyist that doesn't embarrass your union or mire it in some sort of scandal. The bottom line is a competent lobbyist can do things that you can't, and that is an unfortunate fact of life in running a union these days. You'll never get used to it, you'll never like it. But you need to do it.

Public Relations Specialists. I've talked in Chapter 13 about the need for a public relations professional in a crisis. On any given news day, there will be some story on the evening news in your local area about the police department or the fire department. Rarely is a public safety entity not reported on, scrutinized, lauded, or criticized about something or another.

So then why consider the long-term services of a public relations specialist? After all, you are already blessed (or cursed) with all the free publicity that you can handle! Well, that's just it. If you were to come into a windfall of money, wouldn't you consider tax and investment advice? Wouldn't you want some professional insights on how to maximize your good fortune? You need to shape the news to your advantage.

Don't forget, most of the public does not differentiate between a police department and a police union, or a fire department and a fire union. In their eyes, it's all cops, firefighters and paramedics. If police and fire unions planned to maximize the benefits of the continuous exposure and the generally positive image put forth by the media, they would be in a position to weather the storm of inevitable controversies and miscues that are on the horizon. A good way to do this is to work up a strategy for long-term image-making and power-building into your strategic plan.

Think of this long-term image as a "bank" of good will. When short-term situations arise, whether in the form of controversies or issue-oriented needs such as a particular legislative goal, think about the good will invested to control those issues as writing a check from your long-term bank. An enviable position for any union is to have enough long-term good will capital to tap into, providing the ability to weather the periodic onslaughts of critical politicians and special interest groups. A public relations specialist can help you maximize this good will and exercise it in a timely and appropriate manner.

The public relations specialist's role can be anywhere from that of a consultant who is hired on a case-by-case basis, to a retained agency that is an integral and involved aspect of your labor organization. A public relations specialist can contract for a poll so that you can get a snapshot of public sentiment regarding a specific issue or to help you establish a baseline regarding how positively or negatively your union is viewed. The public relations specialist can help you interpret poll results and best apply the information that you just gained. With that information, the public relations specialist will guide you in crafting the appropriate message, to the appropriate audience, through the appropriate medium.

Don't lose sight of the fact that a long-term relationship engendered with a public relations firm can provide access to the official and unofficial opinion molders in a community. Like the lobbyist who helps you hone your message, the public relations expert will help you educate and inform those folks in the community who are often sought out for their opinions by the media and decision makers. They'll even set up regular meetings with the editorial boards of local news media. The public relations specialist will help you build bridges between your organization and non-profits and businesses that might share a common interest or intent. It is music to the ears of a police or fire union president when members of the Chamber of Commerce refer to your union collectively as "the cops" or "the firefighters," not differentiating the union from the Department or its management, and providing the kind of credibility very few other unions can so readily attain. It is the public relations expert who can help transcend your organization from an entity that is viewed solely as a labor interest to one that is viewed as having a respected professional opinion regarding community and public safety issues.

While the public relations specialist will help you keep your finger on the pulse of public opinion regarding your union, there is an inherent danger in allowing public relations concerns drive your union's decision-making process. That is why an early decision must be made regarding the role of public relations in your union. A cardinal rule is this: Public relations must be a tool to further your union's policy and philosophy, not a basis for the formation of that policy and philosophy. There will be times when your organization will have to go against the prevailing public sentiment to accomplish a goal that is beneficial to your members, and how you have managed your public relations in the past and how well you respond in the crafting of your message in the present will impact the outcome.

Like many other professionals, public relations specialists can be retained on either an hourly or a retainer basis. In making the decision as to which fee struc-

Public relations must be a tool to further your union's policy and philosophy, not a basis for the formation of that policy and philosophy.

ture to use, your union should assess the scope of the project and the potential benefits of a long-term relationship with the specialist or the agency.

CHAPTER 17

COMPUTERS, THE INTERNET AND SOCIAL MEDIA

It's easy to get overwhelmed by technology. Even if you grew up with it, the rate of change in technology is almost blinding, and it's easy to feel uncomfortable with even dipping the figurative big toe in the technology pond.

My overriding message is to not let your reservations stand in the way of getting your organization in front of, and not behind, the technology curve. Computers today mean information management, and today as always, information is power. You need systems in place that are more powerful and more flexible than those of your employer.

There are three general rules that apply to all information technology, no matter whether you are dealing with a stand-alone computer system or building a Facebook presence:

- Identify your needs.

- Be willing to invest. Software and programmers cost money so you have to be willing to spend it. Just make sure you're not buying more than you need.

- Be willing to learn. You don't need to be an expert, but you should know basic terminology and concepts.

THE STARTING AND ENDING POINT – BACKING UP YOUR FILES.

I want to start the discussion of computers in what might seem like an unusual place – the need to backup your files. As more and more of a union's organizational history is stored electronically, there is a greater risk that history can be lost if the union does not take basic and (almost) free steps.

Let's start with some basic propositions. Backups should be made as easy as possible so they are more likely to get done, and automated backups are the best. The more frequent the backups, the better. Backing up information every Friday may not help you if you lose your data on Thursday.

The simplest backup system is to buy an external hard drive. Hard drive storage has become incredibly inexpensive over the last few years. Today, it is possible to obtain a one-terabyte external hard drive for as little as $100. One terabyte of data will store all of your union's files unless, for some reason, your union stores many, many very large video files. Buy two of these external hard drives, use the software that comes with the hard drive to set up daily backups, plug them in, and you're almost set. All you need to do now is to remember to rotate your hard drives, always storing one off-site to hedge against the danger of fire. If you find the program that comes with the hard drive difficult to navigate, both the Windows and Apple operating systems come with backup utilities that can be used in place of your hard drive software.

Backups should be made as easy as possible so they are more likely to get done, and automated backups are the best.

What about CDs, DVDs, and flash drives? The storage on CDs and DVDs is extremely limited. Not only are your data files likely much larger than could be contained on a single CD or DVD, it's also impossible to automate backup operations with CDs or DVDs, and CDs and DVDs degrade over time. Flash drives have better storage, and are rapidly increasing in size, but they still do not approach the storage capacities of external hard drives. Plus, flash drives are easy to misplace or lose, and this whole exercise is about the security of your backup operations.

If your union computers are networked, you should back up your files in two ways. First, set up your network in such fashion that files are routinely backed up on one of the network's servers. Once again, this is likely easy to do with your networking software, and the Apple and Windows operating systems have backup utilities that will allow you to schedule network backups. You should also take the basic steps of backing up your files to either a server located in a separate facility or to an external hard drive. Make sure each of the computers on your network are regularly backed up.

There are also any number of on-line backup systems. Amazon's S3 is a good example. As of the writing of this book, Amazon charges $0.125 per gigabyte for the first terabyte of storage. Prices get even cheaper as you store more information, but it's very unlikely that you will need more than one terabyte of storage. The list of on-line backup services is a long one, and is getting longer. Here is a fair sampling:

Service	Price	Free Plan?
Backblaze	$50 per year	15-day trial
Carbonite	$230 per year, 250GB	15-day trial
CrashPlan	$120 per year per 1 PC, 50GB	30-day trial
IDrive	$49.75 per year per 100GB per 1 PC	5GB free account
Jungle Disk	$4 per month plus storage fees	First 10GB free per user
KineticD	$6 per GB per year plus $3.95 per month license fee	14-day trial
MiMedia	$49 per year per 100GB Unlimited PCs	7GB free account
MozyPro	$220 per year, 50GB	30-day free trial
Nomadesk	$10 per month per user	30-day free trial
Norton Online Backup	$50 per 25GB per 5 PCs	30-day 5GB trial
SOS Online Backup	$100 per year per user, 100GB	14-day trial, 50GB
SpiderOak	$100 per year, 100GB, unlimited PCs	2GB

SECURITY OF YOUR INFORMATION.

With your backup system in place, it's time to turn to the next basic requirement of the computer system – security. A good starting point is to have a written
policy on the basics of computer and network security. The policy should mandate
the use of passwords, and specify that the union president and at least one other
officer should have access to all passwords for all union computers. I'd recommend
your policy cover at least these other points:

Access To Internet. Your policy should prohibit the downloading or trading
of copyright material. To avoid the possibility of a harassment suit or worse, your
policy should make pornographic web sites off limits. I'd also recommend that the
policy prohibit access to piracy sites and web pages maintained by hate groups.
When thinking these things through, always ask yourself the question, "If our
computer use files were subpoenaed, would I be embarrassed?"

Wi-Fi. Wireless networks are everywhere, which means that hackers trying to
penetrate wireless networks are everywhere. If your union has a wireless system,
take some basic steps. Use a strong password consisting of a mixture of upper
and lower case letters and numbers. If you're the Springfield Police Association,
for heaven's sake don't set your password as SpringfieldPolice or SpringfieldPolice
Association. Don't get cute with your wireless password, get complicated. You
should encrypt your wireless by using the enterprise mode of WPA or WPA2 security so passwords aren't visible in case a desktop or laptop computer is stolen. Since
it's easy for a visitor to reset a wireless router to remove encryption, make sure the
hardware on your wireless system is physically secure.

Networks. If you use a network, set "permissions" so that only the right people have access to the right folders or files. For example, your bookkeeper may
need access to your financial files, but does he need access to your grievance folders? You might want to allow some users to be able to read files, but not to copy,
delete, or modify them. All of this can be done through the setting of "permissions."

Speak With An IT Pro. As public safety employees, we're likely to have some
knowledge about computer systems, but the chances that we're a full-blown IT
specialist are minimal. You should find such a person. It may be someone you
need to hire for a few hours, or someone in your bargaining unit may have the
necessary skills. Discuss some computer basics with the IT professional. Talk
about viruses and worms, whether you're adequately protected, and how you need
to train your users to avoid the most common attacks. Ask about whether attachments to e-mails should be allowed and, if so, what kinds of attachments. Should
you filter content and set up firewalls? Should you create a VPN or virtual private
network and, if you do, who should have access to it and how? All of these questions and many more can be answered by a qualified IT professional. Believe me,
it's worth the investment to protect your union's files.

Specialized Computer Programs. Most of us are reasonably conversant in
basic computer programs such as word processors, spreadsheets, and presentation

Have a written policy on the basics of computer and network security.

If you use a network, set "permissions" so that only the right people have access to the right folders or files.

software. There are three types of specialized programs you might wish to consider. The first is a database-driven program that can track your grievances, send you reminders when it's time to act on a grievance, and allow you to query your files to look for information relevant to grievances. The most popular grievance-tracking software is marketed by Grievance Manager, though other vendors exist.

The second type of specialized software is written for specific functions in which your union engages. Once again, this is usually database-driven software, and will require you to hire a programmer. For example, the Portland Police Association handles the assignment of off-duty work to its members, and needed a database to track information for special duty employers (contact names, phone numbers, email, etc); special duty jobs (employer, location, date, time, number of officers needed, special skills required); and officer information (name, telephone, email, special skills). The database also had to track each officer's special duty work history, automatically generate a list of officers to contact, and generate reports on demand for individual officers' special duty work history and total special duty assignments in a given time period. The Association worked with Marc Fuller of LRIS to create such a program, and has used it to efficiently administer its off-duty work operations.

The third type of specialized program is a member database. The program should allow you to track as much information about your members as they'll provide you, and as your Board deems appropriate. At a minimum, a member database should have dates of hire, seniority dates (if they're different from dates of hire), job classification, assignments, first and last names, home address, phone numbers (work, cell, home) and email addresses. A member database can track the member's participation in optional union benefits such as insurance, the member's grievance history, and the member's experience with the union. Member databases can be extremely useful when political season rolls around and you need to know which of your members lives in the district of a particular senator.

A good rule to remember about databases is "garbage in, garbage out." Databases can be wonderfully designed and have immense capabilities, but can be useless unless the information in them is routinely updated.

Social Media.

Should your union have a social media presence? Let me answer that question with a question. How many of your members, particularly your newer members, use social media as a form of communication? As their primary form of communication? A 2012 study by the Pew Research Center found that 69% of American adults use social media. If you're without a social media presence, you're not doing the job you should of communicating with your members, and with whole swaths of the public.

Social media are an efficient and inexpensive way to engage your members, the public and the media. Social media is two-way communication, and you should focus on listening, not just broadcasting your message. Social media isn't like a press release or newspaper ad.

One of the first things you're going to have to decide when you start using social media is how you are going to deal with comments. Some applications such as Facebook do not allow you to turn all comments off, but do allow you to delete comments once they've been made. All social media applications allow you to respond to comments. When you're setting your "comment policy," keep a couple of things in mind. On one hand, social media are not about controlling the message; they're about encouraging communication. On the other hand, you can be positive that the traditional media will be following your social media account, and imagine what might happen if someone posted a racist, sexist, or otherwise offensive comment to your Facebook post. All in all, I favor allowing comments (after all, we're pretty used to offensive comments on the websites of the traditional media), but recommend that your union have a system for promptly reviewing and responding to comments in a timely fashion.

Use your social media presence to share information. If you see an interesting tweet then re-tweet it. "Like" or share useful Facebook posts. Post or tweet original ideas. This will set your union up as an authority on the issues. Share photos and video. Images grab people more than text. Photos help to humanize your union, especially photos from charitable events and meetings.

You should monitor the social media accounts of others, particularly those of the traditional media and local bloggers. Local news stations often ask viewers to comment on stories through Twitter or Facebook. Don't miss this opportunity.

Make sure you don't over-extend your resources. Focus on the social media outlets your members use. You can argue that Google Plus is better than Facebook but don't bother with a Google Plus account if your members are all on Facebook. Keep your posts relevant. Users can hide updates from friends or fan pages. Make sure your posts are interesting, topical and relevant so they don't get blocked.

Above all, be patient, be diligent, and be careful. Don't expect to set up a Facebook page and Twitter account and then have hundreds of followers in a week. It takes time and effort to build a following. Have a social media policy! Your Executive Board and staff should know what is acceptable to post and what isn't. If possible, your members should also be trained to follow this policy.

Finally, here are a few tips about the most popular social media sites. You should use Facebook Pages not Facebook Groups. Pages allow you to interact with users' News Feed, Groups do not. Facebook's Page Insights gives you demographic metrics on your Facebook fans and their activity on your page. You can see how many people "liked" or shared a post and other details. Facebook Pages must be linked to an individual account. This can be a personal account or a business account.[1] Be aware that Facebook has a strict policy prohibiting users from having more than one account.

As to Twitter, say you don't know a @ from a #? Twitter has a concise and easy-to-understand overview of the basics on its website.[2] Follow Twitter trends. Know what people are saying about your union and your employer. The easiest way to do this is to use Twitter's search function. Remember, with Twitter you need to follow to be followed. You're not Lady Gaga or Shaq so people won't follow you blindly. Don't just follow other unions. Search for bloggers, economists, attorneys, journalists and others in the Twitterverse with something interesting to say. Be careful to avoid spam. Spammers love Twitter. Because of the tiny URLs used in Tweets it is often difficult to know where a link goes. You don't want you or your followers to click on a link for a porn site or a site that is infected with malware.

Almost all of us have seen dozens, hundreds, or thousands of videos on YouTube. But have you thought about using YouTube as a communication device for your union? Video adds a human face to your organization. Setting up a YouTube channel is free and simple. You can share videos from others or upload and share your own content. Be careful what you share. That funny traffic stop video may get a laugh out of your members, but it might offend the public. You don't need to be Steven Spielberg. Anyone with a decent cell phone can take video and post it to YouTube.

Finally, don't forget about email! Facebook and Twitter haven't replaced it, at least not yet. If you're using Outlook or something similar for email campaigns then you're doing it wrong. Sending large numbers of emails with Outlook is inefficient, annoying to the recipient and could cause your email account to be suspended for spamming. For large numbers of emails, use a third-party program that allows you to track things like who opens the email, who is forwarding it to others, and which links are being clicked. Examples of these programs are MailChimp, Campaign Monitor, and Constant Contact. There's also a great and free ebook on the subject by Alex White, *Introduction To Email Campaigning For Unions* (www.alexwhite.org).

Keep The Information Flowing: Your Own Web Page.

Recognize that your organization's website might provide the first opportunity for you to impact someone's perception of your union.

The Internet has provided public safety unions with a way to get information to their members and the public alike. Recognize that your organization's website might provide the first opportunity for you to impact someone's perception of your union. After all, a well-organized, professional website will provide an initial perception of a well-organized, professional union, and can undoubtedly go a long way to reinforce that perception to your own members. A key to this is accessing the services of a good webmaster. This person can help you design your website or work with a web designer to design a website that reflects your union's values and articulates your issues. In Chapter 13 we mention in a bit more detail why your website is a great place to craft your message and plant appropriate information for digestion by politicians and the public. A user-friendly design and easy accessibility will aid in the dissemination of appropriate information that can help your general membership stay updated on issues.

While there are innumerable "how to" resources devoted to the design and maintenance of web-sites, I'd like to share a few do's and don'ts of a public safety union's web-site. Key: Remember who we are. What follows will make perfect sense if you keep that in mind:

- *Do* have a "Members Only" section.

- *Do* keep the interface within the "Members Only" section simple.

- *Do* keep the "Members Only" section updated so your members will remain engaged with it.

- *Don't* ever think that what is put in the "Members Only" section will actually stay in the "Members Only" section and not be circulated to the media, the public, or to politicians who cultivate special relationships with disgruntled or self-serving members.

- *Don't* assume that members will not post diatribes or post personal attacks against management in the publicly accessible sections. That in the least will exacerbate tensions and in the worst case, could cost that particular bonehead their job.

- *Do* have a good administrator for your website.

- *Do* expect to have to monitor member and public entries for vicious rumors and inappropriate comments.

- *Don't* let the publicly accessible content become stale and dated. Out of date material and non-pertinent postings diminish your union's credibility. The web-site is your bully pulpit. Use it responsibly and effectively. Folks wouldn't click on it if they weren't interested in what your organization had to say.

A good webmaster will keep up with technological developments, making sure your website works well with different browsers. He will keep files trimmed so that download times are minimized. He will monitor the website for problems and work to fix them. Most importantly, a good webmaster will keep your website updated and pester you to provide the appropriate information and content to do just that.

NOTES

[1] Read about differences in account types at http://www.facebook.com/note.php?note_id=117376211655809.

[2] http://business.twitter.com/en/basics/what-is-twitter/.

CHAPTER 18

LOOKING AHEAD: STRATEGIC PLANNING

Your organization needs a strategic plan. I don't care how big or small your union is; I don't care how diverse your membership is; I don't care if you are a police officer, firefighter, paramedic, or dispatcher. If you are a member of a public safety union, you must ensure that your union develops a strategic plan. The most difficult part of planning for the future is coalescing your union's reason for existing into a mission, encapsulating your union's desire for success into a vision, and getting an honest perspective from your members on how they see fit to achieve both. The most difficult part of making a strategic plan meaningful is implementing the strategies, updating the overall plan as your organization moves ahead within the parameters of the plan, and measuring the progress.

Strategic planning for a public safety union is a dynamic process that transcends the routine, day-to-day business of running the union. Assessing where the organization is, where it wants to go, and how it is going to get there is the essence of what any strategic plan will address.

Just like anything else you try to get done with your union, you will have to engage that usual group of committed members who can be counted on to ramrod something through, steering it through the special interests and around those who are set in their ways. These folks should make up your steering committee. Above all, the steering committee must have credibility with your rank and file or you are wasting your time.

Mission Statement. Before you can steer your union on a path to anywhere, your members need to recognize and agree on a mission statement. In one direct, concise, and clearly-written sentence you should be able to sum up your union's reason to exist. Here is an example:

> "The mission of the Springfield Police Association is to ensure the optimum wages, hours, and working conditions for its members while maintaining an effective and efficient organization focused on preservation of bargaining rights and support of the best interests of the General Membership."

Okay, you say, that's pretty straight forward. So how do the good folks in Springfield begin to accomplish their mission? Just what are you building to get you to the point of accomplishing the mission? Here is where a vision statement comes in.

Vision And Values. You can't just make up a vision statement. Credible vision statements are developed from your members' input. Vision statements generally answer questions such as stating the nature of your union, the scope of the services provided, and the overall aim of your organization. The vision statement will provide your union with the ultimate answer to the question "Where are we going as an organization?"

So, if you can't make up a vision statement, then how the heck do you develop one? It's not easy, but it's not all that difficult. It just takes a little bit of time.

According to Hugh Davidson in his book *The Committed Enterprise*, engaging in a strategic debate with your members forces everyone to think deeply about

Strategic planning for a public safety union is a dynamic process that transcends the routine, day-to-day business of running the union.

the future.[1] The debate should involve members from diverse representative sections of your union. The discussions should be facilitated to ensure that everyone is heard and each opinion regarding the direction the union should take is given due regard. Ultimately, the vision that results will be a product that your union leadership and general membership can agree upon and are willing to commit to and, utilizing the values that your union espouses, have the will to progress towards. An example of a vision statement by your union might read something like this:

> "To provide for the highest wages and benefits and to maintain collective bargaining rights for all our members, while cultivating our professional standing in the community."

Simple. Attainable. Positive. Supported by a menu of values that provide a foundation to achieve the general outcome.

Values can be generally described as the guiding beliefs and practices of your union. High minded and politically correct values may be admirable, but if they are not relevant to your union they are at best meaningless. At worst, they erode the credibility of your union's vision, so any efforts put forth previously to develop the vision could very well be undone by hokey values.

Values can be generally described as the guiding beliefs and practices of your union.

For instance, if you state your union's values as diversity, employee recognition, and empowering individuals, then I would ask, "Do these values move your union forward?" Maybe more appropriate values for a public safety union would be proper compensation for members, maximizing workplace safety, job proficiency, taking care of our members, timely and honest communications, and a commitment to activism in politics and the community. All of these values, if adhered to in applied strategies, can move your union forward.

Goals. The general statements that become your union's goals should be attainable and seen as much as a process as an end state. The strategic plan should have no more than four or five goals stated. Consider some suggested goals for the folks in Springfield:

1. Improve the Public's Perception of the Springfield Police Association.

2. Improve Wages, Hours, and Working Conditions Through Bargaining.

3. Project and Prioritize the Union's Capital Needs.

4. Advance the Union's Use of Technology.

For every goal, it is important to have an explanation as to why the particular goal is important and the necessity of attaining it. In Goal No. 2 above, there is nothing more foundational to a union than maintaining its collective bargaining rights and to always be moving ahead when it comes to wages, hours and working conditions. The manner in which goal achievement will be measured should also be explained. This is called metrics. Once the goals are identified, the next step is to further subdivide the strategic plan into objectives that move the union toward the attainment of the goal.

Objectives. Continue to develop the strategic plan by deciding on attainable objectives that move your union closer to the attainment of the goal. Objectives are more specific than goals, and therefore there will be many more of them. Each objective should also be accompanied by an explanation. Let's take the Springfield Police Association's last goal, "Advance Union's Use of Technology" and determine some examples of appropriate objectives.

For starters, let's format it like this:

> Goal 4: Advance the Union's Use of Technology
>
> There is no money budgeted in the Springfield Police Association to keep technology current. The union is operating in a maintenance mode and not in an innovation mode, which limits the opportunities to maximize the benefits of technology as they present themselves. Metrics: Backlog, accuracy of data entry, and workflow and communications efficiencies should be monitored.
>
> Objective 4.1: Formalize a plan for future technology applications:
>
> The union's vision must include a plan to proactively analyze, plan and implement technological innovations to effectively and efficiently serve our members.
>
> Objective 4.2: Improve the union's use of technology:
>
> Improved processes and systems will increase the union's efficiency and record keeping.

It's easy to see then that if you think of the objectives as logical subsets of the goal, the development of the objectives can be deduced as steps necessary to attain the goal. But it is only through specific strategies that progress can be made on the objectives.

Strategies. The plan's goals and objectives are supported by a framework of strategies that are designed to ensure attainment of each objective. Think of the strategies as mechanisms to bridge the gap between planning and implementation. It is key that opportunities for the initiation of objective-oriented strategies are constantly being identified and assessed. Let's try some strategies for attaining the objectives outlined above. We will use the same relative formatting to underscore the deductive nature of the strategies relative to the objectives. Note that the 4th Goal, 1st Objective, 1st Strategy will be written 4.1.1 as shown below, and so on:

The union's vision must include a plan to proactively analyze, plan and implement technological innovations to effectively and efficiently serve our members.

> 4.1.1: Initiate a study of technology practices and uses being employed by other comparable unions.

Think of the strategies as mechanisms to bridge the gap between planning and implementation.

4.1.2: Develop ways to upgrade and improve existing hardware and software.

4.1.3: Develop a life-cycle replacement plan for the union's technology equipment.

Objective 4.2: For technology to work for the union, it must increase organizational efficiency by reducing traditional paper handling tasks.

4.2.1: Purchase and implement software and hardware that allows direct entry of data and ease of use.

4.2.2: Develop and update procedures that provide backups, recovery plans, and audit trails if data is not accessible or if there is a technology glitch.

4.2.3: Develop and update the union's website so it becomes an efficient medium for the transmission of information to and from the general membership and the public.

SUMMARY.

Okay, this should be enough to get you started. Formatting aside, there is so much benefit to crafting a strategic plan for your union. Entire books are dedicated to the development of strategic plans.[2] But as I mentioned previously in this book, I am a great advocate of stealing from unions that have successfully accomplished anything. So find a union that has successfully constructed a strategic plan and steal as much as you can. But don't just write something down and let it collect dust on a shelf or sit static on a website. Hand it out. If you wind up doing a strategic plan, keep it alive, have your steering committee meet regularly, and measure your union's progress. If you are serious about strengthening your organization, providing it with a plan for the future, and bringing together rank-and-file members who otherwise might have no interest in working together, developing and maintaining a strategic plan is a useful tool to "get there from here." And as an added benefit, chances are your union will have a strategic plan and your department's administration will not.

NOTES

[1] Davidson, Hugh "The Committed Enterprise," Butterworth Heineman, 2002, p.32.

[2] I like *Weil's Turning the Tide: Strategic Planning for Labor Unions* (Xanedu 2002), Bradford and Tarcy's *Simplified Strategic Planning: The No-Nonsense Guide for Busy People Who Want Fast Results* (Chandler House 2000) and Goodstein, Nolan and Pfeiffer's *Applied Strategic Planning: How To Develop A Plan That Really Works* (McGraw-Hill 1993). A good on-line resource can be found at http://www.afscme2010.org, in a document titled "Local Union Strategic Planning."

APPENDIX A

CONSTITUTION AND BYLAWS

CONSTITUTION AND BY-LAWS
OF THE
ANCHORAGE POLICE DEPARTMENT EMPLOYEES ASSOCIATION

ARTICLE I

NAME, AFFILIATION AND HEADQUARTERS

Section 1. Name.

The name of this organization shall be the Anchorage Police Department Employees Association. The headquarters of the Association shall be in Anchorage, Alaska.

ARTICLE II

OBJECTIVES

It shall be the purpose of the Association to secure improved wages, medical benefits, hours, working conditions and other advantages for its members through negotiations and collective bargaining, and through other lawful methods.

ARTICLE III

MEMBERSHIP AND DUES

Section 1. Eligibility.

All full-time employees of the Anchorage Police Department who are members of the Association's collective bargaining unit shall be eligible to be members of this Association. The regular membership shall constitute the principal body of the Association.

Section 2. Dues and Initiation Fees.

The initiation fee for the Association shall be the equivalent of 10% (ten percent) of the employee's hourly wage multiplied by 160. The initiation fee will not be assessed to members hired after January 1st, 2014. Dues, assessments, and any fees, including initiation fees, shall be set by the Executive Board and ratified by a majority vote of the membership present at a regular or special general meeting of the Association.

Section 3. Payment of Dues and Initiation Fees.

Membership dues shall be payable bi-weekly. Initiation fees must be paid in full within thirty (30) days of date of hire by the Municipality of Anchorage. Members with service related/occupational or non-occupational disabilities or who are activated by orders into the United States Military who are no longer receiving wages from the Municipality of Anchorage shall have their dues waived until they return to work. Employees who retire from and are subsequently rehired to the Municipality shall be required to pay an initiation fee upon their rehire.

Section 4. Non-Payment of Dues.

A. All members whose dues are paid as per Section 3 of this Article shall be in good standing. Any member whose dues are not paid as per Section 3 of this Article shall be automatically suspended.

B. Members suspended for non-payment of dues or initiation fees shall be denied all benefits and privileges until reinstated by the Executive Board. Before being reinstated to membership, they shall be required to pay a reinitiation fee as set by the Executive Board, in addition to all delinquent dues, fines, and assessments.

C. The Executive Board shall have complete discretionary power to waive penalties for non-payment of dues in cases of sickness and injury. The exercise by the Executive Board of this power shall not set a past practice requiring the exercise of the power in a future case.

Section 5. Fair Share.

A. Fair share members of the Association shall not be entitled to voice or vote in the Association, nor to participate in any of the Association's activities.

B. If a member of the bargaining unit refuses to join the Association, he or she will be assessed his or her fair share of the costs germane to the collective bargaining process. This amount will be determined by the Association's Executive Board after an independent auditor has examined the Association's detailed budget for the year. The accounting must designate the amount of funds which are to be clearly used for ideological purposes, those which are clearly to be used for cost germane to the collective bargaining process, and those which are not clearly in either category. This accounting must also include all funds sent to state or national organizations and affiliates. The Association will then inform the employer to deduct from fair share members the amount equal to all funds not clearly to be used for ideological purposes or for negotiations or administering the collective bargaining agreement. The Association will place in escrow the amount which is not clearly either for ideological purposes or for negotiating or administering the collective bargaining agreement. The amount which is clearly to be used for negotiating and administering the contract may be used immediately by the Association. The amount in escrow can only be used after fair share members have had an opportunity to register their objections by utilizing the appeal process described below.

C. All fair share members shall be provided with a copy of the budget along with an explanation of the amount of dues to be deducted from their paychecks. They will also be provided with a copy of the procedures described in this Article whereby they may register their objections to the amount deducted.

D. Fair share members will have thirty (30) days to join the Association as fair share members after their date of employment, or sixty (60) days after the effective date of the collective bargaining agreement if they are currently an employee. If they fail to join, the Association will instruct the employer to deduct their fair share of dues in accordance with the procedures outlined in this Article.

E. A fair share member will have fifteen (15) days from the date they receive the information described in this Article, to inform the Association in writing that they object to the amount being deducted from their wages, and the reasons for these objections. Failure to inform the Association in a timely manner will be considered a waiver of the right to so object.

F. Upon receipt of this objection, the Association's Executive Board will review the objection and inform the member within thirty (30) days of its decision. If the Board agrees with the fair share member, the dues will be adjusted accordingly. If the Board rejects the fair share member's objection, then the fair share member has ten (10) days in which to inform the Board that he or she desires to have the dispute settled by arbitration.

G. Upon receipt of a request for arbitration, the Association will request, as soon as possible, a list from the American Arbitration Association of the names of five (5) arbitrators to be submitted to the Association and the fair share member. Within ten (10) days of the receipt of the list, the Association representative will meet with the fair share member and each will alternatively strike names until a single arbitrator is left. The Association will inform the arbitrator of his or her selection and schedule a hearing as soon as possible. The arbitrator will have thirty (30) days from the date of the hearing to render his or her decision. The decision will be final and binding upon both parties. The cost of the arbitrator will be borne by the Association.

H. If the arbitrator sustains the objection by the fair share member, then the Association will refund to the fair share member the appropriate amount. If the arbitrator rejects the objection and supports the Association, then the remainder of the fair share member's dues deducted and in escrow may be withdrawn and used by the Association.

ARTICLE IV

MEETINGS

Section 1. Meetings.

General membership meetings shall be held at least quarterly at dates and times as shall be set by the Executive Board. Members of the Association shall be given at least two week's notice prior to the date of the regularly-scheduled general membership meetings. An agenda for the general membership meeting shall be simultaneously posted when the notice of a general membership meeting is posted. Twenty-five (25) members, including the officers of the Association, shall constitute the quorum necessary to conduct Association business.

Section 2. Special Meetings.

Special general membership meetings may be called by the Association's President, the Association's Executive Board, or by petition filed with the President and signed by ten (10) percent of the members of the Association, and shall be called for specifically listed purposes. Transactions at a special general membership meeting shall be limited to the purposes listed in the call for the special general membership meeting.

Section 3. Rules of Order.

Meetings shall be conducted in an orderly and businesslike manner.

Section 4. Members Not in Good Standing.

Members not in good standing shall be denied attendance at the meetings of the Association.

Section 5. Sanctions.

A member may be sanctioned by a majority vote of the Executive Board if said member through gross negligence or unlawful act, exposes the Association to financial loss, releases confidential information or commits any act deemed by the Board to cause significant harm to the Association. Prior to any decision regarding sanctions, the member shall be notified in writing no less than ten days prior to the Board meeting when the sanction will be discussed. The member may appear at the Executive Board meeting to offer evidence to mitigate or prevent the proposed sanction. The member will be given written notice of the Executive Board's final decision within three working days of the Executive Board's decision. The membership will be notified of the details of the sanction in approved meeting minutes.

The decision to sanction a member shall not be subject to appeal.

Sanctioned members will not be allowed to run for any office or act as a shop steward for a two-year period from the date the sanction is imposed.

Section 6. Intoxicating Liquors.

There shall be no intoxicating liquors of any kind served or consumed during an Association meeting. Any member entering a meeting in a state of intoxication shall be ejected from the meeting.

ARTICLE V

OFFICERS, NOMINATIONS, ELECTIONS AND CONTRACT RATIFICATION

Section 1. Titles.

Officers of this Association shall be a President, a Vice President, a Recording Secretary, a Treasurer, and ten (10) Trustees, and that shall be the order of succession to the office of the Presidency. These officers shall constitute the Executive Board.

Section 2. Terms of Office.

The term of office of all officers shall be for two (2) years. The President, Treasurer, and half of the Trustees shall be elected on each even-numbered year. The Vice-President, Recording Secretary, and half of the Trustees shall be elected on each odd-numbered year.

Section 3. Nominations and Elections.

A. Nominations for elections shall be made during the month of November prior to the conclusion of an Association general membership meeting. Only members in good standing may be nominated, and nominated candidates must accept nominations at the time made, either in person, or, if absent, in writing before the end of the meeting. Candidates may accept nomination for only one (1) office. If a question is raised concerning the eligibility of a candidate, the Elections Committee shall investigate the eligibility of the candidate. The Committee shall report its findings to the Executive Board, which shall have the authority to disqualify any ineligible candidate.

B. On all ballots, the names of the candidates for each position shall be listed in alphabetic order. Write-in candidates shall be allowed, provided the candidates are members in good standing of the Association.

C. Elections shall be held during the first two (2) weeks of December. A seven (7) day notice of election shall be given. If an electronic ballot is used, members will be given a seven (7) day voting period. If a paper ballot is used, voting shall occur on a single day, as set by the Elections Committee.

D. The candidates for the position of Trustee receiving the most votes cast in election for the Trustee position shall be the winners of the election for the open Trustee positions. The candidates for the four officer positions of President, Vice President, Treasurer, and Recording Secretary receiving the majority of the votes cast in the elections for their office shall be the winners of the election for that office. In the event that no candidate for an officer position receives a majority of the votes, a run-off election between the two candidates for that position receiving the most votes shall be conducted no later than the conclusion of the fourth week in December.

E. If there is a tie for the most votes received, there shall be a runoff election between the candidates receiving the most votes. The runoff election shall be held no later than the conclusion of the fourth week in December, and the candidate receiving the most votes cast in the runoff election shall be the winner of the election.

F. The terms of office of the officers who are elected shall commence on January 1 of the year following their election to office.

Section 4. Vacancies In Office.

Vacancies in trustee shall be filled for the remainder of the unexpired term with the candidate(s) receiving the most votes from the prior election. If the top two vote recipients received the same number of votes, the Executive Board shall select, through using random selection, which of the two recipients shall be appointed. Vacancies in officer positions will be filled by a special ballot held within thirty (30) days of the vacancy. Provided, however, that if the vacancy in an officer's term is less than six months in length, the vacancy may be filled by vote of the Executive Board.

Section 5. Contract Ratification.

All collective bargaining agreements shall be subject to ratification by the general membership by secret ballot. The balloting shall be so conducted as to afford all members a reasonable opportunity to vote. At least five (5) days advance notice shall be given the membership prior to holding the ratification vote, and the Association shall conduct at least one (1) informational meeting prior to the ratification vote.

Section 6. Procedure for Special Balloting.

Special balloting on any issue other than those described above may be called by the Executive Board. Special balloting shall be held under the same conditions as indicated in Section 3 of this Article.

Section 7. Elections Committee.

In January of each year, the President shall appoint three Association members to serve as the Election Committee for that year. The Committee shall have charge of the polls during all elections and balloting in that year. No member of the Elections Committee may be a candidate for office in the election held in that year. The Committee shall report the results of the election to the Recording Secretary as soon as the vote is tabulated.

Section 8. Balloting Challenges.

In the event any member protests the conduct of balloting or certain ballots, such protest shall be sent in writing by registered or certified mail within forty-eight (48) hours or via email to the Elections Committee, setting forth the exact nature and specification of the protest and his/her claim as to how the protested practice or ballots affected the outcome of the election. The Executive Board will resolve the protest at its next meeting, and the decision of the Executive Board shall be appealable to the general membership at the next general membership meeting. The decision of the general membership on appeal shall be final and binding.

Section 9. Absentee Ballots.

Absentee ballots shall be permitted in all balloting and elections conducted under this Constitution and By-Laws with the exception of elections held electronically or elections where notice is insufficient to provide absentee ballots. The Executive Board shall establish the procedures for absentee ballots.

ARTICLE VI

DUTIES OF OFFICERS AND EXECUTIVE BOARD

Section 1. Duties Common to All Executive Board Members.

Members of the Executive Board shall perform faithfully not only those duties with which they are specifically charged under this Constitution and By-Laws, but shall also perform such other duties as ordinarily pertain to their office or such as the Association may from time to time impose.

Section 2. President.

A. The President shall be the chief executive and administrative officer of the Association, and shall conduct the affairs of the Association in accordance with its constitution and in accordance with policy decisions of the membership and the Association's Executive Board. The President shall be an ex-officio member of all committees, shall issue the call for regular and special meetings, shall preside at general membership meetings, and shall have the right to vote in any general membership or Executive Board decisions where the President's vote is necessary to break a tie. The President shall, with the Executive Board's approval, procure suitable offices for the transaction of the Association's business. The President shall, with the approval of the Executive Board, engage such technical and professional services, including legal counsel, labor representative, accounting, and other services as may be required. The President shall have full authority to appoint and remove all shop stewards, and to appoint members to committees created by the Executive Board. The President shall report on his/her actions at regular or special meetings to the Executive Board.

B. The responsibilities of the President may not be delegated, but the President may delegate to a member or members the execution of the President's duties, subject to the limitations of this Constitution and By-Laws. The President shall have the non-delegable authority to sign all checks, authorizations for expenditures, contracts, and other official documents of this Association.

C. Should the President elect not to seek reelection, or should the President be defeated for reelection, at the conclusion of the President's term of office the President shall, for a one (1) month period of time, assist the newly-elected President in executing the duties and functions of the President. The outgoing President shall be provided full-time release and receive reimbursement as specified in subsection D for the one (1) month period.

D. Upon the ratification by the APDEA membership of an agreement between the Municipality and the APDEA calling for a full-time APDEA President, the APDEA shall reimburse to the Municipality such salary and fringe benefit costs as required by the agreement.

Section 3. Vice President.

It shall be the duty of the Vice-President to assist the President in preserving order at meetings, to preside over Executive Board meetings, and to carry out the delegable duties of the President in the absence of the President or in cases of a vacancy in the Office of President.

Section 4. Treasurer.

The Treasurer shall receive and receipt for all monies of the Association, and deposit such monies in accounts or investments in the Association's name. The types of funds in which the Association's monies are invested as well as the percentage allocation of the Association's monies among those funds shall be subject to the approval of the Executive Board, which shall set the investment policies of the Association unless overridden by a vote of the general membership. Monies so deposited or invested shall be withdrawn only upon written authorization signed by two (2) Officers, one (1) of whom shall be the Treasurer if the Treasurer is available. The Treasurer shall keep an accurate record of receipts and disbursements and shall submit to the Executive Board an annual budget and a quarterly operating statement of the financial transactions of the Association. The Treasurer shall act as custodian of all properties of the Association. The Treasurer, subject to the approval of the Executive Board, shall engage a certified public accountant to perform an annual independent audit or review of the Association's books, and the result of the audit or review shall be reported to the Executive Board.

Section 5. Recording Secretary.

It shall be the duty of the Recording Secretary to keep a correct and impartial account of the proceedings of each meeting of the Association and of the Executive Board, and to preserve the same at all times ready for inspection by any member of the Association. The Recording Secretary shall post the results of all balloting conducted under this Constitution and By-Laws within twenty-four (24) hours of the conclusion of the balloting.

Section 6. The Executive Board.

A. The Executive Board shall possess all the legislative and policy-making authority of the Association except the power to amend the Constitution and By-Laws. The Executive Board shall have the authority to make final and binding interpretations of this Constitution and By-Laws. The Executive Board shall have the authority to make binding interpretations and enter into memoranda of exception or understanding of the collective bargaining agreement, and to create committees. The policies, rulings and decisions of the Executive Board shall remain in full force and effect unless reversed by the Association at votes at two (2) consecutive special or general membership meetings. The members of the Executive Board shall be required to attend all general and Executive Board meetings of the Association. Any Executive Board member who misses three (3) consecutive regularly scheduled Executive Board meetings without an excused absence, as determined by the Executive Board, will be removed from the Board by the President.

B. The Executive Board shall meet at the call of the President or a majority of the members of the Executive Board upon seven (7) days notice unless an emergency situation dictates otherwise. All meetings of the Executive Board shall be open to all members of the Association. Meetings may be closed by a majority vote of the Board. Minutes of closed meetings of the Executive Board may not be removed from the Association office and may not be copied.

C. At the conclusion of his/her term of office, an Executive Board member shall deliver to his/her successors all records, funds, and properties of the Association entrusted to their care.

D. A voting quorum shall consist of no less than seven (7) voting members of the Executive Board present at a specific and notified meeting.

E. Members of the Executive Board shall serve the term for which they are elected unless removed in accordance with these provisions for failure to attend meetings pursuant to Section A, above, or for incompetency, neglect of duty, or dishonesty. If any member in good standing believes that an Executive Board member should be removed from office for incompetency, neglect of duty, or dishonesty, the member must present his/her concerns to the Executive Board. If, in the opinion of a majority of the Executive Board, the challenged member should be removed from office, the Executive Board shall present its concerns to the general membership at a special meeting, to be held no more than seven and no less than fourteen days after the Executive Board meeting. A recall election shall be conducted no more than seven and no less than fourteen days after the special meeting. If the majority of those voting in the recall election agree that there is cause for removal, then the Executive Board member shall be immediately removed from duty.

In cases of emergency, a member of the Executive Board may be temporarily suspended pending the completion of the recall process. No member of the Executive Board may be temporarily suspended unless three-quarters of the members of the Executive Board voting on the recall recommendation to the general membership vote for such a suspension.

If a member is recalled from office, the member shall not be able to run for office or serve as a shop steward for a two-year period following the effective date of the recall.

F. The exercise of discretion by the Executive Board in a particular case or cases shall not constitute a past practice or in any way bind the Association to act in an identical or similar manner in the future.

ARTICLE VII

ASSOCIATION FUNDS

Section 1. Sources of Funds.

The funds of the Association shall be derived from initiation fees, reinitiation fees, dues, assessments, fines, donation, rents, interest, dividends, and from other lawful sources.

Section 2. Expenditures.

The funds of the Association may be expended in furthering the object of this Association, in the assistance of other Unions, in proper deposits and investments, and for such other purposes as this Constitution and By-Laws provide. No investments over $1,000 shall be made until the same have been investigated and approved by the Executive Board.

Section 3. Financial Dealings With Association Members.

No loans shall be authorized to any Association member or employee. Except upon dissolution of the Association, the funds of the Association shall not in any manner be divided among its members.

ARTICLE VIII

MISCELLANEOUS PROVISIONS

Section 1. Power to Bind Association.

Except to the extent specified in this Constitution and By-Laws, no officer of the Association shall have the power to act as agent for or otherwise bind the Association in any way whatsoever. No member or group of members or other persons shall have the power to act on behalf of or otherwise bind the Association except to the extent specifically authorized in writing by the President or by the Executive Board of the Association.

Section 2. Receipts and Expense Accounts.

All receipts and other evidence of expenditures on behalf of the Association shall be made available for inspection by any Association member eligible to vote in Association elections. Members who wish to review receipts or other evidences of expenditures shall do so in the presence of the President, the Vice-President, and the Treasurer.

Section 3. Surety Bonds and Insurance.

Any member having authority to sign checks on behalf of the Association or having access to the Association's funds shall be covered by surety bonds or insurance purchased by the Association.

Section 4. Funds Produced By Games Of Chance And Contests Of Skill.

Upon the dissolution of the Association, any remaining net proceeds from the APDEA's conduct of Games of Chance and Contests of Skill shall be distributed to charities as defined in AS 05.15.690(5).

ARTICLE IX

CONTRIBUTIONS POLICY

All Association contributions shall be made under one of the following categories:

A. Professional. Contributions to organizations for the purpose of improving law enforcement. The amount shall be determined on a case-by-case basis by the Executive Board.

B. Association Athletics: Contributions to athletic teams and events organized for the benefit of Association members. The maximum contribution shall be $600 and shall not exceed $30 per involved Association member. An additional contribution of up to $500 may be made once during any three-year period for the purchase of equipment and/or uniforms.

C. Hospitality Rooms: Activities organized for the purpose of entertaining Association members and/or members of other law enforcement agencies with the provision of food and beverage. The maximum contribution shall be $500.

D. Youth Activities: Contributions to activities organized for the benefit of young people such as Scouts, athletic teams and School Safety Patrol. The maximum contribution shall be $400.

E. Gifts to Individuals: Gifts other than the retirement honorarium purchased for individuals as an expression of Association appreciation. The maximum expenditure per individual gift shall be $200.

F. Political: All political contributions will be made in accordance with the rules established by the Alaska Public Offices Commission.

G. All Others: All other contributions will be determined by the Executive Board not to exceed $250. The contributing limits specified herein may be waived by unanimous vote of the Executive Board.

H. The contributing limits specified herein may be waived by vote of nine Executive Board.

I. Applicants will fill out an Association contribution request form and submit it to the Association office. The request will be submitted to the Executive Board at the next meeting. Before the next Executive Board meeting, the Treasurer shall review the completed form and forward a copy to each member of the Executive Board. In the event time does not permit a copy being sent in advance, the copies will be made available to Board members at the beginning of the Executive Board meeting.

J. (1) The APDEA shall pay a dues refund to any Anchorage Police Department employee hired prior to January 1st, 2014 and who terminates service with the Anchorage Police Department with 15 years of service or more, or who retires from employment with the Anchorage Police Department.

(2) The dues refund shall be in the amount of $50.00 per year of membership in the Anchorage Police Department Employees Association.

(3) The dues refund shall not be paid to an employee who is terminated for just cause. If a terminated employee challenges the termination through the arbitration process, the decision on whether to pay the dues refund shall be made by the Executive Board at its meeting next following the final resolution of the employee's grievance challenging the termination.

K. Employee Assistance: Members may request financial assistance when unforeseen hardships arise. Members requesting assistance will submit the request in writing to the Treasurer for review. Requests for payments shall be made by the impacted member himself/herself. The Treasurer shall present the request for payments to the Board for action. The Executive Board will have complete discretion as to whether to approve or reject requests for payments, and to set the amount of any payment.

L.   Academic Award Program:

(1)   Each year, the Association shall provide up to five (5) one-thousand dollar ($1,000) academic awards to children of active members.

(2)   Taking into consideration the recommendations of the Academic Award Committee, the Board shall establish the qualifications for the awards and approve award application forms.

(3)   The Association President or designee shall publish the Academic Award Program qualifications, submission deadlines, and application forms. It shall be sufficient if publication occurs in the minutes of a Board meeting.

4.   The Academic Award Committee shall review all applications and provide a list of eligible candidates to the Board.

5.   The Board shall have the discretion to determine the means of selecting award recipients provided that the recipients are selected by chance. The names of the award winners shall be published no later than August 15 and award recipients shall be notified no later than August 31.

ARTICLE X

AMENDMENTS

Proposed amendments to this Constitution and By-Laws must be read at two regular or special general meetings of the Association. This Constitution and By-Laws may be amended by a majority of the members voting in the election. Written balloting subsequent to the meeting at which the amendments were read shall be required in elections to amend this Constitution and By-Laws. Such balloting shall be completed as specified under Article V, Section 3, Nominations and Elections.

Adopted this 5th day of December, 2009.

Derek Hsieh, President
Anchorage Police Department Employees Association

APPENDIX B

GRIEVANCE FILING FORM

GRIEVANCE FORM FOR AGREEMENT BETWEEN ANCHORAGE POLICE DEPARTMENT EMPLOYEES ASSOCIATION AND THE MUNICIPALITY OF ANCHORAGE

GRIEVANCE INFORMATION

Please complete this form to best of your ability, so the appropriate parties will be made familiar with the important aspects of the case and your position.

1.   Case Number:

2.   Name and duty assignment of individual(s) involved:

3.   Name of Union Representative Handling Grievance:

4.   Indicate that part of the contract and/or practice you believe was violated:

5.   Indicate the date the alleged violation first occurred:

6.   Remedy sought:

Information Pertaining To Grievance Status

1.   Indicate the date the grievance was presented to the Executive Board:

2.   Date the grievance was accepted by the Executive Board:

3.   Indicate the date provided to the Chief of Police or his designee and the date a response is required by:

APPENDIX C

SHOP STEWARD'S MANUAL

SHOP STEWARD'S MANUAL

Anchorage Police Department
Employees Association

2013

TABLE OF CONTENTS

I.

THE IMPORTANCE OF SHOP STEWARDS

Shop stewards play several critical roles in the enforcement of the collective bargaining agreement between the APDEA and the Municipality. Perhaps most importantly, shop stewards are the first line of defense against any violations of the collective bargaining agreement. By being on the scene and understanding and applying the contract, shop stewards can often defuse potentially troublesome situations. Shop stewards can also immediately bring contract violations to the APD's attention, insuring that the APDEA's contract rights are protected and documented.

In addition to enforcing the contract, shop stewards also guard against violations of the APDEA's collective bargaining rights. Shop stewards are usually the first to be aware of the Municipality's plan to make any change in wages, hours, and working conditions. By asserting the APDEA's right to collective bargaining over "mandatory" subjects of bargaining, a shop steward can insure that the Municipality complies with its statutory obligation to collectively bargain.

A third important role played by shop stewards is the representation of employees in the disciplinary process and in other interactions with the Municipality. Shop stewards are usually primarily charged with investigating the background of disciplinary charges made against an employee, and representing employees in the initial interview process. Shop stewards also often represent employees at pre-disciplinary due process hearings, and work with the APDEA's attorneys in preparing for disciplinary arbitrations.

By aggressively investigating charges made against employees and preparing the best defense against those charges at an early point in the disciplinary process, shop stewards can play an invaluable role in not only assisting employees, but in preventing the Municipality from making an incorrect disciplinary decision.

Shop stewards also frequently act as intermediaries between employees and supervisors in non-disciplinary settings where, for whatever reasons, communication has broken down. The shop steward's role in this setting is to do as much as possible to get relationships back on track and to try to deescalate situations.

II.

ENFORCING THE CONTRACT

A. INTRODUCTION.

The importance of the role of a shop steward in enforcing the collective bargaining agreement cannot be overstated. Shop stewards are often the only individuals who are in a position to be aware of violations of the collective bargaining agreement. Since the strength of a collective bargaining agreement is directly related to the willingness of the APDEA to enforce the contract, the shop steward's role becomes all the more important.

In enforcing the contract, there are five areas of information any shop steward should possess: (1) A working knowledge of the provisions of the contract; (2) Knowledge of how the grievance procedure works; (3) Knowledge of the time limits imposed by the grievance procedure for the processing of grievances; (4) Awareness of how to best write a grievance; and (5) Knowledge of how to process the grievance through the steps in the grievance procedure.

B. UNDERSTANDING THE COLLECTIVE BARGAINING AGREEMENT.

The first task of any shop steward should be to read the entire collective bargaining agreement. When reading the contract, the shop steward should jot down notes about provisions of the contract that may be unclear. These notes should later be reviewed with members of the APDEA's Executive Board and/or attorney to insure that the shop steward has the correct working understanding of the rights guaranteed by the collective bargaining agreement.

In addition to the initial reading of the contract, each shop steward should, on at least an annual basis, reread the most important portions of the collective bargaining agreement. These portions include, at a minimum, articles 5 through 9 of the contract, which cover such critical areas as employee rights, hours of work, overtime, and seniority.

C. THE CONTRACT'S GRIEVANCE PROCEDURE.

The grievance procedure in the APDEA's contract with the Municipality contains a three-step process culminating with final and binding arbitration. The steps can be summarized as follows:

Step 1 – The Pre-Executive Board Step. Immediately after the employee becomes aware of a possible violation of the contract, the employee should contact one of the APDEA's officers or a shop steward with respect to the potential filing of the grievance. Under the APDEA's contract, a grievance is only formalized if the APDEA's Executive Board votes to accept it.

If the employee approaches the shop steward directly, and the shop steward wishes to handle the potential grievance, the shop steward should contact the President or Vice-President of the APDEA for approval to work on the potential grievance. Once the approval is received, the shop steward can begin the process of investigating the potential grievance and representing the employee.

After the shop steward's investigation is complete, and at least 10 days before the Executive Board meeting at which the grievance will be considered, the shop steward should write a draft grievance. The draft grievance should state the facts of the grievance, the contract article alleged to be violated, and the remedy sought. It's a good practice for a shop steward to sit down with the employee when drafting a grievance. In that way, both the employee and the shop steward will have a good idea what provisions of the contract may or may not apply to the situation.

In all cases except where an employee has been terminated, the grievance must be accepted and filed by the Executive Board within 60 days of its occurrence. Where an employee has been terminated, the grievance must be accepted and filed in 30 days. These strict time limits make it incumbent upon the shop steward to complete a timely investigation.

If at any time a shop steward feels there exists a possibility that the case will not be ready to submit to the Executive Board within these time limits, the shop steward should immediately speak with the APDEA's President or Vice President to see if an extension of time can be obtained from the Municipality. Until the shop steward has been told that an extension of time has been granted, the shop steward should assume that the original time deadlines are still in effect.

Step 2 – The APD Step. If the grievance is accepted by the Executive Board, the APDEA must immediately submit the grievance to the Anchorage Police Department. The grievance must be filed within 60 days of the date the employee first became aware of the violation, and within 30 days of any termination from employment. When the APDEA files a grievance with the Department, it must simultaneously send a copy of the grievance to the Municipality's Labor Relations Department.

Step 3 – The Municipality Step. If the Chief denies the grievance or does not respond to it within 14 days (7 days in the case of a termination from employment), the APDEA has the right to refer the grievance to the Mayor or his designee. The grievance must be appealed to Step 3 within 10 days after the response from APD is due or the date the response is actually received, whichever occurs first. The Municipality must respond in writing to the APDEA within 5 days of receipt of the grievance.

If the grievance still remains unresolved, the APDEA has the right, within 20 days of when the response from the Municipality is due, to notify the Municipality of its intention to arbitrate the grievance.

The grievance and arbitration procedure between the APDEA and the Municipality can be found in Article 5 of the collective bargaining agreement.

D. A SPECIAL CASE – CHANGES IN PAST PRACTICES.

Whenever the Municipality makes a change in a past practice in a subject which is mandatorily negotiable, the APDEA has the right to challenge the change through an expedited grievance procedure found in Article 5(2)(n) of the contract. Under the expedited grievance procedure, the APDEA must challenge a change in a past practice within 3 days of the time it becomes aware of the changed past practice. These time limits are so strict that it is imperative that whenever a shop steward even hears a rumor that a past practice may be changed, the shop steward should immediately discuss the issue with one of the APDEA's officers.

E. TIME LIMITS IN THE GRIEVANCE PROCEDURE.

As can be seen above, the grievance procedure contains very specific time limits for the advancement of grievances from one step to another. It is critically important that all shop stewards understand these time limits. If a grievance is not advanced within the time limit specified by the contract, the grievance is forever lost and cannot be reactivated (except in the limited circumstances when the grievance is of a continuing nature). If you ever have any doubts about time limits, get in touch with an officer of the APDEA for immediate advice.

F. HOW TO INVESTIGATE AND WRITE A GRIEVANCE.

How well a grievance is investigated and written often determines whether or not the grievance is won or lost. When investigating a grievance, it is important that a shop steward follow at least the following basic steps:

Interview the employee. In all cases, the grieving employee should be interviewed prior to the writing of the grievance. In the course of the interview, the shop steward should make sure to ask questions that will reveal both the strengths and weaknesses of the grievance. The items that should be covered in the interview of the employee are the following:

(1) Why does the employee believe there has been a grievance;

(2) What section of the contract has been violated;

(3) When did the grievance happen;

(4) What remedy to the grievance is the employee seeking;

(5) Where did the grievance happen, and who was involved in the grievance.

(6) Who does the employee think might be a witness to the actions giving rise to the grievance.

(7) Who does the employee believe might be able to provide background information, either about the actions leading to the grievance, or as to the general contract issues involved in the grievance.

(8) What does the employee believe the Municipality's motivation was for the actions which led up to the grievance.

(9) Does the employee know of any similar situations in the past either involving the employee or other employees. The similar situations may have been handled the same way by the Municipality, or may have been handled in a different manner.

Examine all records. Before the grievance is written, the shop steward should examine all records relevant to the grievance. This should include records possessed by the employee, and records which the Municipality may have in its possession.

Speak with the Municipality's representatives. Before writing the grievance, the shop steward should attempt to get the Municipality's side of the grievance. To do this, the shop steward should speak with any supervisors who may have knowledge of why the Municipality took the action which resulted in the grievance.

Speak with witnesses. Try to speak with as many witnesses as possible, not only those who support the employee's version of events, but also those who might have a different point of view.

Speak with other APDEA representatives. Another important step to follow prior to writing the grievance is to speak with other APDEA representatives to determine whether or not they have encountered a similar problem and, if so, how they were able to successfully resolve the problem.

Call the APDEA's attorney, if authorized by the APDEA. The APDEA has contracted with the law offices of Will Aitchison to provide representation at all steps in the grievance procedure. Whenever you are considering filing a grievance, call the APDEA President. The President will then review the facts of the grievance with you and will assist you with specific wording to be placed into the grievance. If the President authorizes it, Mr. Aitchison will contact you with regard to the grievance.

G. HOW TO PROCESS A GRIEVANCE.

Under the APDEA's organizational scheme, shop stewards are given the responsibility to physically process grievances through the Executive Board step of the grievance procedure. This requires that shop stewards be aware of all time limits imposed by the grievance procedure, and that shop stewards move the grievance through the grievance procedure in compliance with those time limits.

H. TAKE NOTES!!!!

At all stages of processing a grievance, particularly when you are interviewing witnesses or the Municipality's representatives, take detailed notes of your conversation. If the flow of the conversation would be interrupted by your taking notes during the conversation, immediately after the conversation is concluded, take the time to write down your recollection of the conversation.

III.

SHOP STEWARDS AND THE APDEA'S RIGHTS TO COLLECTIVELY BARGAIN

A. INTRODUCTION.

Under the law, the APDEA is given the right to collectively bargain over wages, hours, and conditions of employment, so called "mandatory" subjects of bargaining. The APDEA's right to bargain over mandatory subjects of bargaining does not end when negotiations for a new agreement are completed. Rather, the APDEA's right to bargain continues throughout the entire time a contract is in place, even after a contract has expired.

This continuing right to bargain can be enforced whenever the Municipality is making a change in a mandatory subject of bargaining. As such, it is important that shop stewards understand what are mandatory subjects of bargaining, and how to best raise the issue of the Municipality's continuing duty to bargain.

B. WHAT ARE MANDATORY SUBJECTS OF BARGAINING?

Mandatory subjects of bargaining can be loosely defined as any matters which touch or concern wages, hours, or working conditions. Virtually anything that involves monetary compensation to an employee, whether in the form of salary, incentive pay, allowances, or reimbursements, is a mandatory subject of bargaining. Thus, whenever an employee's overall compensation is affected by a change in the practices of the Municipality, shop stewards should be aware that there may be mandatory bargaining issues inherent in the change.

For example, if an employer has been calculating overtime in the past on the basis of an assumption that employees work 2080 hours in a work year, and if the employer decides to change this method of overtime calculation to the assumption that employees work 2088 hours in a work year, the resulting effect will be a reduction in the employee's overtime rate. Since the employee's "wages" have been affected by a change the employer has made, the organization representing the employees would have a right to bargain over the change before the change is implemented.

Mandatorily negotiable changes in hours of work practices are also fairly easy to identify. Wherever an employer makes any change in the times when employees are required to work, it is likely that the change is mandatorily negotiable. For example, if the employer changes the starting times for shifts, or the length of a work shift, or the way in which the work shift rotates, mandatorily negotiable "hours of work" issues have been affected. In each case, the organization representing the employees has the right to demand that the employer bargain over the changes in the hours of work before the changes are implemented.

Mandatorily negotiable working conditions or "conditions of employment" are not as easy to identify as "wages" and "hours of work." In order to be mandatorily negotiable, a working condition must be one which has a substantial effect on an employee. The effect can be on the employee's day to day job activities or on restrictions placed on the employee's off-duty life. The following have all been held to be mandatorily negotiable working conditions:

(1) A decision to institute drug testing;

(2) Changes in the criteria used to make job assignments;

(3) Changes in take-home car policies;

(4) Restrictions on what type of second jobs employees may take in their off-duty time;

(5) The utilization of reserves, and other forms of subcontracting;

(6) Changes in shift scheduling;

(7) Changes in whether an employer will defend and indemnify employees for claims made against employees for action taken on the job (tort claim defense and indemnification); and

(8) Safety considerations, ranging from the type of safety equipment furnished by the employer to the circumstances under which employees are required to do certain tasks.

(9) New disciplinary rules or procedures.

(10) Changes in the types of employee records that are released to the public.

As is the case with mandatorily negotiable "wages" and "hours of work," an employer may not make any change in mandatorily negotiable "conditions of employment" without first negotiating with the employees' labor organization.

C. THE SHOP STEWARD'S ROLE IN PROTECTING THE APDEA'S BARGAINING RIGHTS.

The shop steward's role in insisting that the Municipality bargain over changes in mandatory subjects of bargaining is a critical one. Often, such changes may be made only in certain areas of the Municipality's operation, or may be instituted so gradually that it would be difficult for the APDEA to gain information that the changes were being made. By keeping a sharp lookout for any changes in mandatory subjects of bargaining, and promptly notifying the APDEA of those changes, shop stewards can insure that the Municipality meets its continuing obligation to bargain with the APDEA.

At the same time as notifying the APDEA, shop stewards should write a memorandum to the APDEA detailing the existing practice before the change, when the change was instituted, and the effects of the change on bargaining unit members. Shop stewards should keep a copy of this memorandum in their own files.

IV.

REPRESENTING EMPLOYEES IN THE DISCIPLINARY PROCESS

A. THE RIGHTS OF APDEA MEMBERS.

The most important part of representing an employee in the disciplinary process is understanding the rights afforded employees of APD under Article 5, Section 1 of the contract. Those rights include:

Individual rights of employees in the Anchorage Police Department shall not be violated. To insure this, the following shall represent the Employee's Bill of Rights:

A. An employee shall be entitled to representation from the Association or its designee at each step of the Grievance Procedure set forth in this Agreement.

B. An employee shall be entitled to representation by the Association or its designee at each stage of a disciplinary proceeding brought against an Association member. Disciplinary proceeding is defined as any action taken against an employee by a superior officer, that may affect his working conditions, integrity, hours or wages, and which results in oral reprimand, written reprimand, suspension, discharge, demotion or disciplinary transfer.

C. No employee shall be required by the Municipality to submit to an interrogation in a disciplinary proceeding unless he is afforded the opportunity of having an Association representative or its designee present. If the Employer has reasonable cause to question an employee's fitness for duty, the Employer may require the employee to undergo a physical or mental examination to determine continued fitness for duty. If the employee disagrees with the results of such examination, or the results of the first examination indicate that a further examination is required, then either the employee or Employer may require a second examination. Should the findings and recommendations of the examining physicians significantly differ, a third opinion from another qualified physician selected jointly by the two physicians shall be obtained. The third opinion shall be followed by the Employer, the Association and affected employee. The first and, where applicable, third examination shall be paid for by the Employer and the second examination shall be paid by the employee (to the extent that such examination is not paid for through the Health and Welfare Plan) if the employee requests the examination, or the Employer if the Employer requires the second examination.

D. In all disciplinary hearings, the employee shall be presumed innocent until proven guilty. This presumption does not increase the Employer's burden to establish just cause in any disciplinary action.

E. An employee shall not be coerced or intimidated or suffer any reprisals either directly or indirectly that may adversely affect his hours, wages, or other terms and conditions of employment as a result of the exercise of his rights under this Agreement.

F. When an employee is (a) under investigation, and (b) subjected to interview by the Department, (c) which could lead to disciplinary action (which is defined as oral reprimand, written reprimand, suspension, discharge, demotion or disciplinary transfer), the interview shall be conducted under conditions listed in this Section.

G. The following provisions shall apply to such interviews:

(1) Interviews shall be conducted at a reasonable hour, preferably when the employee is on duty, unless the seriousness of the investigation requires otherwise.

(2) Employees shall be compensated if the interview occurs off-duty, at the appropriate overtime rate of pay.

(3) Employees under non-criminal investigation shall be informed of the nature of the investigation and provided a copy of the written complaint, if one exists, within four (4) working days of when the complaint is received. Employees on leave status shall be notified within four (4) working days of returning to duty. Where known, employees shall be advised of the name of the complainant. Employees shall be informed of all details of the investigation which are necessary to reasonably apprise the employee of the factual background of the complaint. When, in the reasonable judgment of the Chief of Police, disclosure of the complaint will seriously jeopardize an investigation of the complaint, the notice requirement under this provision shall not apply.

(4) Interview sessions shall be for a reasonable period and under reasonable conditions. Save when in the reasonable judgment of the Chief of Police prior notice of an interview will seriously jeopardize an investigation, an employee under investigation for a non-criminal

offense shall be provided with a minimum of twenty-four (24) hours notice of any non-criminal interview.

(5) Employees being interviewed shall be informed that failure to answer questions directly related to the investigation can result in disciplinary action, which includes discharge, unless the incident is being investigated as a criminal act, in which case, no employee shall be required to answer any questions and no disciplinary action can be taken for failure to answer under these circumstances. No promise of reward shall be made as an inducement to answering questions.

(a) If the incident may result in either a civil suit and/or a criminal action, the employee may have an attorney, at his own cost, in addition to an Association Representative, be present at all steps of the investigation, provided the attorney does not obstruct the course of the investigation.

(6) The interview may be recorded, and if it is, the employee shall have access to the tape, if any further proceedings are contemplated, or prior to any further interviews at a subsequent time. The employee that is being interviewed shall also have the right to bring his own recording device and record any and all aspects of the interview and, if he does, the employee shall provide access to the tape to the Municipality. No recording device may be used by any party unless the Association and the Municipality are made aware of the fact prior to such interview. Employees shall be entitled to a transcribed copy of any notes made by a stenographer.

(7) If prior to or during the interview of an employee, it is determined that he may be charged with a criminal offense, he shall immediately be informed of this fact.

(8) Interviews shall be conducted under circumstances devoid of abuse.

H. All disciplinary matters will be removed from the personnel file at the following times and under the following conditions:

Oral Reprimand, Written Reprimand, Suspension, Demotion or Disciplinary Transfer: One year after the date of imposition of an oral reprimand or written reprimand, and two (2) years after the imposition of a suspension, demotion or disciplinary transfer. Any similar violations occurring during the above time periods will cause the existing disciplinary action(s) to be maintained in the personnel file for an additional one (1) year period.

At any time after the effective date of this Agreement, employees shall have the opportunity to notify the Municipality of any disciplinary records that are subject to the provisions of this section. In all cases where the Municipality receives such notification, and in all cases where discipline is imposed after the effective date of this Agreement, the Municipality shall remove the disciplinary matters from the employee's file on the time schedule set forth in this section, and shall provide the employee with the original of the documents removed from the file.

I. Unless otherwise described herein, all investigations will be conducted in accordance with State and Federal law.

J. Except where obligated by law or with prior written consent of the affected employee, the Municipality will not release information which is not otherwise a public record from an employee's personnel file to any third party not associated with or acting on behalf of the Municipality. Where release is required by law, the employer will make a reasonable effort to notify the employee prior to release of the information.

Before representing any employee in a disciplinary interview, the shop steward should reread Article 5, Section 1 of the contract so as to be familiar with the process and the protections provided therein.

B. THE EMPLOYEE'S RIGHT TO REPRESENTATION – THE *WEINGARTEN* RULE.

Irrespective of any provisions in the collective bargaining agreement, employees are guaranteed the right to representation whenever an employee is being questioned under circumstances which may lead to discipline. These rights, so called *Weingarten* rights because of the name of the Supreme Court decision in which they were first described, apply in a variety of settings. In each case, however, the employee is entitled to representation only if the employee requests representation. Absent a request from the employee, the employer has no obligation to notify the employee of the employee's right to request representation.

Because *Weingarten* rights turn on an employee's request for representation, shop stewards should make sure that all employees with whom they work understand that they have the right to an APDEA representative whenever they are being interrogated about a matter which they believe could result in discipline. At a minimum, *Weingarten* rights exist under the following circumstances:

(1) Any disciplinary interview concerning a citizen's complaint;

(2) Any disciplinary interview concerning a department-initiated complaint;

(3) Any situation where the employee is required to give an oral or written report about the use of force.

Remember, *Weingarten* rights only come into existence when the employee requests representation. It's important that all APDEA members understand that the first thing they should do when faced with questioning that could result in discipline is to request a shop steward.

Lastly, though the issue hasn't arisen with the Municipality in several years, the Municipality may take the position that "witnesses" are not entitled to APDEA representation during questioning. Such an argument would almost certainly be wrong under *Weingarten*, but it clearly violates Article V, Section 1(C), which provides: "No employee shall be required by the Municipality to submit to an interrogation in a disciplinary proceeding unless he is afforded the opportunity of having an Association representative or its designee present."

C. AN EMPLOYEE'S RIGHT TO IMMUNITY – *GARRITY* RIGHTS.

Apart from the Municipality's internal affairs procedures and the *Weingarten* rule, there is one other important set of principles which shop stewards should keep in mind whenever they are representing an employee in the disciplinary process. The Supreme Court has held that if an employer orders an employee to answer a question, the employee's answer and the fruits of that answer cannot be used against the employee in a subsequent criminal proceeding. This rule, known as the *Garrity* rule, is named after the case in which the United States Supreme Court first enunciated the rule. In Alaska, the scope of immunity is probably even greater under the Alaska Constitution, with employees not just being granted immunity from the use of their statements and the fruits of their statements, but also receiving complete immunity from any prosecution whatsoever.

The impact of the *Garrity* rule is that a shop steward should insure that whenever an employee is being asked a question about alleged misconduct, the employee always solicits an order prior to voluntarily responding to the questions. A good rule of thumb is that when an employee is being interviewed in a disciplinary setting, the employee should be advised that the first words out of the employee's mouth should be: "Am I being ordered to answer this question?"

If the employee is informed that he or she is not being ordered to answer the question, then the employee should respectfully decline to proceed with the interview. If the employee is informed that he or she is being required to answer the question, then the employee should cooperate fully with the investigation (the employee could be charged with insubordination if he or she does not answer the questions), bearing in mind that the statements made cannot be used against the employee in a criminal setting.

Though it is rare to find a police officer charged with any criminal law violations, invoking an employee's *Garrity* rights should nonetheless be part and parcel of the shop steward's role in the disciplinary process. The old bromide that "an ounce of prevention is worth two ounces of cure" is rarely truer than with the invocation of *Garrity* rights.

D. DISCIPLINARY STANDARDS – WHAT TO LOOK FOR.

When representing an employee in the disciplinary process, it is important to understand what it is arbitrators look for in a discipline case. In all discipline cases, arbitrators impose a burden upon the employer to prove that it had just cause to discipline an employee. Generally, the standard of proof will be proof by clear and convincing evidence.

In the book *The Rights of Law Enforcement Officers*, the author sets forth 12 factors considered by arbitrators in evaluating police discipline cases:

1. Have the charges against the employee been factually proven. Courts and arbitrators have held that a variety of standards of proof are required to sustain an employer's disciplinary decision. Some have ruled that the employer must substantiate a disciplinary decision by a preponderance (or a majority) of the evidence. Yet others have held that the higher standard of proof by clear and convincing evidence must be met by an employer, particularly in cases where the employee has been discharged. Some arbitrators have held in cases where the alleged conduct of the employee, if proven, would constitute evidence of criminal wrongdoing, that an employer must prove its disciplinary case beyond a reasonable doubt -- the same burden of proof applied in criminal trials.

Where an employer lodges specific factual charges against an employee, it must prove all of the elements of the charges it brings. For example, in one case an employer charged an employee with becoming involved in an "intoxicated altercation" with a doorman employed by a bar. A court reversed the employer's discipline, finding that there was no showing that the employee's intoxication was a factor in the incident with the doorman. The court also found that while a confrontation occurred between the employee and the doorman, the confrontation did not rise to the level of a "vehement quarrel" -- the dictionary definition of an "altercation."

2. Was the punishment imposed by the employer disproportionately severe under all the circumstances: This element of just cause requires that punishment be proportionate to the offense, taking into account factors such as harm to the department resulting from the employee's conduct and the underlying seriousness of the conduct.

3. Did the employer conduct a thorough and complete investigation into the incident? Particularly in cases involving discipline of law enforcement employees, courts and arbitrators tend to require that an employer's investigation of misconduct be just as thorough and complete as would the employer's investigation in a criminal case. Such an investigation should, at a minimum, include examining all investigatory leads and personal interviews with witnesses.

4. Were other employees who engaged in conduct similar or identical to that of the discipline employee treated as harshly by the employer? Commonly referred to as the "disparate treatment" defense, this question focuses on the employer's pre-existing pattern of discipline imposed in identical or similar cases. If an employer substantially varies from prior sanctions in similar cases where there is no significant difference in the work records of the employees involved, the harsher discipline is likely to be set aside or modified. At the heart of the defense is the notion that an employer's pattern of discipline puts employees on notice as to the sanctions the employer believes are appropriate in a given case, and that to vary from such a pattern of discipline without prior notice to employees is inherently unfair.

5. Was the employee's misconduct the product of action or inaction by the employer? This defense which encompasses an increasingly wide variety of theories, including claims that the employee was not adequately trained or that supervisors contributed to the atmosphere which led to the employee's misconduct.

6. Did the employer take into consideration the employee's good or exemplary work history? This defense focuses on the notion that an employer is obligated not just to consider the nature of the employee's conduct, but also the character of the employee as demonstrated through the employee's work history.

7. Did the employer take into consideration mitigating circumstances? Mitigating circumstances which an employer is required to take into account prior to imposing discipline include employee's state of mind at the time of the alleged misconduct, the employee's physical condition, and whether the employee was provoked into the misconduct.

8. Was the employee not subjected to progressive or corrective discipline? The principle of progressive or corrective discipline mandates that punishment be meted out in increasingly severe doses in an effort to correct (as opposed to punish) the behavioral problems of an employee.

9. Was the employer motivated by anti-union bias? An employer's decision to impose discipline cannot be based on the improper motivation of bias against a labor organization. This defense is commonly raised where the target of discipline is a union officer or activist, where there is a pattern of more lenient discipline for similar offenses in the past, and where the relationship between the labor organization and the employer is a difficult one.

10. Are the employer's rules clear and understandable? Before an employer may apply its rules to discipline employees, it must establish that its rules are understandable by the average police employee. If a rule is reasonably capable of more than one interpretation, discipline imposed under the rule will likely be overturned. However, even broadly written rules such as rule forbidding the use of "excessive force" or "obscene language" are enforceable if they are readily understandable by the average employee.

11. Is the employee likely to engage in similar misconduct in the future? Usually only in cases of termination, courts and arbitrators will inquire as to whether the employee is or can be rehabilitated, or whether the conduct was an aberration from the type of conduct normally displayed by the employee.

12. Was the employee accorded procedural due process in the disciplinary investigation? In this context, due process means not only constitutional due process but also what is termed "industrial due process." Industrial due process is a broader notion than constitutional due process, and includes not only concepts such as fair pre-disciplinary hearings but also a ban on basing a disciplinary decision solely on hearsay in cases where complaining witnesses are not called to testify, a requirement that employees be allowed representation during disciplinary interviews, and a prohibition against punishing an employee twice for the same offense. The difference between constitutional and industrial due process is best seen in cases where the employer's investigation has been delayed. While even as much as a five-year delay in completing an investigation may not be enough to violate constitutional due process, delays of one year or less violate industrial due process and often result in the reversal of discipline.

The above 12 factors are a good checklist to use in every discipline case. When investigating the case, shop stewards should discuss each factor with the employee in order to determine what possible defenses exist.

E. HOW TO ACT WHILE REPRESENTING EMPLOYEES IN A DISCIPLINARY SETTING.

The extent to which shop stewards can participate in disciplinary interviews is not yet settled in the law. At a minimum, it is known that shop stewards have the right to be present during any disciplinary interview. Additionally, shop stewards are granted the right to determine what the charges against the employee are before the interview commences. At the conclusion of the interview, the representative can offer mitigating circumstances or other facts helpful to the employee.

What is not so clear is the extent to which a shop steward may participate in a disciplinary interview beyond these limits. Some cases argue that a shop steward should have the right to object to blatantly improper questions. Others suggest that, apart from consulting with the employee, the shop steward should merely be a "fly on the wall" in the disciplinary interview and should not be involved.

Given all these considerations, the best advice for a shop steward would be to participate as actively in an interview as necessary to insure that the employee's rights are protected. If the Municipality's representative begins asking inappropriate or "trick" questions, the shop steward should not hesitate to interject objections to the question, and even to rephrase the questions in a way that is more acceptable. If the Municipality's representative takes on an unprofessional or threatening manner, shop stewards should not hesitate to note this fact for the record.

APPENDIX D

DUTY OF FAIR REPRESENTATION INSURANCE POLICY

.

DIRECTORS AND OFFICERS LIABILITY POLICY
DECLARATIONS

Corporate Office
945 E. Paces Ferry Rd.
Suite 1800
Atlanta, GA 30326

C.	ANY SYMBOL	POLICY PREFIX & NUMBER	RENEWAL OF
	N	HP651255	NHP646124

●THIS IS A CLAIMS MADE POLICY. PLEASE READ IT CAREFULLY.●

THIS POLICY IS ISSUED BY: RSUI Indemnity Company (hereinafter referred to as the Insurer)

ITEM 1.   INSURED'S NAME AND MAILING ADDRESS   PRODUCER'S NAME AND ADDRESS

ANCHORAGE POLICE DEPARTMENT EMPLOYEES
ASSOCIATION (APDEA)

P.O. BOX 230330

ANCHORAGE, AK 99523-0330

IN CONSIDERATION OF THE PAYMENT OF THE PREMIUM, IN RELIANCE UPON THE STATEMENTS HEREIN OR ATTACHED HERETO, AND SUBJECT TO ALL THE TERMS OF THIS POLICY, THE INSURER AGREES TO PROVIDE THE INSURANCE AS STATED IN THIS POLICY.

ITEM 2. POLICY PERIOD:

FROM   4/26/2013   TO   4/26/2014   12:01 AM Standard Time at the Insured's address as stated herein

ITEM 3. LIMIT OF LIABILITY:

$ 1,000,000   Aggregate Limit of Liability each policy period

ITEM 4. RETENTION:

$ 0   Insuring Agreement A

$ 25,000   Insuring Agreement B

$ 25,000   Insuring Agreement C   Service Fee-$250

$ 75,000   Employment Practices Claim

ITEM 5. PREMIUM:

$ 15,930.00

ITEM 6. POLICY FORM AND ENDORSEMENTS MADE A PART OF THIS POLICY AT THE TIME OF ISSUE:
SEE RSG 200007 0204 - SUPPLEMENTAL DECLARATIONS - SCHEDULE OF ENDORSEMENTS; RSG 211003 0609 - DIRECTORS AND OFFICERS LIABILITY POLICY - NOT FOR PROFIT ORGANIZATION - 2009

THESE DECLARATIONS TOGETHER WITH THE COMPLETED, SIGNED AND DATED APPLICATION, POLICY FORMS AND ENDORSEMENTS, IF ANY, ISSUED TO FORM A PART THEREOF, COMPLETE THE ABOVE NUMBERED POLICY.

ntersigned: _____   April 10, 2013   _____
                                                                    DATE   AUTHORIZED REPRESENTATIVE

RSG 200006 0204

A member of Alleghany Insurance Holdings LLC

DIRECTORS AND OFFICERS LIABILITY POLICY
SUPPLEMENTAL DECLARATIONS

POLICY NUMBER: NHP651255

SCHEDULE OF ENDORSEMENTS

TITLE	FORM NUMBER
Disclosure Pursuant to Terrorism Risk Insurance Act	RSG 204123 0108
Alaska - Coverage Extension - Labor Organization	RSG 212062 0110
Alaska - Full Severability	RSG 212029 0606
Alaska Changes	RSG 202070 0205
Alaska Changes - Cancellation and Nonrenewal	RSG 203054 0506
Amended Notice of Claim or Circumstance	RSG 204090 0204
Amended Settlement Clause	RSG 204091 1210
Bilateral Discovery	RSG 204080 0204
Cap on Losses From Certified Acts of Terrorism	RSG 204081 0108
Exclusion - Prior and or Pending Litigation Backdated	RSG 206071 0204
Modified Insured vs. Insured Exclusion (Carve Back Former D&O's)	RSG 216020 0609
Predetermined Allocation	RSG 204132 0205
Severability of the Entity	RSG 214049 0407
Side A Non-Rescindable Coverage	RSG 204136 0606

RSG 200007 0204

APPENDIX E

ONLINE NEGOTIATIONS RESOURCES

Perhaps no area of public sector collective bargaining is changed as much as the availability of online resources. Information that once cost thousands of dollars to amass, and months to gather, is now instantly available without cost over the Internet. Even the smallest of organizations can now have access to information that once was the province of organizations with greater resources.

We have compiled a list of the online resources that we have found to be helpful. There are many more web pages that could be of assistance; all it takes to locate them is time, energy, and imagination.

THE LAW

Cornell University Law School has a well-organized on-line clearinghouse where one can find the **constitutions**, **statutes** and **codes** for all 50 states, as well as the federal government. http://www.law.cornell.edu/statutes.html. The **regulations** issued by federal agencies such as the Department of Labor can be found at the Government Printing Office's web site, http://www.gpoaccess.gov/cfr/, as well as through other sites. http://www.law.cornell.edu/cfr/.

The decisions of the **United States Supreme Court** can be found on the Court's web site, http://www.supremecourt.gov/. A wealth of information about the Supreme Court, including the briefs filed in cases as well as recordings of oral arguments, can be found at The Oyez Project. http://www.oyez.org/. The decisions of **lower federal courts**, as well as those of **state courts**, can quickly be located at Findlaw. http://www.findlaw.com/casecode/. Findlaw, like the Cornell University law school webpage, is an excellent general legal portal for a variety of different sources of the law.

For many years, one of the most difficult things to find on-line were the **codes** for various municipalities and counties. Thanks to the Municode website, more than 1,100 local codes are now online. http://www.municode.com/. In addition, State and Local Government on the Net, http://www.statelocalgov.net/, is a broad portal to state and local government web pages.

EMPLOYMENT LAW NEWSLETTERS AND BLOGS

Employment law newsletters and blogs have proliferated in the last two years. Where once there were a handful, now there are hundreds. Among the best are:

• *Labor Relations Information System*, www.LRIS.com. A thrice-weekly free e-mail newsletter containing information about public sector wage settlements, court decisions, and statutory and regulatory changes.

• *Employment Law Information Network*, http://www.elinfonet.com/. Publishes a five-day per week free newsletter on private and public sector labor developments.

HOW TO NEGOTIATE

There is seemingly no end to the advice contained on the Internet as to how to best negotiate. The more accessible web pages include:

• *Everyone Negotiates*, http://www.negotiatingguide.com/. Contains negotiating advice, and on-line tests of negotiating skills and style, books and audio materials, and a free monthly newsletter devoted to negotiations tactics.

• *How To Negotiate*, http://www.how-to-negotiate.com/. A blog devoted to the development of negotiations skills.

• *The Negotiations Experts*, http://www.negotiations.com/article/. A good collection of articles about effectively negotiating any type of agreement.

• *Top 10 Negotiations Tips*, http://meetingsnet.com/negotiating/tips/meetings_top_negotiating_tips_4/. A straightforward list of many of the important things to do (and avoid) when negotiating. A greatly expanded list, together with many negotiations catch-phrases, can be found at *Changing Minds*, http://changingminds.org/disciplines/negotiation/tactics/tactics.htm.

DEMOGRAPHIC AND ECONOMIC DATA

From the standpoint of public sector negotiators, perhaps the greatest riches to be found on the Internet is in the area of economic and demographic data. Not that long ago, compiling this sort of information would require the services of an expert and the expenditure of a significant amount of money. Today, the information is not only available without cost, but is increasingly found on web sites with easy-to-use interfaces.

• *Census Bureau*, http://www.census.gov/. One could spend days on the Census Bureau's web site and not completely explore all the information helpful in the collective bargaining process. The Bureau compiles a Fact Sheet for every city and county in the country. The information on those Fact Sheets, including (among others) population, median family income, and home values, are useful in selecting comparable jurisdictions. Where some of the data on the web site are figures produced by the decennial census, and can be dated depending upon when they are viewed, the Bureau also conducts an annual American Community Survey with more recent information.

• *Bureau of Labor Statistics*, http://www.bls.gov/. The BLS tabulates, among other things, the Consumer Price Index, as well as information on the demographics of employment, safety, wages, earnings, and benefits. The BLS's web site is well laid out, and even a neophyte can determine the cost of living or the effects of long-term inflation in a particular area using BLS's cost of living calculator. Those interested in more detail will not leave unsatisfied; for example, information on the relative rates of change of different components of the CPI is easy to access.

• *Bureau of Justice Statistics*, http://ojp.usdoj.gov/. An essential for negotiations involving law enforcement groups, the BJS web site contains crime and policing data allowing jurisdiction-to-jurisdiction comparison of matters such as officers per 1,000 population and relative crime rates. The BJS web site also contains information on more specific issues such as the relationship between law enforcement wages and levels of higher education.

• *Congressional Budget Office*, http://www.cbo.gov/. The CBO's web site contains the federal government's forecasts of changes in the Consumer Price Index and other key economic indicators.

- *Bureau of Economic Analysis*, http://www.bea.gov/. Economic trend analysis, including estimates of key aspects of the national and regional economy.
- *FedStats*, http://www.fedstats.gov/. The federal government's FedStats web site contains links to a variety of statistics collected by over 100 government agencies.
- *The Dismal Scientist*, http://www.dismal.com/. A British historian once referred to economics as the "dismal science." The Dismal Scientist web page is one of the best economics web pages on the Internet, containing an extremely thorough collection of economic indicators including ranking of states and metropolitan areas on 130 different statistical criteria.
- *Economagic*, http://www.economagic.com/. Economagic's web site contains over 400,000 data files, charting a wide range of economic time series data on such things as the Gross Domestic Product, changes in personal income, and interest rates.
- *EconData*, http://www.econdata.net. EconData has over 1,000 links to socioeconomic data sources, arranged by subject and provider, links to the Internet data collections, and a list of the ten best sites for finding regional economic data.

REGIONAL COST OF LIVING CALCULATORS

If wage comparisons are made to jurisdictions that are geographically distant, it may be appropriate to make adjustments for regional differences in the cost of living. There are any number of "cost of living calculators" on the Internet. One should use these calculators with caution – few disclose their methodology, and one can enter the same figures into the calculators on different web sites and get wildly disparate results. Among the most popular of the calculators are:

- *Bankrate*, http://www.bankrate.com/calculators/savings/moving-cost-of-living-calculator.aspx.
- *Sperling's BestPlaces*, http://www.bestplaces.net/col/.
- *MySalary*, http://swz.salary.com/costoflivingwizard/layoutscripts/coll_start.asp.
- *CNNMoney*, http://cgi.money.cnn.com/tools/costofliving/costofliving.html.

MEDICAL INFORMATION

With medical and other insurance occupying an increasing amount of the total compensation package, it is important to obtain information about projected increases in medical care and about insurance trends. These websites all contain valuable health care information.

- *Kaiser Family Foundation*, http://www.kff.org/. The KFF web site – published by a foundation and not the HMO – provides historical and projected information on health insurance trends, including costs and benefit structures.
- *Health Affairs*, http://www.healthaffairs.org/. Health Affairs is the on-line version of the leading journal on health policy issues, and contains peer-reviewed articles on topics such as evidence-based health care and health care reform.
- *Almanac of Policy Issues*, http://www.policyalmanac.org/health/index.shtml, is chock full of links to articles on health insurance and public health issues.

• *Health Policy Gateway*, http://ushealthpolicygateway.wordpress.com/. Health Policy Gateway is probably the richest portal site for Internet links to health policy issues, covering dozens of topics from health care spending to health demographics to health care regulation and reform.

• *Retiree Health Cost Calculator*, https://powertools.fidelity.com/healthcost/intro.do. Published by Fidelity Investments, this is one of many sites allowing the user to calculate the savings necessary to pay for post-retirement health insurance.

NATIONAL LABOR ORGANIZATIONS.

The websites for national labor organizations have some information that is useful in the collective bargaining process, though the amount of helpful information that is available outside of password-protected portals varies from organization to organization. Most of the web sites are focused on the organizations' structure, history, and activities, and contain only a modicum of information useful in the collective bargaining process.

• The *AFL-CIO*, http://www.aflcio.org/. Primarily general information about the AFL-CIO's legislative efforts, though the "Facts and Stats" database has interesting general information on topics such as worker safety and pension coverage.

• *American Federation of State, County and Municipal Employees*, http://www.afscme.org/. The "Collective Bargaining Tool Kit," containing everything from a compendium of state laws to tips on budget analysis, is one of the more helpful sections of any union or employer website.

• *American Federation of Teachers*, http://www.aft.org/. A well-designed web page that, apart from AFT's annual Public Employee Compensation Survey, does not contain much information helpful to the collective bargaining process.

• *Combined Law Enforcement Associations of Texas*, http://www.cleat.org/. Since CLEAT largely operates in a non-collective bargaining environment, its web site does not contain much current information helpful to the bargaining process.

• *Fraternal Order of Police*, http://www.grandlodgefop.org/. The FOP has what is surely the most sophisticated collective bargaining-related applications on any union or management web site, including features that select comparable jurisdictions based on demographic characteristics, analyze total compensation, and calculate inflation-adjusted wages. However, those features are all behind a password-protected portal, and the rest of the FOP's web site is fairly standard for a labor organization.

• *International Association of Fire Fighters*, http://www.iaff.org/. The public sections of the IAFF's web site contain the usual fare for a union web site, with sections devoted to organizational structure, pending legislation, and the various programs offered by the organization.

• *International Union of Police Associations*, http://www.iupa.org/. The public portions of IUPA's web page, like the IAFF's, is focused almost exclusively on organizational issues and pending legislation.

• *National Association of Police Organizations*, http://www.napo.org/. Since NAPO is a lobbying organization rather than a true labor union, its web page is predictably short on collective bargaining information.

• *National Education Association*, www.nea.org. The public portions of NEA's web site are long on classroom issues such as lesson plans and educational strategies and shy on collective bargaining information.

• *Service Employees International Union*, http://www.seiu.org/index.php. The "Members" section of SEIU's web site, which is not password protected, has some basic advice on employee rights issues such as the *Weingarten* rule.

NATIONAL EMPLOYER ORGANIZATIONS.

• *Americans For Effective Law Enforcement*, http://www.aele.org/. There may be more freely-available content on AELE's web site than that of any other national organization. Though the user interface could use updating, the "Library" alone is worth visiting the web site, with hundreds of references to articles relevant to public sector negotiations. Several free periodicals offer updates on caselaw. Don't be deterred by the law enforcement-related name of AELE – most of the materials on the web site apply to all public sector employees.

• *National League of Cities*, http://www.nlc.org/. NLC has posted some valuable information about general economic conditions, located in the Research Reports section of its web site. The web site also contains legislative updates, and the Governance section of the web site contains some thoughtful publications on the upcoming challenges municipal governments face.

• *National Association of Counties*, http://www.naco.org/. The County Resource Center on NACO's web site contains some studies that are helpful in the collective bargaining process, particularly a study of health insurance trends.

• *National Public Employer Labor Relations Association*, http://www.npelra.org/. NPELRA is the largest organization representing employer labor relations professionals. To the extent its web page contains collective bargaining information, it is only found behind password-protected portals.

• *National School Boards Association*, http://www.nsba.org/default.aspx. The NSBA's web page contains much more information on national legislative priorities than it does on collective bargaining issues.

NEWS ARTICLE "TRAWLERS."

No organization about to embark on bargaining should be without at least one news article Internet "trawler." Trawlers set up user-defined searches of news sources, and produce results on a regular basis. A trawler can be set up so that each day, one receives published articles on "the cost of living in Chicago," or "Long Beach budget," or "teacher or firefighter layoffs in New York." Many trawlers are now quite easy to use, and allow the user not only to define one or dozens of search strings, but also the frequency with which results are received. Among the best of the trawlers is Google News, http://news.google.com/, which touts itself as a "computer-generated news site that aggregates headlines from news sources worldwide, groups similar stories together and displays them according to each reader's personalized interests." Yahoo News also has a polished news trawler, http://news.yahoo.com/.

APPENDIX F

TOTAL COMPENSATION SURVEY

TOTAL COMPENSATION SURVEY

Jurisdiction: _____

Bargaining Unit: _____

Positions Covered: _____

Period Covered: _____

WAGES.

1. For the classification of **Police Officer** or **Deputy Sheriff**, please provide wage information for the following levels of service. (Please <u>do not</u> include longevity payments in these amounts.)
   Years to Top Step: _____

_____	_____	_____		_____	_____	_____
Year	Entry	Top Step		Year	Entry	Top Step

   Source/Date: _____

2. For the classification of **1st Line Supervisor**, please provide the following wage information. (Please <u>do not</u> include longevity payments in these amounts.)
   Job Title: _____ Years to Top Step: _____

_____	_____	_____		_____	_____	_____
Year	Entry	Top Step		Year	Entry	Top Step

   Source/Date: _____

3. For the classification of **2nd Line Supervisor**, please provide wage information for the following levels of service. (Please <u>do not</u> include longevity payments in these amounts.)
   Job Title: _____ Years to Top Step: _____

_____	_____	_____		_____	_____	_____
Year	Entry	Top Step		Year	Entry	Top Step

   Source/Date: _____

4. For the classification of **3rd Line Supervisor**, please provide the following wage information. (Please <u>do not</u> include longevity payments in these amounts.)
   Job Title: _____ Years to Top Step: _____

_____	_____	_____		_____	_____	_____
Year	Entry	Top Step		Year	Entry	Top Step

   Source/Date: _____

5. What is the monthly top step detective pay?

_____	_____	+	_____	+	_____		_____	_____	+	_____	+	_____
		+		+					+		+	
Year	Base		$ Premium		% Premium		Year	Base		$ Premium		% Premium

   Source/Date: _____

6. Please list the effective dates and amounts of any known future wage increases.

_____	_____		_____	_____
Date	Amount		Date	Amount

   Source/Date: _____

7. What longevity payments (if any) do employees receive in addition to the wages listed above:

    5 Years _____   *10 Years* _____   *15 Years* _____

    20 Years _____   *25 Years* _____   *30 Years* _____

    Source/Date: _____

8. Please provide the details of any education incentive program which rewards employees for obtaining college education:

Level of Education	Education Incentive Benefit
2 Years of College	_____
Bachelor's Degree	_____
Master's Degree	_____

    Source/Date: _____

9. Please provide the details of any POST certification program that rewards employees for obtaining peace officer standards and training certification:

Level of Certification	Certification Incentive Benefit
Basic Certificate	_____
Intermediate Certificate	_____
Advanced Certificate	_____

    Source/Date: _____

10. Can the employee receive both POST and education incentive payments? ☐ Yes ☐ No ☐ N/A

    Source/Date: _____

11. Can the employee receive both longevity payments and POST/education premium payments?
☐ Yes ☐ No ☐ N/A

    Source/Date: _____

12. What is the maximum amount of physical fitness incentive pay received by employees?

    _____

    Source/Date: _____

13. Does the employer pay a patrol officer premium? ☐ Yes ☐ No If so, how much?

    _____

    Source/Date: _____

14. What other types of incentive pay can be received by employees (SWAT, K-9, FTO, etc.)?

    _____

    _____

    _____

    _____

    Source/Date: _____

15. What types of incentive pay are received by all employees, or a majority of employees?

    _____

    Source/Date: _____

LEAVE BENEFITS.

16. How many hours of vacation per year are received by employees at the following levels of tenure?

5 Years _____   10 Years _____   15 Years _____

20 Years _____   25 Years _____   30 Years _____

      Source/Date: _____

17. Do employees receive sick leave in addition to vacation? ☐ Yes ☐ No   If yes, how many hours of sick leave do employees receive per year?
_____

      Source/Date: _____

18. Do employees receive holiday hours? ☐ Yes ☐ No
   If yes, how many holiday hours do employees receive per year? (Premium hours are hours when an employee receives a premium rate of pay, in addition to hours off, when the hours are worked).
   Premium Hours: _____   Non-Premium Hours: _____   Premium Amount: _____
   If no, what compensation do they receive in lieu of hours?
_____

      Source/Date: _____

19. How many personal leave hours per year do employees receive in addition to vacation and holidays?
_____

      Source/Date: _____

RETIREMENT.

20. What is the monthly contribution to the employee's pension plan? If possible, please provide the information as a percentage of the employee's salary. ☐ State System   ☐ Local System

Year	Employer	Pickup	Employee	Year	Employer	Pickup	Employee
_____	_____	_____	_____	_____	_____	_____	_____

      Source/Date: _____

21. How much, if anything, does the <u>employer</u> match or contribute to the employee's deferred compensation account?
   ☐ Match   ☐ Contribution   _____
   Source/Date: _____

22. Does the employer contribute to the employee's Social Security (other than the basic Medicare contribution)? ☐ Yes ☐ No   If not, does the employer contribute to Municipal Employees Beneficial Trust (MEBT), or any other Social Security replacement fund? ☐ Yes ☐ No ☐ N/A   If so, how much?
_____

      Source/Date: _____

23. Which of the following incentive payments are included in retirement contribution calculations:

	Longevity Incentives	Education Incentives	POST Incentives	Patrol Premiums	Detective Premiums
Retirement	☐	☐	☐	☐	☐
Deferred Compensation	☐	☐	☐	☐	☐
MEBT (or other program)	☐	☐	☐	☐	☐

      Source/Date: _____

INSURANCE.

24. What is the dollar amount that the ***employer*** contributes towards insurance premiums for the most commonly used plan for? Is this a flexible spending account? ☐ Yes ☐ No
If this is a flat amount (not related to the actual premium) please make a note.

Effective Dates:								
One Party:								
Two Party:								
Full Family:								
Composite:								
	Medical	Dental/Ortho	Vision	Prescription	Medical	Dental/Ortho	Vision	Prescription

Source/Date: _____   _____

Effective Dates:								
One Party:								
Two Party:								
Full Family:								
Composite:								
	Medical	Dental/Ortho	Vision	Prescription	Medical	Dental/Ortho	Vision	Prescription

Source/Date: _____   _____

25. What is the dollar amount that the ***employee*** contributes towards insurance premiums for the most commonly used plan for full family coverage?

Effective Dates:								
One Party:								
Two Party:								
Full Family:								
Composite:								
	Medical	Dental/Ortho	Vision	Prescription	Medical	Dental/Ortho	Vision	Prescription

Source/Date: _____   _____

Effective Dates:								
One Party:								
Two Party:								
Full Family:								
Composite:								
	Medical	Dental/Ortho	Vision	Prescription	Medical	Dental/Ortho	Vision	Prescription

Source/Date: _____   _____

Page 4

26. What forms of <u>disability</u> and <u>life</u> insurance are provided by the **employer**, and what are the corresponding monthly dollar amounts paid by the employer for these premiums?

_____   _____
_____   _____
_____   _____
_____   _____

      Type of Insurance   *Monthly Employer Cost*
         Source/Date: _____

27. How much, if anything, does the <u>employer</u> contribute to retiree health insurance on a monthly basis?

      Source/Date: _____

CLOTHING ALLOWANCES.
28. Does the employer provide uniforms? ☐ Yes ☐ No
      Source/Date: _____

29. Does the employer provide cleaning of the uniform? ☐ Yes ☐ No
      Source/Date: _____

30. Does the employer provide a uniform or cleaning allowance? ☐ Yes ☐ No If so, how much?

      Source/Date: _____

31. Does the employer provide a plainclothes allowance? ☐ Yes ☐ No If so, how much?

      Source/Date: _____

32. Can an officer receive both the uniform/cleaning and the plainclothes allowance? ☐ Yes ☐ No ☐ N/A
      Source/Date: _____

33. Does the employer furnish and replace uniforms when damaged or worn? ☐ Yes ☐ No
      Source/Date: _____

HOURS OF WORK.
34. Describe the work shift for patrol officers, listing the length of work days and the shift configuration
    a.   Number of hours worked per day:

    b.   Number of Days in a Work Cycle:

    c.   Days worked in a Work Cycle:

    d.   Annual hours off to account for schedule:

      Source/Date: _____

35. How often are employees paid? (i.e. bi-weekly, semi-monthly)

      Source/Date: _____

NOTES.

APPENDIX G

SAMPLE BUDGET

Anchorage Police Department Employees Association
Profit & Loss Budget vs. Actual
January through December 2013

	Jan - Dec 13	Budget	$ Over Budget
Ordinary Income/Expense			
Income			
400 · Dues Income			
664 · Retirement Honorariums	-36,250.00	25,000.00	-61,250.00
400 · Dues Income - Other	576,279.84	679,250.00	-102,970.16
Total 400 · Dues Income	540,029.84	704,250.00	-164,220.16
Total Income	540,029.84	704,250.00	-164,220.16
Gross Profit	540,029.84	704,250.00	-164,220.16
Expense			
611e · Union Officer Expense	1,567.57		
694 · Scholarships	5,000.00	5,000.00	0.00
632 · Honor Guard Support	1,276.26	2,000.00	-723.74
682 · Finance Charges	81.65		
606 · Training	1,832.89	5,000.00	-3,167.11
698 · Lobbyist	36,000.00	36,000.00	0.00
683 · External Communications			
693 · Advertising / Public Relations	21,673.53	36,000.00	-14,326.47
699 · Legislative Affairs			
691 · Travel, Lodging, and Meals	4,011.68	10,000.00	-5,988.32
699 · Legislative Affairs - Other	111,750.00	250,000.00	-138,250.00
Total 699 · Legislative Affairs	115,761.68	260,000.00	-144,238.32
601 · PSA's / Polling	2,000.00	10,000.00	-8,000.00
683 · External Communications - Other	4,756.92	25,000.00	-20,243.08
Total 683 · External Communications	144,192.13	331,000.00	-186,807.87
604 · Full Time Administrative Staff	24,837.51	33,000.00	-8,162.49
603 · Licenses & Fees	20.00		
500 · Professional Service			
602 · PERS Education	6,082.50	10,000.00	-3,917.50
655 · Accounting Fees	17,556.58	20,000.00	-2,443.42
656 · Legal - A&V	147,795.90	245,000.00	-97,204.10
657 · Legal - Other	11,725.05	15,000.00	-3,274.95
658 · Arbitrators/Consultants	9,002.62	25,000.00	-15,997.38
Total 500 · Professional Service	192,162.65	315,000.00	-122,837.35
611 · Meetings & Meals			
611d · Meals Legislative	2,713.02		
611c · Meals Political	474.25		
611b · Meals Board Meetings	3,105.36		
611a · Meals Arbitrators / Legal	1,284.75		
611 · Meetings & Meals - Other	0.00	5,000.00	-5,000.00
Total 611 · Meetings & Meals	7,577.38	5,000.00	2,577.38
620 · Membership Dues & Subscriptions	468.40	2,500.00	-2,031.60
634 · Office Expense			
633 · Telephone/Internet	8,921.92		
605 · Bank Fees	0.00	1,000.00	-1,000.00
634 · Office Expense - Other	6,199.29	15,000.00	-8,800.71
Total 634 · Office Expense	15,121.21	16,000.00	-878.79
645 · Insurance	22,056.20	22,000.00	56.20
6560 · Payroll Expenses	95.61	.	
680 · Miscellaneous Expense			
999 · Suspense	4,760.34		
680 · Miscellaneous Expense - Other	0.00	1,000.00	-1,000.00
Total 680 · Miscellaneous Expense	4,760.34	1,000.00	3,760.34
684 · Charitable Contributions-Dues	8,900.00	10,000.00	-1,100.00
689 · Education, Seminars & Travel	14,682.59	25,000.00	-10,317.41
903 · Union President Stipend	100,281.60	100,000.00	281.60
Total Expense	580,913.99	908,500.00	-327,586.01
Net Ordinary Income	-40,884.15	-204,250.00	163,365.85
Other Income/Expense			
Other Income			
1001 · Interest Income	105.56		
410 · PAC Revenues	24,098.00		
460 · Rental Investment Income	87,867.60		
Total Other Income	112,071.16		
Other Expense			
910 · PAC expense	11,000.00		

Anchorage Police Department Employees Association
Profit & Loss Budget vs. Actual
January through December 2013

	Jan - Dec 13	Budget	$ Over Budget
800 · Building Expense			
810 · Building Snowplowing	7,670.00		
809 · Building Janitorial	10,240.80		
808 · Building Property Taxes	26,791.20		
802 · Building Repairs & Maint	5,203.70		
804 · Building Insurance	8,971.00		
801 · Building Utilities	23,018.16		
Total 800 · Building Expense	81,894.86		
665 · Other Membership Benefits			
662 · Memorial Tributes	6,813.73	5,000.00	1,813.73
673 · Police Memorial Picnic	2,500.00	2,500.00	0.00
661 · Flowers/Other	1,150.00	2,000.00	-850.00
669 · Annual Picnic	14,396.51	15,000.00	-603.49
672 · Police Navidad			
672b · Expenses	0.00	50,000.00	-50,000.00
Total 672 · Police Navidad	0.00	50,000.00	-50,000.00
665 · Other Membership Benefits - Other	3,292.44	2,500.00	792.44
Total 665 · Other Membership Benefits	28,152.68	77,000.00	-48,847.32
806 · Charitable Contributions-Events	1,500.00		
Total Other Expense	122,547.54	77,000.00	45,547.54
Net Other Income	-10,476.38	-77,000.00	66,523.62
Net Income	-51,360.53	-281,250.00	229,889.47

INDEX

A

B

C